Java™ Collections

John Zukowski

Apress™

Java™ Collections
Copyright ©2001 by John Zukowski

ISBN (pbk): 1-893115-92-5

Printed and bound in the United States of America 12345678910

Trademarked names may appear in this book. Rather than use a trademark symbol with every occurrence of a trademarked name, we use the names only in an editorial fashion and to the benefit of the trademark owner, with no intention of infringement of the trademark.

Editorial Directors: Dan Appleman, Gary Cornell, Karen Watterson
Technical Editor: Kim Topley
Developmental Editor and Copy Editor: Kiersten Burke
Production Editor: Kari Brooks
Compositor: Impressions Book and Journal Services, Inc.
Indexer: Carol Burbo
Cover Designer: Karl Miyajima

Distributed to the book trade in the United States by Springer-Verlag New York, Inc., 175 Fifth Avenue, New York, NY, 10010
and outside the United States by Springer-Verlag GmbH & Co. KG, Tiergartenstr. 17, 69112 Heidelberg, Germany

In the United States, phone 1-800-SPRINGER; orders@springer-ny.com; http://www.springer-ny.com
Outside the United States, contact orders@springer.de; http://www.springer.de; fax +49 6221 345229

For information on translations, please contact Apress directly at 901 Grayson Street, Suite 204, Berkeley, CA, 94710
Phone: 510-549-5938; Fax: 510-549-5939; info@apress.com; http://www.apress.com

Brief Contents

Contents

Acknowledgments

Writing this book has been an interesting experience. So much has changed from when I started until now, it's almost hard to believe. No more "Focus on Java" at About.com, no more employment by jGuru (though I still consult for them), and I'm now off on my own with JZ Ventures, Inc. If you're in need of strategic Java consulting. . .

As always, it's time to thank everyone who helped take my horrible writing and awful drawings into the book you're holding today.

At Apress, I'd like to thank Gary Cornell for the book's concept, without which this may have ended up being just another book on JavaServer Pages, XML, or some other already-covered topic. I would especially like to thank Kiersten Burke for putting up with me, Grace Wong for her roll as mediator, as well as Kari Brooks and Stephanie Rodriguez for their help in shaping up what you are holding today. Special thanks to technical editor Kim Topley who not only straightened me out on some technical lapses, but also helped me to fill in some gaps. Any remaining technical inaccuracies are mine alone.

For their continued encouragement along the way, I'd like to personally acknowledge my brother-in-law, Scott Pross, for joining the ranks of geekhood, even if it is with certification from that other software company; my cousin Rachel Goodell, the traveling nurse—it was fun having you in Boston for a change; and Ted Behr, my personal coach, for reminding me that there is more to life than Java (`http://www.makingalife.com/coaches/tedbehr.htm`). And, of course, all the readers and jGuru Collections FAQ contributors (`http://www.jguru.com/faq/Collections`) whose ideas, questions, and encouragement should make this edition much better.

As always, I am grateful to my wife, Lisa, for her patience and support in jumpstarting JZ Ventures, and our playful three-year old pup, Jaeger, who thinks it's more important for him to be amused than me to be productive. Thanks to Mom and Dad, too, may they enjoy their computer.

CHAPTER 1

Java Collections Framework: An Overview

When learning a new computer programming language, one of the first things you tend to ask is how to work with large groups of data. This topic is often covered in the second course of the standard curriculum for Computer Science as part of a class typically called Data Structures. If you were to look at the class syllabus, you'd likely see topics such as linked lists, queues, stacks, and binary trees, among many other data structures. In Java, these structures are part of the Java Collections Framework.

Collections are typically used in a business environment for short-term management of information. This information may have been retrieved from a database, acquired over the network, or just entered by a user. Their primary purpose though is to help the data persist over the lifetime of a program, in a structure that is efficient for the data's purpose. Different collections offer different purposes with quick insertions and deletions but slower fetches, or the reverse, or something in between. Your typical computer science text describes this information in what is called Big O notation and states how fast or slow operations take for each data structure.

What Is This Book About?

This book is about Java's support for dealing with groups of data. Prior to the Java 2 release, the only standard support for data structures and algorithms was a few fairly basic options available through arrays, hash tables, and vectors. Many people either created their own standard data structure library or reused one of several libraries introduced to deal with collections like the Generic Collection Library for Java (JGL) from ObjectSpace. Aside from rolling their own libraries or reusing those created by others, the Collections Framework (beginning with what came with the early beta release of the Java 2 platform, version 1.2) introduced support into the core Java APIs for manipulating data collections. This book describes how to use this Collections Framework. We'll also look at some of the common alternate frameworks available.

A *JavaWorld* survey back in the summer of 1998 asked readers whether Sun should scrap its Collections API in favor of the more robust JGL (the results are posted at *JavaWorld*, `http://www.javaworld.com/jw-08-1998 /jw-08-pollresults.html`). At the time, the Java 2 release wasn't final yet, and as Figure 1-1 shows, most people wanted Sun to dump the Collections Framework in favor of licensing JGL.

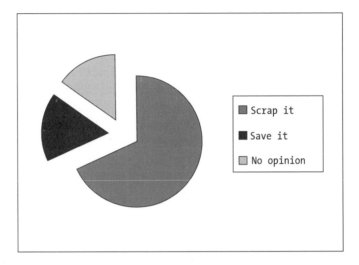

Figure 1-1. The 1998 JavaWorld *survey results.*

While there hasn't been a new survey since, many people find the Collections Framework much easier to use. In addition, since the framework is a core API, not a third-party library, you do not need to redistribute the library with your application. Of course, even Sun doesn't use their own Collections Framework in things like the Swing component set yet, whereas all the internal data models are still using the historical collection classes. And for what its worth, ObjectSpace hasn't released a new version in close to two years. As of this writing in early 2001, they just recently removed a reference from their Web site to the 1.2 release of Java being in limited beta testing, months after the release of 1.3.

> **NOTE** *Given the name of the JGL library, you might think the acronym was coined when someone spent too much time at the pub. It actually comes from an earlier name for the library that violated Sun's Java trademarks. After a friendly letter from the legal department at Sun, the product name was changed but the acronym remained. Most of the time you only see the acronym with no mention of its illogical expansion.*

Is This Book for You?

This book is not meant to be a textbook for a second course in computer science. It does not cover the material in ACM's *Curriculum '78*, its revised version in '84, or even in the combined ACM/IEEE *Computing Curricula 1991*! In fact, I've never read any of those.

This book will not teach you how to program in Java. If you need to learn, there are many good books. While I would like everyone to learn from my *Mastering Java 2* book (Sybex, 1998), other good learning books are *Core Java 2, Volume 1: Fundamentals* (Prentice Hall, 2000); *Beginning Java 2* (Wrox, 2000); *The Java Tutorial* (Addison-Wesley, 2000); *Thinking in Java* (Prentice Hall, 2000); and *Learning Java* (O'Reilly, 2000). Which one is right for you depends upon your specific background. If you are truly new to programming, consider getting *Java Programming: from the Beginning* (Norton, 2000). If you can program with Java but you don't understand interfaces yet, you may have some trouble getting through the material in this book.

So what does that leave? This book *will* teach you about the Java Collections Framework. If you'd like to learn more than the single chapter's coverage of the Collections Framework found in most Java books, this book will provide you with a great deal more. In addition, this book describes several of the alternate collection libraries, such as the JGL Libraries from ObjectSpace; Doug Lea's util.concurrent package; and the Colt Distribution for high performance computing. With each of these other libraries, we'll take a quick look at what they offer and I'll introduce you to the collections-related support available from each.

While this book isn't meant to be a computer science curriculum text, I *do* describe concepts like the details of balanced trees and hash tables. An understanding of how each concept works helps you to decide which collection implementation class is appropriate.

You will, of course, need a Java development environment. The latest JDK from Sun is sufficient, although you might find yourself more productive with one of the visual development tools like JBuilder or Forté for Java. Of course, since the collections library is not meant to be visually programmed, any old text editor like emacs will do.

How Is This Book Structured?

This book is broken down into three parts and three appendices. The first part introduces the historical collection classes; the second part describes the Java Collections Framework; and in the third part you'll find descriptions of the alternate collection libraries. In most cases, you don't need to read the book from start to finish; you can just go directly to the particular data structure, class, or interface you wish to learn more about. The exception would be cases such as working with hash tables. Instead of describing them in multiple sections, with both Hashtable and HashMap you'll find the deepest description in the first Hashtable chapter and less in the HashMap chapter. Feel free to flip back and forth as necessary.

The Historical Collection Classes

Part One of the book provides you with everything you ever wanted to know about the historical collection classes. While most people know how to do most of the basic array, vector, and hash table operations, we'll also dig into some of the less commonly discussed tasks, such as array reflection and optimization techniques.

The Java Collections Framework

Part Two deals with the Java Collections Framework. This framework was introduced with the release of the Java 2 Standard Edition, version 1.2. With minor changes, it remains relatively the same in the 1.3 release of the Standard Edition (and *is* the same in the 1.2 release of the Enterprise Edition). The framework provides enhanced support to manipulate groups of data and allows you to easily separate storage from access. We also explore using the framework with the earlier 1.1 release of the JDK.

Alternative Collection Libraries

In Part Three, we'll discuss some of the other collection libraries out there. While the JGL Libraries seemed like a de facto collection library years ago, its usage seems to be slipping of late. We'll introduce it here, along with Doug's library and Colt.

NOTE *Originating from work by Alexander Stephanov at Hewlett-Packard in 1979, the C++ Standard Template Library, or STL as it is commonly known, is a standard part of the ANSI (American), ISO (International), BSI (British), and DIN (German) adopted C++ standard of November 14, 1997. While this book doesn't cover the STL, if you are interested in learning more about it, you can read "Mumit's STL Newbie's Guide" available at* http://www.xraylith.wisc.edu/~khan/software/stl/STL.newbie.html. *Keep in mind that the document is for the C++ developer and not the Java developer.*

The Appendices

There are three appendices in this book. Appendix A provides an API reference to the core Java classes of the Collections Framework. You'll find both a class-level API reference as well as an alphabetical class, method, and field reference. In Appendix B you'll find a list of resources to help you become more productive with the book's contents. Appendix C describes support for parameterized types, a prelude to something that could become a Java standard soon, possibly as early as the 1.4 release.

The Source Code

This book does not include a CD. However, the source code from the book is freely available from the Apress Web site at `http://www.apress.com/`. With nearly universal Internet access, at least for those programming with Java, I hope that this will not be an issue for anyone.

How Do I Read the Diagrams?

In all three parts of the book, I've used UML to diagram the design of the classes and processes. If you're already familiar with UML, you should have no problem understanding the diagrams. If you're not yet familiar with the UML, consider reviewing *The Unified Modeling Language User Guide* (Addison-Wesley, 1998) or *UML Distilled* (Addison-Wesley, 1999) for a complete tutorial on the subject.

In the next chapter, you'll take a long look at array support in Java. Beginning with basic access and creation, you'll quickly move into multi-dimensional array support, initialization, cloning, and immutability.

Part One

The Historical
Collection Classes

CHAPTER 2

Arrays

Arrays are the only collection support defined within the Java programming language. They are objects that store a set of elements in an order accessible by *index,* or position. They are a subclass of `Object` and implement both the `Serializable` and `Cloneable` interfaces. However, there is no `.java` source file for you to see how the internals work. Basically, you create an array with a specific size and type of element, then fill it up.

> **NOTE** *Since arrays subclass* `Object`, *you can synchronize on an array variable and call its* `wait()` *and* `notify()` *methods.*

Let's take a look at what we can do with array objects—beginning with basic usage and declaration and moving through to copying and cloning. We'll also look at array assignment, equality checking, and reflection.

Array Basics

Before going into the details of declaring, creating, initializing, and copying arrays, let's go over a simple array example. When creating a Java application, the `main()` method has a single argument that is a `String` array: `public static void main(String args[])`. The compiler doesn't care what argument name you use, only that it is an array of `String` objects.

Given that we now have the command-line arguments to our application as an array of `String` objects, we can look at each element and print it. Within Java, arrays know their size, and they are always indexed from position zero. Therefore, we can ask the array how big it is by looking at the sole instance variable for an array: `length`. The following code shows how to do this:

```
public class ArrayArgs {
  public static void main (String args[]) {
    for (int i=0, n=args.length; i<n; i++) {
      System.out.println("Arg " + i + ": " + args[i]);
    }
  }
}
```

> **NOTE** *Array indices cannot be of type* long. *Because only non-negative integers can be used as indices, this effectively limits the number of elements in an array to 2,147,483,648, or 2^{31}, with a range of indices from 0 to $2^{31}-1$.*

Because an array's size doesn't change as we walk through the loop, there is no need to look up the length for each test case, as in: for (int i=0; i<args.length; i++). In fact, to go through the loop counting down instead of up as a check for zero test case is nominally faster in most instances: for (int i=args.length-1; i>=0; i-). While the JDK 1.1 and 1.2 releases have relatively minor performance differences when counting down versus counting up, these timing differences are more significant with the 1.3 release. To demonstrate the speed difference on your platform, try out the program in Listing 2-1 to time how long it takes to loop "max int" times:

Listing 2-1. Timing loop performance.

```java
public class TimeArray {
  public static void main (String args[]) {
    int something = 2;
    long startTime = System.currentTimeMillis();
    for (int i=0, n=Integer.MAX_VALUE; i<n; i++) {
      something = -something;
    }
    long midTime = System.currentTimeMillis();
    for (int i=Integer.MAX_VALUE-1; i>=0; i-) {
      something = -something;
    }
    long endTime = System.currentTimeMillis();
    System.out.println("Increasing Delta: " + (midTime - startTime));
    System.out.println("Decreasing Delta: " + (endTime - midTime));
  }
}
```

This test program is really timing the for-loop and not the array access because there is no array access.

NOTE *In most cases, the numbers calculated on my 400 MHz Windows NT system were in the low 11,000s for JDK 1.1 and 1.2. However, under JDK 1.3 with the -classic option (no JIT), the timing numbers increased to around 250,000. Even using the HotSpot VM with 1.3, the numbers were between 19,000 and 30,000.*

If you ever try to access before the beginning or after the end of an array, an ArrayIndexOutOfBoundsException will be thrown. As a subclass of IndexOutOfBoundsException, the ArrayIndexOutOfBoundsException is a runtime exception, as shown in Figure 2-1. Thankfully, this means that you do not have to place array accesses within try-catch blocks. In addition, since looking beyond the bounds of an array is a runtime exception, your program will compile just fine. The program will only throw the exception when the access is attempted.

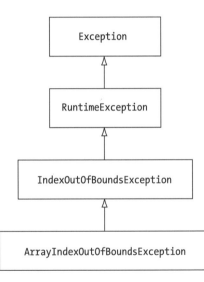

Figure 2-1. The class hierarchy of ArrayIndexOutOfBoundsException.

NOTE *You cannot turn off array bounds checking. It is part of the security architecture of the Java runtime to ensure that invalid memory space is never accessed.*

The following code demonstrates an improper way to read through the command-line array elements:

```
public class ArrayArgs2 {
  public static void main (String args[]) {
    try {
      int i=0;
      do {
        System.out.println("Arg " + i + ": " + args[i++]);
      } while (true);
    } catch (ArrayIndexOutOfBoundsException ignored) {
    }
  }
}
```

While functionally equivalent to the earlier ArrayArgs example, it is bad programming practice to use exception handling for control flow. Exception handling should be reserved for exceptional conditions.

Declaring and Creating Arrays

Remember that arrays are objects that store a set of elements in an index-accessible order. Those elements can either be a primitive datatype, such as an int or float, or any type of Object. To declare an array of a particular type, just add brackets ([ ]) to the declaration:

```
int[] variable;
```

For array declaration, the brackets can be in one of three places: int[] variable, int []variable, and int variable[]. The first says that the variable is of type int[]. The latter two say that the variable is an array and that the array is of type int.

> **NOTE** *This might sound like we're arguing semantics. However, there is a difference when you declare multiple variables depending upon which form you use. The form* int[] var1, var2; *will declare two variables that are* int *arrays, whereas* int []var1, var2; *or* int var1[], var2; *will declare one* int *array and another just of type* int.

Once you've declared the array, you can create the array and save a reference to it. The new operator is used to create arrays. When you create an array, you must specify its length. Once this length is set, you cannot change it. As the following demonstrates, the length can be specified as either a constant or an expression:

```
int variable[] = new int[10];
```

  or

```
int[] createArray(int size) {
  return new int[size];
}
```

> **NOTE**   *If you try to create an array where the length is negative, the run-time* NegativeArraySizeException *will be thrown. Zero-length arrays, however, are valid.*

You can combine array declaration and creation into one step:

```
int variable[] = new int[10];
```

> **WARNING**   *In the event that the creation of an array results in an* OutOfMemoryError *being thrown, all dimension expressions will already have been evaluated. This is important if an assignment is performed where the dimension is specified. For example, if the expression* int variable[] = new int[var1 = var2*var2] *were to cause an* OutOfMemoryError *to be thrown, the variable* var1 *will be set prior to the error being thrown.*

Once an array has been created, you can fill it up. This is normally done with a for-loop or with separate assignment statements. For instance, the following will create and fill a three-element array of names:

```
String names = new String[3];
names[0] = "Leonardo";
names[1] = "da";
names[2] = "Vinci";
```

Arrays of Primitives

When you create an array of primitive elements, the array holds the actual values for those elements. For instance, Figure 2-2 shows what an array of six integers (1452, 1472, 1483, 1495, 1503, 1519) referred to from the variable life would look like with regards to stack and heap memory.

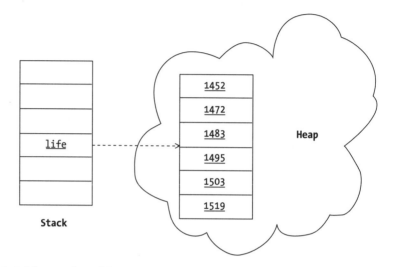

Figure 2-2. The stack and heap memory for an array of primitives.

Arrays of Objects

Unlike an array of primitives, when you create an array of objects, they are not stored in the actual array. The array only stores references to the actual objects, and initially each reference is null unless explicitly initialized. (More on initialization shortly.) Figure 2-3 shows what an array of Object elements would look like where the elements are as follows:

* Leonardo da Vinci's country of birth, Italy

* An image of his painting *The Baptism of Christ*

* His theories (drawings) about helicopters and parachutes

* An image of the *Mona Lisa*

* His country of death, France

The key thing to notice in Figure 2-3 is that the objects are not in the array: only references to the objects are in the array.

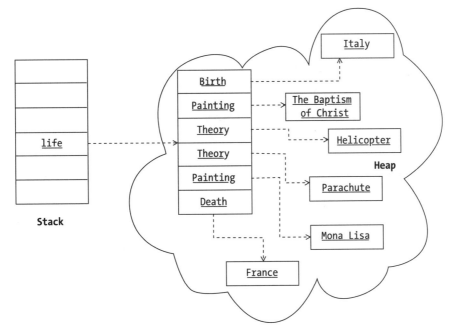

Figure 2-3. The stack and heap memory for an array of objects.

Multidimensional Arrays

Because arrays are handled through references, there is nothing that stops you from having an array element refer to another array. When one array refers to another, you get a *multidimensional array*. This requires an extra set of square brackets for each added dimension on the declaration line. For instance, if you wish to define a rectangular, two-dimensional array, you might use the following line:

```
int coordinates[][];
```

As with one-dimensional arrays, if an array is one of primitives, you can immediately store values in it once you create the array. Just declaring it isn't sufficient. For instance, the following two lines will result in a compilation-time error because the array variable is never initialized:

```
int coordinates[][];
coordinates[0][0] = 2;
```

If, however, you created the array between these two source lines (with something like `coordinates = new int[3][4];`), the last line would become valid.

In the case of an array of objects, creating the multidimensional array produces an array full of null object references. You still need to create the objects to store in the arrays, too.

Because each element in the outermost array of a multidimensional array is an object reference, there is nothing that requires your arrays to be rectangular (or cubic for three-dimensional arrays). Each inner array can have its own size. For instance, the following demonstrates how to create a two-dimensional array of floats where the inner arrays are sized like a set of bowling pins—the first row has one element, the second has two, the third has three, and the fourth has four:

```
float bowling[][] = new float[4][];
for (int i=0; i<4; i++) {
  bowling[i] = new float[i+1];
}
```

To help visualize the final array, see Figure 2-4.

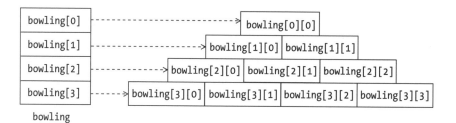

Figure 2-4. A triangular, bowling-pin-like array.

When accessing an array with multiple dimensions, each dimension expression is fully evaluated before the next dimension expression to the right is ever examined. This is important to know if an exception happens during an array access.

> **NOTE** *While you can syntactically place square brackets before or after an array variable when it is for a single dimension (`[index]name` or `name[index]`), you must place the square brackets after the array variable for multiple dimensions, as in `name[index1][index2]`. Syntactically, `[index1][index2]name` and `[index1]name[index2]` are illegal and will result in a compile-time error if found in your code. For declarations, it is perfectly legal to place the brackets before (`type [][]name`), after (`type name[][]`), or around (`type []name[]`) the variable name.*

Keep in mind that computer memory is linear—when you access a multidimensional array you are really accessing a one-dimensional array in memory. If you can access the memory in the order it is stored, the access will be most efficient. Normally, this wouldn't matter if everything fit in memory, as computer memory is quick to hop around. However, when using large data structures, linear access performs best and avoids unnecessary swapping. In addition, you can simulate multidimensional arrays by packing them into a one-dimensional array. This is done frequently with images. The two manners of packing the one-dimensional array are row-major order, where the array is filled one row at a time; and column-major order, where columns are placed into the array. Figure 2-5 shows the difference between the two.

Two-dimentional

bowling[0][0]	bowling[0][1]	bowling[0][2]
bowling[1][0]	bowling[1][1]	bowling[1][2]
bowling[2][0]	bowling[2][1]	bowling[2][2]

row major

bowling[0][0]	bowling[0][1]	bowling[0][2]	bowling[1][0]	bowling[1][1]	bowling[1][2]	bowling[2][0]	bowling[2][1]	bowling[2][2]

column major

bowling[0][0]	bowling[1][0]	bowling[2][0]	bowling[0][1]	bowling[1][1]	bowling[2][1]	bowling[0][2]	bowling[1][2]	bowling[2][2]

Figure 2-5. Row-major versus column-major order.

> **NOTE** *In many of the image processing routines, such as* setPixels() *of the* ImageFilter *class, you'll find two-dimensional image arrays flattened into row-major order, where Pixel (m, n) translates into a one-dimensional position, n * scansize + m. This reads top-down, left-to-right through the image data.*

Initializing Arrays

When an array is first created, the runtime-environment will make sure that the array contents are automatically initialized to some known (as opposed to undefined) value. As with uninitialized instance and class variables, array contents are initialized to either the numerical equivalent of zero, the character equivalent of \u0000, the boolean false, or null for object arrays, as shown in Table 2-1.

Table 2-1. Array Initial Values

DEFAULT VALUE	ARRAY
0	byte
	short
	int
	long
0.0	float
	double
\u0000	char
false	boolean
null	Object

When you declare an array you can specify the initial values of the elements. This is done by providing a comma-delimited list between braces [{ }] after an equal sign at the declaration point.

For instance, the following will create a three-element array of names:

```
String names[] = {"Leonardo", "da", "Vinci"};
```

Notice that when you provide an array initializer, you do not have to specify the length. The array length is set automatically based upon the number of elements in the comma-delimited list.

> **NOTE** *The Java language syntax permits a trailing comma after the last element in an array initializer block, as in {"Leonardo", "da", "Vinci",}. This does not change the length of the array to four, but keeps it at three. This flexibility is primarily for the benefit of code generators.*

For multidimensional arrays, you would just use an extra set of parenthesis for each added dimension. For instance, the following creates a 6 × 2 array of years and events. Because the array is declared as an array of Object elements, it is necessary to use the Integer wrapper class to store each int primitive value inside. All elements within an array must be of the array's declared type, or a subclass of that type, in this case, Object, even though all of the elements are subclasses.

```
Object events[][] = {
    {new Integer(1452), new Birth("Italy")},
    {new Integer(1472), new Painting("baptismOfChrist.jpg")},
    {new Integer(1483), new Theory("Helicopter")},
    {new Integer(1495), new Theory("Parachute")},
    {new Integer(1503), new Painting("monaLisa.jpg")},
    {new Integer(1519), new Death("France")}
};
```

NOTE *In the event the type of the array is an interface, all elements in the array must implement the interface.*

Starting with the second dot-point Java release (Java 1.1), the concept of *anonymous arrays* was introduced. While it was easy to initialize an array when it was declared, you couldn't reinitialize the array later with a comma-delimited list unless you declared another variable to store the new array in. This is where anonymous arrays step in. With an anonymous array, you can reinitialize an array to a new set of values, or pass unnamed arrays into methods when you don't want to define a local variable to store said array.

Anonymous arrays are declared similarly to regular arrays. However, instead of specifying a length within the square brackets, you place a comma-delimited list of values within braces after the brackets, as shown here:

```
new type[] {comma-delimited-list}
```

To demonstrate, the following line shows how to call a method and pass to it an anonymous array of `String` objects:

```
method(new String[] {"Leonardo", "da", "Vinci"});
```

You'll find anonymous arrays used frequently by code generators.

Passing Array Arguments and Return Values

When an array is passed as an argument to a method, a reference to the array is passed. This permits you to modify the contents of the array and have the calling routine see the changes to the array when the method returns. In addition, because a reference is passed around, you can also return arrays created within methods and not worry about the garbage collector releasing the array's memory when the method is done.

Copying and Cloning Arrays

You can do many things when working with arrays. If you've outgrown the initial size of the array, you need to create a new larger one and copy the original elements into the same location of the larger array. If, however, you don't need to make the array larger, but instead you want to modify the array's elements while keeping the original array intact, you must create a copy or clone of the array.

The arraycopy() method of the System class allows you to copy elements from one array to another. When making this copy, the destination array can be larger; but if the destination is smaller, an ArrayIndexOutOfBoundsException will be thrown at runtime. The arraycopy() method takes five arguments (two for each array and starting position, and one for the number of elements to copy): public static void arraycopy (Object sourceArray, int sourceOffset, Object destinationArray, int destinationOffset, int numberOfElementsToCopy). Besides type compatibility, the only requirement here is that the destination array's memory is already allocated.

> **WARNING**   *When copying elements between different arrays, if the source or destination arguments are not arrays or their types are not compatible, an* ArrayStoreException *will be thrown. Incompatible arrays would be where one is an array of primitives and the other is an array of objects; or the primitive types are different; or the object types are not assignable.*

To demonstrate, Listing 2-2 takes an integer array and creates a new array that is twice as large. The doubleArray() method in the following example does this for us:

Listing 2-2. Doubling the size of an array.

```java
public class DoubleArray {
  public static void main (String args[]) {
    int array1[] = {1, 2, 3, 4, 5};
    int array2[] = {1, 2, 3, 4, 5, 6, 7, 8, 9};
    System.out.println("Original size: " + array1.length);
    System.out.println("New size: " + doubleArray(array1).length);
    System.out.println("Original size: " + array2.length);
    System.out.println("New size: " + doubleArray(array2).length);
  }
  static int[] doubleArray(int original[]) {
    int length = original.length;
    int newArray[] = new int[length*2];
```

```
System.arraycopy(original, 0, newArray, 0, length);
    return newArray;
  }
}
```

After getting the length of the original array, a new array of the right size is created before the old elements are copied into their original positions in the new array. After you learn about array reflection in a later section, you can generalize the method to double the size of an array of any type.

When executed, the program generates the following output:

```
Original size: 5
New size: 10
Original size: 9
New size: 18
```

> **NOTE** *When copying arrays with* arraycopy( )*, the source and destination arrays can be the same if you want to copy a subset of the array to another area within that array. This works even if there is some overlap.*

Since arrays implement the Cloneable interface, besides copying regions of arrays, you can also clone them. *Cloning* involves creating a new array of the same size and type and copying all the old elements into the new array. This is unlike *copying*, which requires you to create and size the destination array yourself. In the case of primitive elements, the new array has copies of the old elements, so changes to the elements of one are not reflected in the copy. However, in the case of object references, only the reference is copied. Thus, both copies of the array would point to the same object. Changes to that object would be reflected in both arrays. This is called a *shallow copy* or *shallow clone*.

To demonstrate, the following method takes one integer array and returns a copy of said array.

```
static int[] cloneArray(int original[]) {
  return (int[])original.clone();
}
```

Array cloning overrides the protected Object method that would normally throw a CloneNotSupportedException with a public one that actually works.

Array Immutability

It is useful to return an array clone from a method if you don't want the caller of your method to modify the underlying array structure. While you can declare arrays to be final, as in the following example:

```
final static int array[] = {1, 2, 3, 4, 5};
```

declaring an object reference final (specifically, an array reference here) does not restrict you from modifying the object. It only limits you from changing what the final variable refers to. While the following line results in a compilation error:

```
array = new int[] {6, 7, 8, 9};
```

changing an individual element is perfectly legal:

```
array[3] = 6;
```

> **TIP** *Another way to "return" an immutable array from a method is to return an* Enumeration *or* Iterator *into the array, rather than returning the actual array. Either interface provides access to the individual elements without exposing the whole array to changes or requiring you to make a copy of the entire array. You'll learn more about these interfaces in later chapters.*

Array Assignments

Array assignments work like variable assignments. If variable x is a reference to an array of y, then x can be a reference to z if a variable of type z can be assigned to y. For instance, imagine that y is the AWT Component class and z is the AWT Button class. Because a Button variable can be assigned to a Component variable, a Button array can be assigned to a Component array:

```
Button buttons[] = {
  new Button ("One"),
  new Button("Two"),
  new Button("Three")};
Component components[] = buttons;
```

When an assignment like this is made, both variables' buttons and components refer to the same heap space in memory, as shown by Figure 2-6. Changing an array element for one array changes the element for both.

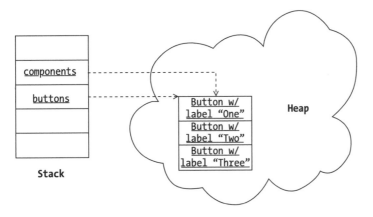

Figure 2-6. Shared memory after an array assignment.

If, after assigning an array variable to a superclass array variable (as in the prior example of assigning the button array to a component array variable) you then try to place a different subclass instance into the array, an `ArrayStoreException` is thrown. To continue the prior example, an `ArrayStoreException` would be thrown if you tried to place a `Canvas` into the `components` array. Even though the `components` array is declared as an array of `Component` objects, because the `components` array specifically refers to an array of `Button` objects, `Canvas` objects cannot be stored in the array. This is a run-time exception as the actual assignment is legal from the perspective of a type-safe compiler.

Checking for Array Equality

Checking for equality between two arrays can be done in one of two manners depending upon the type of equality you are looking for. Are the array variables pointing to the same place in memory and thus pointing to the same array? Or are the elements of two arrays comparatively equivalent?

Checking for two references to the same memory space is done with the double equal sign operator `==`. For example, the prior `components` and `buttons` variables would be equal in this case since one is a reference to the other:

```
components == buttons // true
```

However, if you compare an array to a cloned version of that array then these would not be equal as far as `==` goes. Since these arrays have the same elements but exist in different memory space, they are different. In order to have a clone of an array be "equal" to the original, you must use the `equals()` method of the `java.util.Arrays` class.

```
String[] clone = (String[]) strarray.clone();
boolean b1 = Arrays.equals(strarray, clone); // Yes, they're equal
```

This will check for equality with each element. In the case where the arguments are arrays of objects, the equals() method of each object will be used to check for equality. Arrays.equals() works for arrays that are not clones, too. For more information on the Arrays class, see Chapter 13.

Array Reflection

If for some reason you are ever unsure whether an argument or object is an array, you can retrieve the object's Class object and ask it. The isArray() method of the Class class will tell you. Once you know you have an array, you can ask the getComponentType() method of Class what type of array you actually have. The getComponentType() method returns null if the isArray() method returns false. Otherwise, the Class type of the element is returned. You can recursively call isArray() if the array is multidimensional. It will still have only one component type. In addition, you can use the getLength() method of the Array class found in the java.lang.reflect package to discover the length of the array.

To demonstrate, Listing 2-3 shows that the argument to the main() method is an array of java.lang.String objects where the length is the number of command-line arguments specified:

Listing 2-3. Using reflection to check array type and length.
```java
public class ArrayReflection {
  public static void main (String args[]) {
    printType(args);
  }
  private static void printType (Object object) {
    Class type = object.getClass();
    if (type.isArray()) {
      Class elementType = type.getComponentType();
      System.out.println("Array of: " + elementType);
      System.out.println(" Length: " + Array.getLength(object));
    }
  }
}
```

> **NOTE** *If* printType() *was to be called with the previously defined* buttons *and* components *variables, each would state that the array is of the* java.awt.Button *type.*

If you don't use the isArray() and getComponentType() methods and you try to print the Class type for an array, you'll get a string that includes a [followed by a letter and the class name (or no class name if a primitive). For instance, if you tried to print out the type variable in the printType() method above, you would get class [Ljava.lang.String; as the output.

In addition to asking an object if it is an array and what type of array it is, you can also create arrays at runtime with the java.lang.reflect.Array class. This might be helpful to create generic utility routines that perform array tasks such as size doubling. (We'll return to that shortly.)

To create a new array, use the newInstance() method of Array, which comes in two varieties. For single dimension arrays you would normally use the simpler version, which acts like the statement new type[length] and returns the array as an object: public static Object newInstance(Class type, int length). For instance, the following creates an array with room for five integers:

```
int array[] = (int[])Array.newInstance(int.class, 5);
```

> **NOTE** *To specify the* Class *object for a primitive, just add* .class *to the end of the primitive type name. You can also use the* TYPE *variable of the wrapper classes, like* Integer.TYPE.

The second variety of the newInstance() method requires the dimensions to be specified as an array of integers: public static Object newInstance(Class type, int dimensions[]). In the simplest case of creating a single dimension array, you would create an array with only one element. In other words, if you were to create the same array of five integers, instead of passing the integer value of 5, you would need to create an array of the single element 5 to pass along to the newInstance() method:

```
int dimensions[] = {5};
int array[] = (int[])Array.newInstance(int.class, dimensions);
```

As long as you only need to create rectangular arrays, you can fill up the dimensions array with each array length. For example, the following is the equivalent of creating a 3 × 4 array of integers:

```
int dimensions[] = {3, 4};
int array[][] = (int[][])Array.newInstance(int.class, dimensions);
```

If, however, you need to create a non-rectangular array, you would need to call the newInstance() method several times. The first call would define the length of the outer array and would have what looks like a funny-looking class argument (float[].class for an array of floats). Each subsequent call would define the length of each inner array. For instance, the following demonstrates how to create an array of floats where the inner arrays are sized like a set of bowling pins: the first row with one element, the second with two, the third with three, and the fourth with four. To help you visualize this, recall the triangular array shown earlier in Figure 2-4.

```
float bowling[][] = (float[][])Array.newInstance(float[].class, 4);
for (int i=0; i<4; i++) {
  bowling[i] = (float[])Array.newInstance(float.class, i+1);
}
```

Once you've created your arrays at runtime, you can also get and set the elements of the array. This isn't normally done unless your square bracket keys on your keyboard aren't working or you're working in a dynamic programming environment where the array names were unknown when the program was created. As shown in Table 2-2, the Array class has a series of getter and setter methods for getting and setting the array elements. Which method you use depends upon the type of array you're working with.

Table 2-2. Array Getter and Setter Methods

GETTER METHODS	SETTER METHODS
get(Object array, int index)	set(Object array, int index, Object value)
getBoolean(Object array, int index)	setBoolean(Object array, int index, boolean value)
getByte(Object array, int index)	setByte(Object array, int index, byte value)
getChar(Object array, int index)	setChar(Object array, int index, char value)
getDouble(Object array, int index)	setDouble(Object array, int index, double value)
getFloat(Object array, int index)	setFloat(Object array, int index, float value)
getInt(Object array, int index)	setInt(Object array, int index, int value)
getLong(Object array, int index)	setLong(Object array, int index, long value)
getShort(Object array, int index)	setShort(Object array, int index, short value)

NOTE *You can always use the* get() *and* set() *methods. If the array is one of primitives, the return value of the* get() *method or the value argument to the* set() *method would be wrapped into the wrapper class for the primitive type, as in an* Integer *with an* int *array.*

Listing 2-4 provides a complete example of how to create, fill up, and display information about an array. Square brackets are used only in the main() method declaration.

Listing 2-4. Using reflection to create, fill, and display an array.

```java
import java.lang.reflect.Array;
import java.util.Random;
public class ArrayCreate {
  public static void main (String args[]) {
    Object array = Array.newInstance(int.class, 3);
    printType(array);
    fillArray(array);
    displayArray(array);
  }
  private static void printType (Object object) {
    Class type = object.getClass();
    if (type.isArray()) {
      Class elementType = type.getComponentType();
      System.out.println("Array of: " + elementType);
      System.out.println("Array size: " + Array.getLength(object));
    }
  }
  private static void fillArray(Object array) {
    int length = Array.getLength(array);
    Random generator = new Random(System.currentTimeMillis());
    for (int i=0; i<length; i++) {
      int random = generator.nextInt();
      Array.setInt(array, i, random);
    }
  }
  private static void displayArray(Object array) {
    int length = Array.getLength(array);
    for (int i=0; i<length; i++) {
      int value = Array.getInt(array, i);
      System.out.println("Position: " + i + ", value: " + value);
    }
  }
}
```

When run, the output will look like the following (although the random numbers will differ):

```
Array of: int
Array size: 3
Position: 0, value: -54541791
Position: 1, value: -972349058
Position: 2, value: 1224789416
```

Let's return to our earlier example of creating a method that doubles the size of an array. Now that you know how to get an array's type, you can create a method that will double the size of any type of array. This method ensures that we have an array before getting its length and type. It then doubles the size of a new instance before copying over the original set of elements.

```
static Object doubleArray(Object original) {
  Object returnValue = null;
  Class type = original.getClass();
  if (type.isArray()) {
    int length = Array.getLength(original);
    Class elementType = type.getComponentType();
    returnValue = Array.newInstance(elementType, length*2);
    System.arraycopy(original, 0, returnValue, 0, length);
  }
  return returnValue;
}
```

Character Arrays

One last thing to mention before we wrap up our look at Java arrays: unlike C and C++, character arrays in Java are not strings. While you can easily go back and forth between a String and a char[] with the String constructor (which takes an array of char objects) and the toCharArray() method of String, they are definitely different.

Byte arrays are another case though. While they too are not strings, trying to go back and forth between a byte[] and a String involves a bit of work, since strings in Java are Unicode-based and 16 bits wide. You need to tell the String constructor what the encoding scheme is. Table 2-3 shows the primary available encoding schemes with the 1.3 platform. For a list of the extended set, see the online list at http://java.sun.com/j2se/1.3/docs/guide/intl/encoding.doc.html. These vary by JDK version.

Table 2-3. Primary Byte-to-Character Encoding Schemes

NAME	DESCRIPTION
ASCII	American Standard Code for Information Interchange
Cp1252	Windows Latin-1
ISO8859_1	ISO 8859-1, Latin alphabet No. 1
UnicodeBig	Sixteen-bit Unicode Transformation Format, big-endian byte order, with byte-order mark
UnicodeBigUnmarked	Sixteen-bit Unicode Transformation Format, big-endian byte order
UnicodeLittle	Sixteen-bit Unicode Transformation Format, little-endian byte order, with byte-order mark
UnicodeLittleUnmarked	Sixteen-bit Unicode Transformation Format, little-endian byte order
UTF16	Sixteen-bit Unicode Transformation Format, byte order specified by a mandatory initial byte-order mark
UTF8	Eight-bit Unicode Transformation Format

If you do specify an encoding, you must place the call to the `String` constructor within a try-catch block because an `UnsupportedEncodingException` can be thrown if the specified encoding scheme is invalid.

If you are working only with ASCII characters, you really don't have to worry much here. Passing a `byte[]` to the `String` constructor without any encoding scheme argument uses the platform's default encoding, which is sufficient. Of course, to be safe, you can always just pass "ASCII" as the scheme.

> **NOTE** *To check the default on your platform, look at the "file.encoding" system property.*

Summary

Arrays in Java seem easy to work with, but there are many things to be aware of to fully utilize their capabilities. While basic array declaration and usage can be considered simple, there are different things to be concerned about when working with arrays of primitives and objects, as well as multidimensional arrays. Array initialization doesn't have to be complicated, but throw in anonymous arrays and things get more involved.

Once you have an array, it takes a little thought to figure out how best to work with it. You need to take special care when passing arrays to methods as they are passed by reference. If you outgrow the original array size, you'll need to make a copy with additional space. Array cloning lets you pass around a copy without worrying about the idiosyncrasies of the `final` keyword. When assigning arrays to other variables, be careful not to run across an `ArrayStoreException` as it can be ugly to deal with at runtime. Equality checking of arrays can involve either checking for the same memory area or checking for equivalently valued elements. Through the magic of Java reflection, you can manipulate objects that happen to be arrays. The last thing you learned in this chapter was how to convert between byte arrays and strings, and how byte arrays are not strings by default as they are in other languages.

In the next chapter, we'll explore the many facets of working with vectors in Java. We'll learn about the inner workings of vectors and how best to deal with concerns like type safety.

The Vector and Stack Classes

Arrays are good when you know the size of your collection and when all the elements in a collection are of the same type. However, what are you to do if you need a dynamically growing structure but you don't necessarily know the final size in advance? This is where the Vector class comes in handy. In addition to the Vector class, Java provides a Stack class for the familiar last-in, first-out data structure.

Figure 3-1 shows the current hierarchy for these two classes. With the Java 2 platform, version 1.2 release, this structure changed considerably with the introduction of the Collections Framework. Figure 3-2 shows the original, more simplified look of the class hierarchy from both Java 1.0 and Java 1.1. The 1.3 release remains the same as the 1.2 release shown in Figure 3-1.

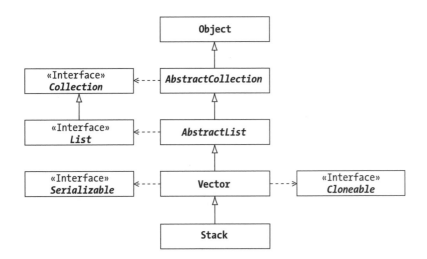

Figure 3-1. The Vector and Stack class hierarchy.

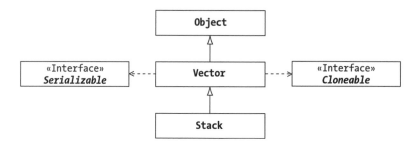

Figure 3-2. The Java 1.0/1.1 Vector and Stack class hierarchy.

Vector Basics

You can think of Java vectors as dynamically sized arrays with synchronized access. They prove to be very useful if you don't know the size of the array in advance, or you just need one that can change sizes over the lifetime of a program. Any object can be stored within a vector: these items are called *elements*. The one exception is that primitive data elements may not be stored in vectors, but since they aren't objects, this isn't really an exception.

The Vector class provides multiple constructors and many different methods to create, access, and modify the data structure. These are listed in Table 3-1.

Table 3-1. Summary of the Vector Class

VARIABLE/METHOD NAME	VERSION	DESCRIPTION
Vector()	1.0 / 1.2	Constructs an empty vector of the appropriate initial size.
capacityIncrement	1.0	Size increment for increasing vector capacity.
elementCount	1.0	Number of elements within a vector.
elementData	1.0	Internal buffer for vector elements.
modCount	1.2	From AbstractList: used by iterator to check for concurrent modifications.
add()	1.2	Adds an element to a vector.
addAll()	1.2	Adds a collection of elements to a vector.
addElement()	1.0	Adds an element to the end of a vector.
capacity()	1.0	Returns the capacity of an internal buffer for a vector.
clear()	1.2	Clears all elements from a vector.
clone()	1.0	Creates a clone of a vector.
contains()	1.0	Checks if the vector contains an element.

containsAll()	1.2	Checks if the vector contains a collection of elements.
copyInto()	1.0	Copies elements of the vector into an array.
elementAt()	1.0	Returns an element at a specific position.
elements()	1.0	Returns an object from the vector that allows all of the vector's keys to be visited.
ensureCapacity()	1.0	Ensures the capacity of an internal buffer is at least a certain size.
equals()	1.2	Checks for equality with another object.
firstElement()	1.0	Returns the first element within a vector.
get()	1.2	Returns an element at a specific position.
hashCode()	1.2	Returns the computed hash code for a vector.
indexOf()	1.0	Searches for an element within a vector
insertElementAt()	1.0	Inserts an element into the vector.
isEmpty()	1.0	Checks if the vector is empty.
iterator()	1.2	Returns an object from the vector that allows all of the vector's elements to be visited.
lastElement()	1.0	Returns the last element within a vector.
lastIndexOf()	1.0	Searches from the end of a vector for an element.
listIterator()	1.2	Returns an object from the vector that allows all of the vector's elements to be visited sequentially.
remove()	1.2	Clears a specific element from the vector.
removeAll()	1.2	Clears a collection of elements from the vector.
removeAllElements()	1.0	Clears all elements from the vector.
removeElement()	1.0	Clears a specific element from the vector.
removeElementAt()	1.0	Clears an element at specific position from the vector.
removeRange()	1.2	Clears a range of elements from the vector.
retainAll()	1.2	Removes all elements from the vector not in another collection.
set()	1.2	Changes an element at a specific position within the vector.
setElementAt()	1.0	Changes an element at a specific position within the vector.
setSize()	1.0	Changes the size of an internal vector buffer.
size()	1.0	Returns the number of elements in a vector.
subList()	1.2	Returns a portion of the vector.
toArray()	1.2	Returns the elements of a vector as an array.
toString()	1.0	Converts vector contents into a string.
trimToSize()	1.0	Trims the capacity of internal buffer to actual size.

With the Java 1.0.x and Java 1.1.x versions of this class, many of the methods were flagged as final. That is no longer the case. You can now subclass Vector and override all methods.

Creating Vectors

You can use one of four constructors to create a Vector. For the first three constructors, an empty vector is created with an initial capacity of ten unless explicitly specified. When that space becomes too small, the vector will double in size unless a different capacity increment is specified.

```
public Vector()
public Vector(int initialCapacity)
public Vector(int initialCapacity, int capacityIncrement)
```

The reason for the different constructors is basically performance. If you know the approximate size beforehand, try to size the vector to that size to start. Otherwise, each time the vector size exceeds its capacity, a new internal array is created, which copies all the original elements to the larger new array. Creating a new array and copying the elements takes time, thus increasing the time it takes to add elements to the array. See the later section "Sizing Vectors" for more information on sizing and capacity.

The final constructor copies the object references in a different collection to initialize the vector:

```
public Vector(Collection c)
```

This effectively makes a shallow copy of the original collection. The new vector is sized to be 10% larger than the number of elements in the original collection.

Basically, you can convert the elements of any collection (that implements Collection) into a Vector. One specialty collection will be mentioned here, though. If you'd like to create a vector from an array, there is a helper method available: The asList() method of the Arrays class will create an object you can pass through to the Vector constructor, as shown here:

```
Vector v = new Vector(Arrays.asList(array));
```

You'll learn more about the Collection interface in Chapter 7 at the beginning of Part Two of this book.

Adding Elements

Once you've created the vector, the next step is to put elements in it. There are six different ways to do this.

Adding at the End

The first set involves the single-argument add() and addElement() methods as you see here:

```
public boolean add(Object element)
public void addElement(Object element)
```

These methods are essentially the same—both add the element to the end of the vector. The difference is that add() will always return true, while addElement() has no return value.

To demonstrate how you might use these methods, the following will fill up an array with all the elements passed from the command line:

```
import java.util.Vector;
public class InsertVector {
  public static void main (String args[]) {
    Vector v = new Vector();
    for (int i=0, n=args.length; i<n; i++) {
      v.add(args[i]);
    }
  }
}
```

> **TIP** *Since an* Object *can be a null reference, the element added to a vector can also be null.*

Adding in the Middle

While the first two methods always add elements to the end of the vector, there are times when you wish to insert elements at arbitrary positions and move the remaining elements down. There are two methods for doing this, shown below, with arguments in the opposite order:

```
public void add(int index, Object element)
public void insertElementAt(Object element, int index)
```

The reason for this duplicity is the reworking of the Vector class to implement the List interface so that it is part of the Collections Framework.

> **NOTE** *An* ArrayIndexOutOfBoundsException *will be thrown if you try to add an element to a negative position or at some point beyond the last position of the vector. Adding an element at an arbitrary position beyond the end of the vector doesn't cause the vector to resize, as some people might think.*

While these methods are useful for inserting elements into the middle of the vector, the operation is not cheap in terms of performance. If you find yourself doing this frequently, the Vector may not be the best data structure to use. Consider using a LinkedList instead, discussed in Chapter 9.

> **TIP** *Like array indices, the index for the first element of a vector is zero.*

When inserting an element into the middle of a vector, as shown in Figure 3-3, the index represents the position to place the new element. All elements from that position forward will have their original index increased by one.

Before

First	Second	Third	Fourth

```
vector.add(2,"Inserted");
```

After

First	Second	Inserted	Third	Fourth

Figure 3-3. Inserting an element into the middle of a vector.

NOTE *Don't confuse the* add() *and* set() *methods. The* set() *method is used to replace the element at a specific position. We'll look at that method shortly in the "Replacing Elements" section.*

Adding Another Collection

The last set of methods to add elements to a vector are both named addAll():

```
public boolean addAll(Collection c)
public boolean addAll(int index, Collection c)
```

They involve copying all the elements from another object into the vector. The elements are copied from a Collection. They can be added either at the end of the current vector or somewhere in the middle, where the index acts just like the one in the add() and insertElementAt() pair.

The order in which the vector adds the elements from the collection is the same order in which the iterator() method for the collection returns the elements. Like the add() and insertElementAt() pair, adding elements into the middle of a vector with addAll() is costly and involves moving the internal elements to their new position. However, one call to addAll() is less costly than multiple add() or insertElementAt() calls as the elements are moved all at once.

WARNING *If the index is invalid (less than zero or beyond the end) an* ArrayIndexOutOfBoundsException *will be thrown. It is also possible to get a* ConcurrentModificationException *thrown, which you'll learn more about in Chapter 7 when we discuss iterators.*

Vectors of Primitives

Because vectors can only store objects, you need to do a bit of extra work if you wish to use primitives and vectors. You must create an instance of the appropriate wrapper class before storing a primitive value within the vector. Table 3-2 shows the familiar wrapper classes for the primitive types. In most cases, the wrapper class name is just the primitive type name capitalized.

Table 3-2. Primitive Wrapper Classes

PRIMITIVE TYPE	WRAPPER CLASS
byte	Byte
short	Short
int	Integer
long	Long
float	Float
double	Double
char	Character
boolean	Boolean

The following shows how one would place the int values one through ten into a Vector as Integer objects.

```
import java.util.Vector;
public class PrimVector {
  public static void main (String args[]) {
    Vector v = new Vector();
    for (int i=1; i<=10; i++) {
      v.add(new Integer(i));
    }
  }
}
```

Then, when getting elements out of the vector, you would need to do the reverse to get back the primitive value. To follow through with the example above, this would involve calling the intValue() method of Integer to get its numerical value as an int.

Printing Vectors

Like all objects in Java, you can call the `toString()` method of a `Vector`, as well:

```
public String toString()
```

One doesn't normally call it directly, instead it gets called as the result of including a vector as an argument to the `println()` method of `System.out`. In the case of a vector, the string generated is a comma-delimited list of the `toString()` results for each element it contains, which is arranged in index order and surrounded by square brackets ([ ]).

If you were to include a line with `System.out.println(v);` in the preceding `PrimVector` program, the following line would be generated:

```
[1, 2, 3, 4, 5, 6, 7, 8, 9, 10]
```

Removing Elements

Like adding elements to a vector, there are many, many different ways to remove them as discussed in the following sections.

Removing All Elements

The simplest removal methods are those that clear out all of a vector's elements: `clear()` and `removeAllElements()`.

```
public void clear()
public void removeAllElements()
```

When you remove all the elements from a vector, the capacity does not change.

Removing Single Elements

Aside from clearing out an entire vector, you can also remove an element at a specific position with `remove()` or `removeElementAt()`:

```
public Object remove(int index)
public void removeElementAt(int index)
```

As long as the index is valid (not less than zero or beyond the end, both of which trigger the throwing of an `ArrayIndexOutOfBoundsException`), the vector capacity stays the same. However, the internal contents shift to fill the vacated space, placing a null element at the end and decreasing the size by one. The difference between the two methods is that `remove()` returns the object removed, while `removeElementAt()` doesn't.

If you don't know where an element is and you just want to remove it, you can pass the object to evict to either of the `remove()` or `removeElement()` methods:

```
public boolean remove(Object element)
public boolean removeElement(Object element)
```

> **NOTE** *The* `equals()` *method is used to check for element equality.*

Functionally equivalent, both methods remove the first instance of the object from the vector. These methods also shift the internal contents to fill the hole left by removing the middle. Both methods return a boolean value to report the success of finding the element to remove. Like the `add()` and `insertElementAt()` methods, there are two because the `Vector` class was reworked to implement the `List` interface.

Removing Another Collection

While the `remove()` and `removeElement()` methods support removal of the first instance of an element, if you find you want to remove all instances of an element, the `removeAll()` method comes in handy:

```
public boolean removeAll(Collection c)
```

The `removeAll()` method takes a `Collection` as an argument, possibly another vector, and removes all instances from the source vector of each element in the collection.

For example, the following helper method is given a vector and an element to remove all instances of the element from the vector:

```
boolean removeAll(Vector v, Object e) {
  Vector v1 = new Vector();
  v1.add(e);
  return v.removeAll(v1);
}
```

This will create a new vector with that one element and then call `removeAll()` to rid the vector of all instances of the element.

The `removeAll()` method is not limited to single elements collections. The collection of elements to remove can be any size. Like the other removal methods, the size of the vector changes. In the case of `removeAll()`, the size changes for each removal from the vector, which causes the internal contents to shift repeatedly if you remove many elements. If you find this happening, perhaps a vector is not the best data structure to use. The `LinkedList` class introduced with the Collection Framework would then be the better data structure.

> **TIP** *If you don't want to remove the first or all instances of an element, you'll have to find the specific position of the element you do want to remove with one of the methods described later in the "Finding Elements" section.*

Retaining Another Collection

The `retainAll()` method is like `removeAll()`, but basically works in the opposite direction:

```
public boolean retainAll(Collection c)
```

In other words, only those elements within the collection argument are kept within the vector. Everything else is removed instead.

Figure 3-4 may help you visualize the difference between `removeAll()` and `retainAll()`. The contents of the starting vector are the first five ordinal numbers repeated a second time. The acting vector for removal and retention consists of the elements 2nd and 3rd.

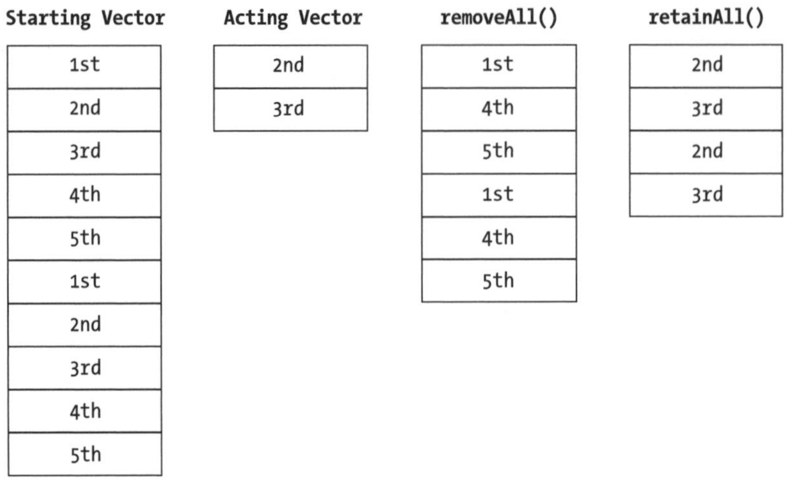

Starting Vector	Acting Vector	removeAll()	retainAll()
1st	2nd	1st	2nd
2nd	3rd	4th	3rd
3rd		5th	2nd
4th		1st	3rd
5th		4th	
1st		5th	
2nd			
3rd			
4th			
5th			

Figure 3-4. The removeAll() method versus the retainAll() method.

Removing a Range of Elements

The last of the removal methods, removeRange(), is protected and only directly callable if you subclass vector:

```
protected void removeRange(int fromIndex, int toIndex)
```

It permits you to remove a whole set of items from the middle of a vector while performing only one shift of all the remaining elements.

Replacing Elements

A vector supports two nearly identical methods, set() and setElementAt(), both of which replace individual elements in an array:

```
public Object set(int index, Object element)
public void setElementAt(Object obj, int index)
```

Both methods take arguments (in different order) of the index and object to replace. The set() method also returns the object being replaced. If the index is invalid, an ArrayIndexOutOfBoundsException will be thrown.

> **TIP** *To help you remember the argument order, the* set() *method works more like an array, where the index is first and what the element is being set to is last.*

Sizing Vectors

So far we've discussed how to modify the contents of the vector, either by adding, removing, or replacing elements. During that discussion, there was mention of storage space for the vector with regards to measurements of *size* and *capacity*. While you may think of a vector as a dynamically growing array, the vector works internally with these two very different length amounts. It is now time to look at these measurements in more detail.

Storage Size

The first length is like the length of an array and is known as the size. It represents the number of elements currently stored in the vector. You retrieve this setting with the size() method and change it with the setSize() method:

```
public int size()
public void setSize(int newSize)
```

If you make the size smaller than the current number of elements, the vector drops elements from the end. Increasing the size adds null elements to the end. Calling setSize(0) removes all elements from the vector. If you set the size to zero or have no elements in the vector, the isEmpty() method returns true:

```
public boolean isEmpty()
```

Storage Capacity

Capacity represents the number of elements a vector can hold before it needs to resize any internal data structures. For performance reasons, it's best to reduce the number of times the internal structure needs to be resized. However, if the capacity is too large, memory goes to waste. To find out the current capacity of a vector, ask by calling the capacity() method:

```
public int capacity()
```

If the size of a vector needs to be larger than the current capacity, the vector will grow dynamically. If you are about to add a large number of elements, it is best to see if the capacity is large enough before adding them, rather than allowing the vector to do the resizing for you. You can use the `ensureCapacity()` method to make sure a vector is large enough before adding elements:

```
public void ensureCapacity(int minCapacity)
```

If the capacity is already large enough, nothing happens. If it isn't, the capacity grows.

When the capacity of a vector needs to grow, how large it grows is determined by how the vector was created. By default, the vector doubles in size when necessary. If, however, you want to grow the capacity in larger or smaller increments, you can set a fixed size as the increment amount. This works out well when you set the initial capacity to be a large amount but you want to increase the capacity in smaller increments when the initial capacity is exceeded. Once you are done adding elements to a vector, it is best to call the `trimToSize()` method:

```
public void trimToSize()
```

This will remove any excess capacity and reduce the capacity to the vector's size.

To help you visualize how size and capacity are related and how this affects the internal length of the vector's data structure, see Figure 3-5. This shows a vector created with the constructor of `new Vector(5, 3)` and also shows what happens when a sixth element is added.

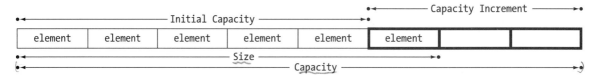

Figure 3-5. A growth chart representing the internal lengths of a vector.

Vector Immutability

If there comes a time when the vector's contents are stable, you may wish to make the vector read-only—this will prevent accidental changes to its contents. The Collections class (described in Part Two, "The Collections Framework") provides this capability with the public static List unmodifiableList(List list) method. Since Vector is a subclass of List, you can pass a Vector as the argument to the method and get a read-only List back, as shown here:

```
Vector v = new Vector();
// fill vector
List l = Collections.unmodifiableList(v);
```

If you truly need an immutable structure, however, it is better to start with one of the structures from the Collections Framework, such as ArrayList. If you are making a vector read-only, access will be unnecessarily synchronized.

> **NOTE** *We'll visit the* List *interface and the* ArrayList *class more fully in Chapter 9.*

Vector Operations

Now that our vector is filled and sized properly, what can we do with it? The Vector class has methods for fetching, finding, and copying, among other secondary tasks we'll also consider.

Fetching Elements

Once you place your elements into a vector, you need to retrieve them. You can retrieve elements by index or position.

Getting by Index

Like most functionality in the Vector class, there are two methods that do this: get() and elementAt(). Both of these methods allow you to fetch the element at a specific index, which is indexed like an array, starting from zero, as shown here:

```
public Object get(int index)
public Object elementAt(int index)
```

When getting an element from a vector, the element is always returned as an `Object`. You need to cast it to the appropriate type in order to work with it as the more specific type. Until Java supports parameterized types, vectors are not restricted to store only certain types. Instead, you always have to work with objects. The following example demonstrates this with a simple `String` object:

```
Vector v = new Vector();
v.add("Hello");
String s = (String)v.get(0);
```

If you wish to visit every element in a vector, you can use a for-loop like this one:

```
Vector v = . . .
for (int i=0, n= v.size(); i<n; i++) {
  process(v.get(i));
}
```

Getting by Position

The `firstElement()` and `lastElement()` helper methods get the element at position 0 and also at the end (position `size-1`):

```
public Object firstElement()
public Object lastElement()
```

Enumerating through the Elements

While the preceding example provides a relatively quick way to go through each element, it isn't particularly flexible if you later decide to change your data structure to something other than a `Vector`. A more flexible way is to use the `Enumeration` returned from the `elements()` method:

```
public Enumeration elements()
```

We'll look at `Enumeration` more in the next chapter. In short, it has two methods: `hasMoreElements()` and `nextElement()`. The first checks to see if there are any more elements in the vector, while the second returns the next element if it is there. You'll get a `NoSuchElementException` thrown if you call `nextElement()` after `hasMoreElements()` returns false.

To perform the same operation to visit all elements of a vector, you can use the following construct:

```
Vector v = . . .
Enumeration e = v.elements();
while (e.hasMoreElements()) {
  process(e.nextElement());
}
```

> **NOTE** *Yet another way to process all the elements of a vector is to copy everything into an array and then loop through the array. We'll look at this later.*

Inherited Methods from AbstractList

When the Java 2 Collections Framework was introduced, the superclass of Vector was changed from Object to AbstractList (which subclasses AbstractCollection, a subclass of Object). Besides the obvious methods inherited from Object, Vector inherits three methods from AbstractList that are not overridden: one iterator() and two listIterator() versions. These methods return an Iterator and ListIterator, respectively:

```
public Iterator iterator()
public ListIterator listIterator()
public ListIterator listIterator(int index)
```

Both interfaces function like the Enumeration interface and let you walk through the elements of a collection.

We'll look more closely at the interfaces in Part Two, "The Collections Framework," but here's the same loop with an Iterator, through all the elements. Basically, the Iterator and Enumeration interfaces are nearly identical with slightly different method names, as shown:

```
Vector v = . . .
Iterator i = v.iterator();
while (i.hasNext()) {
  process(e.next());
}
```

A `ListIterator` permits you to go forward and backward through the elements, too.

Multidimensional Vectors (Vectors of Vectors)

No special support is needed to provide multidimensional vectors. Since each element of a vector can be any object type, simply create the appropriate structure first: one vector for the first dimension, and individual vectors for each element of the second dimension. For instance, in order to create a vector of four vectors (where each internal vector contains four elements), you would need to create five vectors before ever putting anything inside. Be sure you truly need the dynamic growth nature of vectors before doing this—there is a lot of overhead involved here. The code also can look ugly when you fetch an element from a multidimensional vector. For instance, the following example would get the element at what might look like `array[3][2]`, if using an array:

```
MyType o = (MyType)((Vector)vector.elementAt(3)).elementAt(2);
```

Or, if you used the shorter named `get()` method:

```
MyType o = (MyType)((Vector)vector.get(3)).get(2);
```

Finding Elements

If, instead of fetching the element at a specific position, you just want to see if an element is in the vector or where in the vector it is, this next set of methods will come in handy.

Checking for Existence

The `contains()` method is the simplest of the searching methods and reports if a specific element is within the vector:

```
public boolean contains(Object element)
```

Checking for Position

If, instead of seeing only whether an element is in the vector, you want to see where it is in the vector, that's where the `indexOf()` methods come in:

```
public int indexOf(Object element)
public int indexOf(Object element, int index)
```

Starting either at the beginning or from some other position, you can find out where in the vector the next instance of a specific element is located.

The indexOf() method uses the equals() method internally to find out if two elements are the same. The equals() method will be called to compare the argument with the vector element. If the element is not found, indexOf() will return –1.

Checking for Position from End

The lastIndexOf() method allows you to search in reverse order from the end or some other position, rather than searching forward from the beginning:

```
public int lastIndexOf(Object element)
public int lastIndexOf(Object element, int index)
```

These methods also use equals() (discussed in the preceding section) to check for equality and return –1 if not found. While the methods start searching from the end, the index reported is from the beginning. To demonstrate the use of indexOf() and lastIndexOf(), the following program in Listing 3-1 reports "where's Waldo" as well as a couple of other names.

Listing 3-1. Finding elements in a vector.

```
import java.util.Vector;
public class FindVector {
  static String members[] =
    {"Ralph", "Waldo", "Emerson",
     "Henry", "David", "Thoreau",
     "Walden", "Pond",
     "Thoreau", "Institute"};
  public static void main (String args[]) {
    Vector v = new Vector();
    for (int i=0, n=members.length; i<n; i++) {
      v.add(members[i]);
    }
    System.out.println(v);
    System.out.println("Contains Society?: " +
      v.contains("Society"));
    System.out.println("Contains Waldo?: " +
      v.contains("Waldo"));
    System.out.println("Where's Waldo?: " +
      v.indexOf("Waldo"));
```

```
    System.out.println("Where's Thoreau?: " +
      v.indexOf("Thoreau"));
    System.out.println("Where's Thoreau from end?: " +
      v.lastIndexOf("Thoreau"));
  }
}
```

Running the program in Listing 3-1 generates the following output:

```
[Ralph, Waldo, Emerson, Henry, David, Thoreau, Walden, Pond, Thoreau, Institute]
Contains Society?: false
Contains Waldo?: true
Where's Waldo?: 1
Where's Thoreau?: 5
Where's Thoreau from end?: 8
```

Notice that lastIndexOf() reports the position from the beginning, but starts at the end.

If you're interested in finding all the positions for a single element, you'll need to call indexOf() or lastIndexOf() multiple times. For instance, the following example allows you to separately process each element contained within the vector that was equal to some value:

```
Vector v = . . .;
Object value = . . .;
int index = 0;
int length = v.size();
while ((index < length) && (index >= 0)) {
  index = v.indexOf(value, index);
  if (index != -1) {
    process(v.get(index));
    index++;
  }
}
```

Checking for Collection Containment

The last of the searching methods is the containsAll() method:

```
public boolean containsAll(Collection c)
```

This method takes a `Collection` as its argument, quite possibly (though not necessarily) a `Vector`, and reports if the elements of the collection are a subset of the vector's elements. In other words, is each element of the collection also an element of the vector? The vector can contain other elements but the collection cannot or `containsAll()` will return false.

Copying and Cloning Vectors

If you need to make a copy of the elements of a vector, there are several different ways to go about it. You can either clone the vector, copy the elements into an array, or create a `List` from a subset of the elements. Which manner you use depends upon what you plan to do with the results.

Cloning a vector with clone() is like making a shallow copy of the vector, similar to calling the `Vector` constructor that accepts a `Collection`. A new vector is created with each object reference copied from the original vector. Because new copies of the objects they refer to are not made, all elements of the two vectors will effectively point to the same set of objects:

```
public Object clone()
```

Cloning is useful if you need to reorder a vector's elements while keeping the vector itself intact. For instance, the following example will clone a vector, then sort the elements of the vector copy.

```
Vector v1 = . . .;
Vector v2 = (Vector)v1.clone();
Collections.sort(v2);
```

If, instead of making a new `Vector` from an old one, you wish to convert the vector to an array, or at least access its elements as an array, you can use either the `toArray()` or `copyInto()` methods:

```
public Object[] toArray()
public Object[] toArray(Object[] a)
public void copyInto(Object[] anArray)
```

Effectively, the three methods (`copyInto()` plus two versions of `toArray()`) do the same thing. However, they are definitely not just renamed versions of the same thing, as explained next.

Copying the Simple Way

The simplest method to call is Object[ ] toArray(). This creates an array of the proper size, fills it with all the elements in the vector, and returns it. This sounds easy enough, but there is a catch. It returns an Object [ ]. Every time you need to get an element out of the array, you need to cast it to the appropriate type. When all elements of a vector are the same type, it is easier for you to work with an array of that specific type.

This is where the second version of toArray() comes in handy: Object[] toArray(Object[] a). With this version of toArray(), you pass as an argument an array of the appropriate type, such as a String[ ]. The method will check to see if the size is large enough for the vector contents. If it is, it fills up the beginning of the array, setting the rest of the elements to null. If it isn't, a new array is created and sized to the current number of elements in the vector. The following example demonstrates the usage of the second version of toArray():

```
Vector v = . . .;
String array[] = new String[0];
array = (String[])v.toArray(array);
```

After calling toArray(), the array will be recreated to the proper size and filled with the vector elements. This effectively wastes the creation of the first version of the array. You can of course size the array right the first time:

```
Vector v = . . .;
String array[] = new String[v.size()];
array = (String[])v.toArray(array);
```

This works fine, but it looks a little awkward to assign the method's returned value to what is passed in as an argument, and also to require a cast. This is where the last method for converting a vector to an array comes in handy: copyInto().

Copying the Smart Way

Instead of requiring an assignment and cast, you can just pass the array into the copyInto() method:

```
Vector v = . . .;
String array[] = new String[v.size()];
v.copyInto(array);
```

Since you've sized it properly and have given it a proper type, this will always work—it will give you an array of the proper type, it doesn't require a cast, and it won't cause a created array to be discarded.

Some runtime exceptions can be thrown from this operation. In the event that the destination array is too small, an `ArrayIndexOutOfBoundsException` will be thrown. If the elements of the vector are not assignment-compatible with the array, an `ArrayStoreException` will be thrown.

Working with Subsets

The last of the cloning and copying methods, `subList()`, involves taking a subset of the vector's elements and referencing them from another `List`:

```
public List subList(int fromIndex, int toIndex)
```

The arguments to `subList()` are a from-index and a to-index. The from-index is inclusive and the to-index is exclusive. So, to copy an entire vector, call with the arguments 0 and `theVector.size()`.

The `subList()` method does not make a clone of the element references. Instead, the original `Vector` and the new `List` reference the same internal data structure. This means that if you replace the element at one of the positions within the sublist, it is replaced in the original vector, too. If you remove something from the sublist, it is also removed from the vector. See Figure 3-6 for a visual aid.

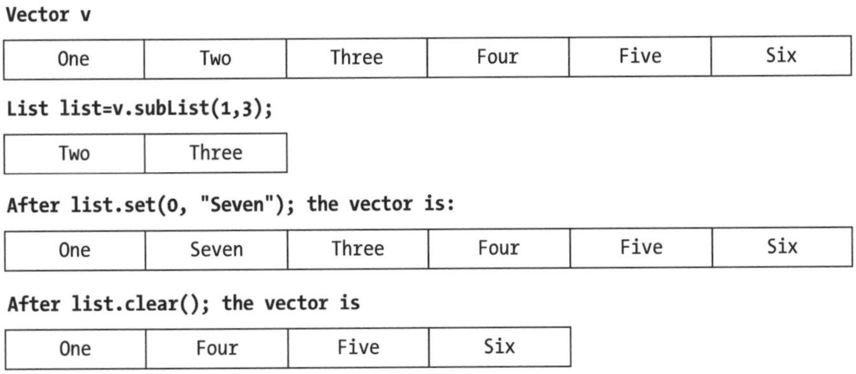

Vector v

| One | Two | Three | Four | Five | Six |

List list=v.subList(1,3);

| Two | Three |

After list.set(0, "Seven"); the vector is:

| One | Seven | Three | Four | Five | Six |

After list.clear(); the vector is

| One | Four | Five | Six |

Figure 3-6. A vector with a sublist.

> **NOTE** *The* List *methods used in Figure 3-6 work like their* Vector *counterparts because* Vector *is a specific type of* List. *Again, for more on the* List *interface, see Chapter 9.*

While changes work fine going from the sublist into the vector, changes to the vector are not necessarily reflected in the list. As long as elements are not added or removed from the vector (replacements are okay), the sublist will continue to work. However, if you modify the size of the vector and then try to access the sublist, a ConcurrentModificationException will be thrown.

Checking Vectors for Equality

The Vector class overrides the equals() method from Object to define equality for vectors, as shown here:

```
public boolean equals(Object o)
```

Two vectors are defined as equals if both vectors are the same size and all elements at corresponding positions are equal. In other words, they contain equivalent elements in identical order.

Hashing Vectors

Besides overriding the equals() method of Object, the Vector class also overrides the hashCode() method:

```
public int hashCode()
```

You'll learn more about hash codes in Chapter 5. Until then, the key requirement with the hashCode() method is that if two objects are equal, they must return the same hash code. Usually when you override equals(), you also need to override hashCode() to ensure this behavior.

Serializing Vector

The Vector class implements the Serializable interface, making instances of the class savable. However, this doesn't mean that all vectors are automatically serializable. A vector is only serializable if all the elements it contains are also serializable. If you try to serialize a vector with elements that are not serializable, you'll get a NotSerializableException thrown.

To demonstrate how to serialize and deserialize a vector, the following program in Listing 3-2 saves the command line arguments to a byte array and then gets them back.

Listing 3-2. Serializing a vector.

```
import java.io.*;
import java.util.*;
public class SaveVector {
  public static void main (String args[]) throws Exception {
    Vector v = new Vector(Arrays.asList(args));
    ByteArrayOutputStream baos = new ByteArrayOutputStream();
    ObjectOutputStream oos = new ObjectOutputStream(baos);
    oos.writeObject(v);
    oos.close();
    ByteArrayInputStream bais = new ByteArrayInputStream(baos.toByteArray());
    ObjectInputStream ois = new ObjectInputStream(bais);
    Vector v2 = (Vector)ois.readObject();
    Enumeration e = v.elements();
    while (e.hasMoreElements()) {
      System.out.println(e.nextElement());
    }
  }
}
```

If you were to run the program in Listing 3-2 with the command line, java SaveVector one two three, the following output would be generated:

```
one
two
three
```

Maintaining Listener Lists with a Vector

Vectors are commonly used to maintain lists of listeners in JavaBean components. Prior to the introduction of the EventListenerList class with Swing, if you wanted to maintain a list of listeners you either had to use the AWTEventMulticaster or roll your own list management and worry about synchronization issues. If your listener wasn't one of the predefined events in java.awt.event, you were forced to roll your own.

To demonstrate, let us define a mechanism to catch exceptions thrown from the run() method of a Runnable. Since you cannot alter an interface to have a method throw an exception that wasn't originally defined, you must notify interested parties through other means. In this particular case, the enclosing ThreadGroup can notify listeners, effectively allowing us to handle unchecked exceptions. So, let us define our own ThreadGroup that does this for us, and defines our own custom event and listener to be notified when the exception is thrown.

First define the event and event listener. As with all JavaBean-oriented events, the event object must subclass java.util.EventObject. Here we'll define a ThreadExceptionEvent, where the event source, a ThreadException, will be the exception thrown from the run() method:

```
import java.util.EventObject;
public class ThreadExceptionEvent extends EventObject {
  public ThreadExceptionEvent(ThreadException source) {
    super(source);
  }
  public Runnable getRunnable() {
    ThreadException source = (ThreadException)getSource();
    return (Runnable)source.getRunnable();
  }
}
```

The ThreadException needs to be a RuntimeException as run() cannot throw an exception that the compiler will force you to catch. While this might imply that you can just catch the exception yourself at the point at which you start the thread, remember that you don't call the run() method of a thread directly. Instead you indirectly startup the thread through its start() method as shown in Listing 3-3.

Listing 3-3. The ThreadException class.

```
public class ThreadException extends RuntimeException {
  Runnable runnable;
  Throwable exception;
  public ThreadException(Runnable r, Throwable t) {
    runnable = r;
    exception = t;
  }
  public ThreadException(Runnable r, Throwable t, String message) {
    super(message);
    runnable = r;
    exception = t;
  }
  public Runnable getRunnable() {
    return runnable;
  }
  public Throwable getSourceException() {
    return exception;
  }
}
```

Now that we have all of our thread event code defined, we can define the listener interface so you can catch the event/exception when it happens in the run() method. Here, we'll define an interface with an exceptionHappened() method that we can listen for.

```
import java.util.EventListener;
public interface ThreadListener extends EventListener {
  public void exceptionHappened(ThreadException e);
}
```

Okay, with the event and listener defined, we come to a point where we need a Vector. In order to catch unchecked exceptions, the thread must execute in a ThreadGroup where you can override the public void uncaughtException(Thread source, Throwable t) method. By overriding the method, you can notify any registered listeners.

The listener registration happens in a pair of add/remove listener methods. In this particular case, they are named addThreadExceptionListener() and removeThreadExceptionListener(). Notification of the registered listeners happens in our fireExceptionHappened() method. Be careful when managing listener lists: the set of list members who were listening when the event happened must be notified; and this set must *not* be modified while you are notifying the listeners. This means that either the add/remove methods modify a list in the background before they replace the listener list, or the notification method makes a copy before notifying the listeners. Our example here performs the latter.

The complete class definition for the ExceptionCatcherThread class is shown in Listing 3-4. Treat it as a Thread, even though it is a ThreadGroup.

Listing 3-4. The ExceptionCatcherThread class.

```java
import java.util.Vector;
public class ExceptionCatcherThread extends ThreadGroup {
  private Runnable runnable;
  private Thread runner;
  private Vector listenerList = new Vector(3);
  /* For autonumbering our group. */
  private static int threadInitNumber;
  private static synchronized int nextThreadNum() {
    return threadInitNumber++;
  }
  public ExceptionCatcherThread(Runnable r) {
    super("ExceptionCatcherThread-" + nextThreadNum());
    runnable = r;
    // Create thread in this group
    runner = new Thread(this, runnable);
  }
  public void start() {
    runner.start();
  }
  /* Listener registration methods */
  public synchronized void
      addThreadExceptionListener(ThreadListener t) {
    listenerList.add(t);
  }
  public synchronized void
      removeThreadExceptionListener(ThreadListener t) {
    listenerList.remove(t);
  }
  public void uncaughtException(Thread source, Throwable t) {
    fireExceptionHappened(t);
    super.uncaughtException(source, t);
  }
  protected void fireExceptionHappened(Throwable t) {
    ThreadException e = (t instanceof ThreadException) ?
      (ThreadException)t : new ThreadException(runnable, t);
    Vector l;
```

```
    synchronized(this) {
      l = (Vector) listenerList.clone();
    }
    for (int i = 0, n = listenerList.size(); i < n; i++) {
      ThreadListener tl = (ThreadListener) l.get(i);
      tl.exceptionHappened(e);
    }
  }
}
```

> **NOTE** *In the* uncaughtException() *method of* ExceptionCatcherThread,
> *you may wish to call* super.uncaughtException() *only if there are no lis-*
> *teners. As currently coded, it is always called.*

We can now create programs using the ExceptionCatcherThread class like a
Thread, register a ThreadListener with it, and deal with the exception handling
outside the run() method. Listing 3-5 demonstrates this capability. It provides a
JTextField, a JTextArea, and a JButton, as seen in Figure 3-7. You are to enter a
URL in the JTextField and then press ENTER. This kicks off a thread to load the
contents specified by the URL in the background, eventually making its way into
the JTextArea. While loading, the GUI is still responsive, which is the sole purpose
of the JButton. If the URL is invalid or an I/O exception happens (in the other
thread), the registered ThreadListener displays an error message popup.

Listing 3-5. A test program for throwing a thread exception.

```
import java.io.*;
import java.net.*;
import javax.swing.*;
import java.awt.*;
import java.awt.event.*;
public class ExceptionCatcherTester {
  public ExceptionCatcherTester() {
    JFrame f = new JFrame("Exception Catcher Tester");
    f.setDefaultCloseOperation(JFrame.EXIT_ON_CLOSE);
    final JTextArea textArea = new JTextArea();
    textArea.setEditable(false);
    JButton button = new JButton("Alive");
    ActionListener buttonListener = new ActionListener() {
      public void actionPerformed(ActionEvent e) {
        System.out.println("I'm Alive");
      }
    };
```

```
button.addActionListener(buttonListener);
final JTextField textField = new JTextField();
ActionListener textFieldListener = new ActionListener() {
  public void actionPerformed(final ActionEvent e) {
    // Code to load URL contents in separate thread
    Runnable r = new Runnable() {
      public void run() {
        textField.setEditable(false);
        String urlString = e.getActionCommand();
        try {
          System.out.println("Loading " + urlString);
          textArea.setText("");
          URL url = new URL(urlString);
          InputStream is = url.openStream();
          InputStreamReader isr = new InputStreamReader(is);
          BufferedReader br = new BufferedReader(isr);
          StringWriter sw = new StringWriter();
          char buf[] = new char[1024];
          int count;
          while ((count = br.read(buf, 0, 1024)) != -1) {
            sw.write(buf, 0, count);
          }
          System.out.println("Done Loading");
          updateTextArea(textArea, sw.toString());
        } catch (IOException e) {
          throw new ThreadException(this, e);
        } finally {
          textField.setEditable(true);
        }
      }
    };
    ExceptionCatcherThread runner = new ExceptionCatcherThread(r);
    // Listener in case of exception
    ThreadListener threadListener = new ThreadListener() {
      public void exceptionHappened(ThreadException e) {
        Throwable t = e.getSourceException();
        final String message = t.getClass().getName() +
          ": " + t.getMessage();
```

```
        Runnable r = new Runnable() {
          public void run() {
            JOptionPane.showMessageDialog(null, message);
          }
        };
        SwingUtilities.invokeLater(r);
      }
    };
    runner.addThreadExceptionListener(threadListener);
    runner.start();
  }
};
textField.addActionListener(textFieldListener);
Container c = f.getContentPane();
c.add(textField, BorderLayout.NORTH);
JScrollPane pane = new JScrollPane (textArea);
c.add(pane, BorderLayout.CENTER);
c.add(button, BorderLayout.SOUTH);
f.setSize(300, 300);
f.show();
}
public void updateTextArea(final JTextArea ta, final String text) {
  // Because file loading happening not blocking event thread
  // We have to set text area in event thread
  Runnable r = new Runnable() {
    public void run() {
      ta.setText(text);
      ta.setCaretPosition(0);
    }
  };
  SwingUtilities.invokeLater(r);
}
public static void main(String args[]) {
  new ExceptionCatcherTester();
}
}
```

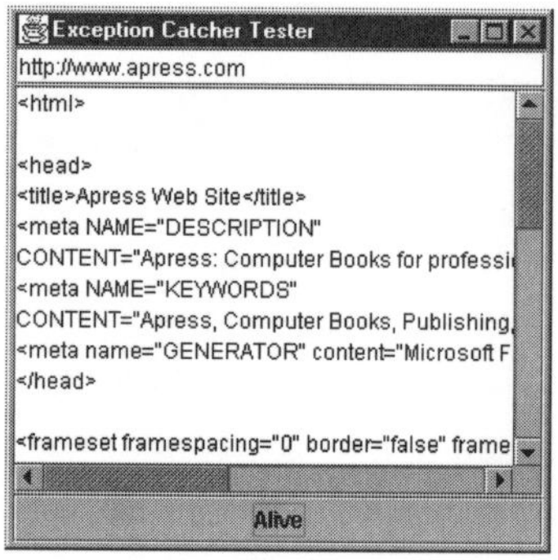

Figure 3-7. A vector listener list management example.

Vector Variables and Constants

The Vector class contains several variables you will likely never use, unless, for some reason, you decide to subclass Vector.

Variables Defined with Vector

Three variables, capacityIncrement, elementCount, and elementData, are defined as part of Vector and are used to maintain the internal buffer that stores the vector elements:

```
protected int capacityIncrement
protected int elementCount
protected Object[] elementData
```

The elements are stored within an object array named elementData. The size of the array, representing the number of elements in it, is stored within the variable elementCount. The actual size of the array is the capacity of the vector. Those array elements beyond the end (from elementCount to the array end) are defined to be null. When the internal structure hits capacity, it will grow in increments of capacityIncrement. If the capacity increment value is less than one, the capacity of the elementData object array doubles when needed.

Variables Defined with AbstractList

The variable modCount is the only one inherited from the parent AbstractList class:

```
protected transient int modCount
```

It is used both by the iterator returned from `iterator()` and when working with a sublist. If the underlying vector changes, the count is modified, which triggers a `ConcurrentModificationException` at the appropriate time. If you subclass vector and introduce any mechanism to modify the vector size, you'll need to increase this value accordingly. The `ConcurrentModificationException` will be discussed more in Chapter 7.

Stack Basics

Java defines a standard `Stack` class, but no queue. The Java class is like the abstract data type (ADT) stack, effectively restricting access to its data structure by permitting elements to be added and removed from only one end. It's a last-in, first-out (LIFO) data structure. You push elements onto and pop elements off of the stack. This is demonstrated in Figure 3-8.

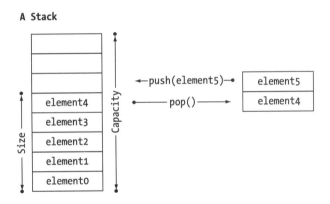

Figure 3-8. Stack visualization.

> **WARNING** *Because* `Stack` *is a subclass of* `Vector`, *it inherits all the methods of* `Vector`, *just as it does for removing elements. These methods should never be called as this would not guarantee the last-in, first-out behavior. The stack-vector relationship should be of the "has-a" variety instead of the "is-a" variety. Unfortunately, this likely will never change.*

The Stack class hasn't changed since first introduced into Java 1.0. Table 3-3 provides a listing of its methods.

Table 3-3. Summary of the Stack Class.

VARIABLE/METHOD NAME	VERSION	DESCRIPTION
Stack()	1.0	Constructs an empty stack.
empty()	1.0	Checks if the stack is empty.
peek()	1.0	Fetches an element at the top of the stack.
pop()	1.0	Removes an element from the top of the stack.
push()	1.0	Adds an element to the top of the stack.
search()	1.0	Checks if an element is on the stack.

Creating Stacks

There is only one constructor for the stack, the default no-argument version:

```
public Stack()
```

This will create a dynamically growable stack, initially sized for ten elements and doubling in capacity as necessary.

Operating Stacks

The stack class provides a variety of methods to support its last-in, first-out behavior.

Adding Elements

To add an element to a stack, call the push() method:

```
public Object push(Object element)
```

This adds the element to the top of the stack or to the end of the vector depending upon how you want to look at things.

Removing Elements

To remove an element from the stack you call the pop() method:

```
public Object pop()
```

This takes the element at the top of the stack, removes it, and returns it. If the stack is empty when called, you will get the runtime EmptyStackException thrown.

To avoid getting an EmptyStackException thrown, you should see if the stack is empty before calling pop(). This is done by calling the empty() method:

```
public boolean empty()
```

If the size of the stack is zero, true is returned; otherwise, false is returned.

Checking the Top

To get a reference to the element at the top of the stack without removing it from the stack, use the peek() method:

```
public Object peek()
```

Like pop(), you'll get an EmptyStackException thrown if the stack is empty.

Searching

To find out if an element is on the stack, ask with the search() method to get its stack position back:

```
public int search(Object element)
```

Unlike working with vectors and arrays, working with this mechanism does not return a zero-based position. Instead, the element at the top of the stack is at position 1. Position 2 is next, then 3, and so on. If the requested object is not found on the stack, –1 is returned.

> **NOTE** *The other place you'll run into a stack when programming in Java is the stack trace when an exception is thrown. This stack represents the call stack and helps you to pinpoint which step in the sequence led to the throwing of the exception. As each method is called, the necessary information to return is pushed onto the stack such that you can pop each level off the stack to return to where you started.*

Stack Example

To demonstrate the use of the Stack class, Listing 3-6 simulates a summer reading list. When you get a new book to read, you add it to a pile. When you have time to read something, you take the top book off the pile. At times, you can look to see what's on top, and if you really like a book you know is in the pile, you can find it, throwing off a few best sellers from the top in the process.

Listing 3-6. Simulating a summer reading list.

```java
import java.util.Stack;
public class StackExample {
  public static void main (String args[]) {
    Stack s = new Stack();
    s.push("Autumnal Tints");
    s.push("A Week on the Concord and Merrimack Rivers");
    s.push("The Maine Woods");
    // Check out what's next to read
    System.out.println("Next: " + s.peek());
    s.push("Civil Disobedience, Solitude and Life Without Principle");
    // Read a book
    System.out.println(s.pop());
    s.push("Walden");
    s.push("The Natural Man");
    // Find that other book
    int count = s.search("The Maine Woods");
    while (count != -1 && count > 1) {
      s.pop();
      count--;
    }
    // Read a book
    System.out.println(s.pop());
    // Anything left?
    System.out.println(s.empty());
  }
}
```

Executing Listing 3-6 generates the following output:

```
Next: The Maine Woods
Civil Disobedience, Solitude and Life Without Principle
The Maine Woods
false
```

That's about all there is to a stack. The only inherited methods that are okay to call are those affecting size and capacity—the other methods really should be avoided.

Summary

This chapter introduced the Vector and Stack classes. You saw the many different ways to manipulate a vector and play with a stack. While you may question some of the duplicate methods in Vector, the redesign to place it into the Collections Framework with the Java 2 platform was well worth it. You'll learn more about these benefits as you progress through the rest of the book.

In the next chapter, we'll take a closer look at the Enumeration interface.

CHAPTER 4

The Enumeration Interface

The Enumeration interface defines a way to traverse all the members of a collection of objects. And although some collections define a specific order of traversal, the Enumeration interface does not. The key tidbit to know is that if you make your way through all the elements, the interface will ensure that each and every element of the collection is visited.

Enumeration Basics

The Enumeration interface follows the Iterator pattern defined by the Gang of Four in *Design Patterns* (Addison-Wesley, 1995). This interface has been around since the beginning of Java time and has been duplicated with extra capabilities in the Iterator interface of the Collections Framework. Chapter 7 covers the Iterator interface in detail. For now, let's look now at the Enumeration interface definition in Table 4-1.

Table 4-1. Summary of Interface Enumeration

VARIABLE/METHOD NAME	VERSION	DESCRIPTION
hasMoreElements()	1.0	Checks for more elements in the enumeration.
nextElement()	1.0	Fetches next element of the enumeration.

Nothing too complicated here: just two methods. When working with an enumeration, the hasMoreElements() method checks to see if there are more elements in the enumeration and then returns a boolean. If there are more elements in the enumeration, nextElement() will return the next element as an Object. If there are no more elements in the enumeration when nextElement() is called, the runtime NoSuchElementException will be thrown.

When working with an Enumeration, the basic structure for walking through the elements is as follows:

```
Enumeration enum = ...;
while (enum.hasMoreElements()) {
  Object o = enum.nextElement();
  processObject(o);
}
```

If you prefer a for-loop, you can do the same thing with:

```
for (Enumeration enum = ...; enum.hasMoreElements(); ) {
  Object o = enum.nextElement();
  processObject(o);
}
```

If followed to the end, both the while-loop and for-loop will visit all members of the original collection. The key difference with the for-loop is that the scope of the enum variable is limited to the looping construct, whereas the enum variable is visible, though somewhat useless, outside the while-loop.

This leaves us with one question. Where do we get the enumeration from? Why, ask the collection, of course! Each of the historical collection classes provides a method to give you the set of elements within them:

* Vector, Stack: elements()

* Dictionary, Hashtable, Properties: elements(), keys()

While we'll explore the Collections Framework more in Part Two, there is one method of the Collections class that should be mentioned here, too:

```
Collection col = ...;
Enumeration enum = Collections.enumeration(col);
```

This allows you to convert from a new collection type to the older enumeration for looping through the elements. You may find this technique necessary when using a third-party library that hasn't yet been upgraded to handle the newer Collections Framework.

> **WARNING** *One should never modify the underlying collection when using an enumeration. This will result in undefined behavior. For safety's sake, place the processing of elements within a synchronized block:* `synchronized (col) { /* get enum & process elements */ }`. *Of course, this only works if other accesses to the underlying collection are synchronized, too, and synchronized on the same object to boot. Thankfully, this access is already synchronized for the historical collections like* Vector *and* Hashtable.

The SequenceInputStream Class

To demonstrate the use of an Enumeration, look at the SequenceInputStream class found in the java.io package. The class has a constructor that accepts an enumeration:

```
public SequenceInputStream(Enumeration enum)
```

To use a SequenceInputStream, create a set of input streams. While we could define our own set, the simplest way to do this would be to create a Vector and then pass the enumeration of elements in the vector to the SequenceInputStream constructor. The elements() method of Vector will give you an Enumeration, and the elements of the enumeration will be used in the order in which they were added (index order).

```
Vector v = new Vector(3);
v.add(new FileInputStream("/etc/motd"));
v.add(new FileInputStream("foo.bar"));
v.add(new FileInputStream("/temp/john.txt"));
```

Once you have filled your vector, you can create the SequenceInputStream and read from it. If you wish to read characters from the combined input stream, you can combine them en masse with an InputStreamReader instead of having to combine individual streams. This is like creating your own SequenceReader class, as shown here:

```
Enumeration enum = v.elements();
SequenceInputStream sis = new SequenceInputStream(enum);
InputStreamReader isr = new InputStreamReader(sis);
BufferedReader br = new BufferedReader(isr);
String line;
```

```
while ((line = br.readLine()) != null) {
  System.out.println(line);
}
br.close();
```

> **NOTE** *When you call the* close() *method of* SequenceInputStream, *all streams are closed.*

StringTokenizer

In most cases, the implementations of the Enumeration interface are done in private classes. There is at least one exception to that rule in the standard Java libraries: the StringTokenizer class, which implements the interface as shown in Figure 4-1.

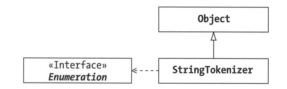

Figure 4-1. The StringTokenizer class hierarchy.

The purpose of the StringTokenizer class is to break apart a string based upon a set of delimiter tokens. You can then call the Enumeration methods to loop through the elements:

```
StringTokenizer tokenizer = new StringTokenizer("This is a test");
while (tokenizer.hasMoreElements()) {
  Object o = tokenizer.nextElement();
  System.out.println(o);
}
```

Besides implementing the Enumeration interface, the StringTokenizer class also provides a second set of methods for the same purpose—hasMoreTokens() and nextToken():

```
StringTokenizer tokenizer = new StringTokenizer("This is a test");
while (tokenizer.hasMoreTokens()) {
  String s = tokenizer.nextToken();
  System.out.println(s);
}
```

While hasMoreTokens() is functionally equivalent to hasMoreElements(), the nextToken() method is slightly different. Instead of returning a generic Object, the nextToken() method returns a String object. Thus, by using the new methods of StringTokenizer, you can avoid making a cast to a String or calling the toString() method if you wish to treat the return value of nextElement() as a String type.

> **NOTE** *There are other public classes in the extension libraries that imple-*
> *ment* Enumeration. *For example,* javax.commerce.base.JCMIterator,
> javax.commerce.database.IndexEnumerator,
> javax.naming.NamingEnumeration, *and*
> javax.smartcard.IFDRegistry.SlotEnumeration. *In most cases, the name*
> *makes it clear what it is.*

Creating Custom Enumerations

In most cases, it isn't necessary to create your own enumerations. Only if you are defining your own collection class or desire to extend the basic functionality of enumerating through a collection (like for filtering) do you need to create a custom enumeration. All of the predefined collections allow you to get back an enumeration to work with. There is one exception to that rule, however—the array. If for some reason you wish to treat an array as an enumeration, you'll either have to store the elements in another collection, like a vector, or define your own array enumeration class. To demonstrate how to create our own Enumeration implementation, we'll do the latter.

Creating a custom Enumeration implementation is no different than implementing any Java interface. Define a class that states it implements the interface. Then provide the implementation. In the case of the Enumeration interface, the implementation takes the form of two methods: boolean hasMoreElements() and Object nextElement() as shown in Listing 4-1. Once you add in a constructor, you're essentially done.

Listing 4-1. The ArrayEnumeration class.

```
public class ArrayEnumeration implements Enumeration {
  private final int size;
  private int cursor;
  private final Object array;
  public ArrayEnumeration(Object obj) {
    Class type = obj.getClass();
    if (!type.isArray()) {
      throw new IllegalArgumentException("Invalid type: " + type);
    }
    size = Array.getLength(obj);
    array = obj;
  }
  public boolean hasMoreElements() {
    return (cursor < size);
  }
  public Object nextElement() {
    return Array.get(array, cursor++);
  }
}
```

> **NOTE** *The* ArrayEnumeration *constructor argument is an* Object, *rather than an* Object[ ]. *Thus, we can work with arrays of primitives, too.*

To demonstrate our new ArrayEnumeration class, we need to create a test program (see Listing 4-2). If you add the following main() method to the class definition, you'll have three good test cases. The first uses the simple String array passed into the main() method. The second creates an int array and then makes an ArrayEnumeration out of that. You should realize that the nextElement() call for this enumeration actually returns Integer objects, not int primitives, even though it is an array of int primitives. This works because we are using reflection to fetch individual elements from the array. The final test case involves an attempt to create an array enumeration from something other than an array. This test case will cause an IllegalArgumentException to be thrown.

Listing 4-2. Testing the ArrayEnumeration.

```java
public static void main(String args[]) {
  Enumeration enum = new ArrayEnumeration(args);
  while (enum.hasMoreElements()) {
    System.out.println(enum.nextElement());
  }
  Object obj = new int[] {2, 3, 5, 8, 13, 21};
  enum = new ArrayEnumeration(obj);
  while (enum.hasMoreElements()) {
    System.out.println(enum.nextElement());
  }
  try {
    enum = new ArrayEnumeration(ArrayEnumeration.class);
  } catch (IllegalArgumentException e) {
    System.out.println("Oops: " + e.getMessage());
  }
}
```

If you were to run the sample program with the following command line:

```
java ArrayEnumeration Do Re Mi
```

You would then get the following output:

```
Do
Re
Mi
2
3
5
8
13
21
Oops: Invalid type: class java.lang.Class
```

Be aware that the ArrayEnumeration class doesn't make a copy of the array to start. This means that the set of elements enumerated over can change in the middle of stepping through.

> **NOTE** *If you're interested in creating your own enumeration, a filtering enumeration is potentially useful. Given some filtering method that returns a boolean, have the enumeration call the filtering method for each element and return only those elements that return true from the filtering method. This example will be revisited when discussing the* Iterator *interface in Chapter 7.*

Summary

In this chapter, we explored traversing through an historical collection with the help of the Enumeration interface. We also showed how to get an Enumeration for one of the new collection classes and how to create our own Enumeration implementations. Finally, we examined the SequenceInputStream and StringTokenizer classes, including how each takes advantage of the Enumeration interface.

In the next chapter, we'll explore the Dictionary class and its subclasses, Hashtable and Properties. Each provides key-value mappings instead of ordered, sequential access.

CHAPTER 5

The Dictionary, Hashtable, and Properties Classes

In this chapter, we'll look at the historical collection classes that offer support to store key-value pairs. Unlike the Vector class where you look up values based upon an integer index, the Dictionary class and its subclasses work with key-value pairs, where an object is the key to look up a value that is also an object. For the most commonly used subclass, Hashtable, both the key and value can be of type Object or any of its subclasses. The Properties class is another implementation. Instead of working with any type of object, the key and value must both be of type String. Figure 5-1 shows a diagram of the hierarchy of these three classes.

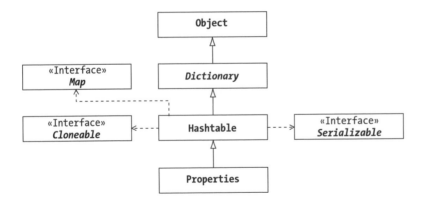

Figure 5-1. Class hierarchy of the Dictionary, Hashtable, and Properties classes.

A dictionary works like a simple phone listing. You look up a friend's phone number by searching for his or her name in a list. The name is the key for the entry in the dictionary, while the phone number is the value. Multiple people can have the same phone number, but any single person in your list can have only one entry. Of course, nowadays with everyone having multiple telephone numbers for cell phones, pagers, and the like, you would need a way to store multiple phone numbers for a single person through some kind of a class structure or multipart key.

Dictionary Basics

The Dictionary is an abstract class with only abstract methods. It is rumored that the class was defined before interfaces existed in the Java language and was never corrected once interfaces were added. Nonetheless, it really should be an interface. Table 5-1 shows the methods defined in this class: to add, delete, and retrieve dictionary values, as well as to find out the dictionary's size.

Table 5-1. Summary of the Dictionary Class

VARIABLE/METHOD NAME	VERSION	DESCRIPTION
Dictionary()	1.0	Empty constructor, implicitly called by subclass.
elements()	1.0	Returns an object from the dictionary that allows all of the dictionary's keys to be visited.
get()	1.0	Retrieves a specific element from the dictionary.
isEmpty()	1.0	Checks if dictionary is empty.
keys()	1.0	Returns a collection of the keys in the dictionary.
put()	1.0	Places a key-value pair into the dictionary.
remove()	1.0	Removes an element from the dictionary.
size()	1.0	Returns the number of elements in the dictionary.

Because Dictionary is an abstract class and you'll likely never use it directly, let's look at a subclass that implements *all* of the abstract methods of the class: Hashtable.

Hashtable Basics

A Hashtable is a specialized Dictionary that relies on a hashing algorithm to convert keys into a mechanism to look up values in the dictionary. The hashing algorithm provides a quick way to convert any object into something that can serve as a look-up mechanism. We'll explore this hashing mechanism more in the upcoming section, "Understanding Hash Tables," later in this chapter. For now, take a look at Table 5-2, which shows a complete method listing for the Hashtable class. Several of these methods provide implementations for the abstract ones defined in the Dictionary class, while others are new to Hashtable.

Table 5-2. Summary of the Hashtable Class

VARIABLE/METHOD NAME	VERSION	DESCRIPTION
Hashtable()	1.0/1.2	Constructs a hash table.
clear()	1.0	Removes all the elements from the hash table.
clone()	1.0	Creates a clone of the hash table.
contains()	1.0	Checks to see if an object is a value within the hash table.
containsKey()	1.0	Checks to see if an object is a key for the hash table.
containsValue()	1.2	Checks to see if an object is a value within the hash table.
elements()	1.0	Returns an object from the hash table that allows all of the hash table's keys to be visited.
entrySet()	1.2	Returns set of key-value pairs in hash table.
equals()	1.2	Checks for equality with another object.
get()	1.0	Retrieves value for key in hash table.
hashCode()	1.2	Computes hash code for hash table.
isEmpty()	1.0	Checks if hash table has any elements.
keys()	1.0	Retrieves a collection of the keys of the hash table.
keySet()	1.2	Retrieves a collection of the keys of the hash table.
put()	1.0	Places a key-value pair into the hash table.
putAll()	1.2	Places a collection of key-value pairs into the hash table.
rehash()	1.0	For increasing the internal capacity of the hash table.
remove()	1.0	Removes an element from the hash table.
size()	1.0	Returns the number of elements in the hash table.
toString()	1.0	Converts hash table contents into string.
values()	1.2	Retrieves a collection of the values of the hash table.

Understanding Hash Tables

Internally, a hash table is a data structure that offers nearly constant time insertion and searching (this is shown as O(1) in Big O Notation). This means that no matter how large or small the structure, it will take roughly the same amount of time to insert or locate any element. How do hash tables do that? And under what conditions is the time not "nearly constant?"

When using the key-value pairs in a hash table, the keys are converted into an integer called a *hash code* by using a hashing algorithm. This hash code is then reduced—based upon the internal storage structure used by the hash table—to serve as an index into this structure (an array). For two equal elements, the hash code must be the same. Two elements are defined as equal if the equals() method returns true when they are compared. For two unequal elements, the hash code may be different *or the same.*

> **NOTE** *The* hashCode() *method is defined in the* Object *class to generate hash codes and is frequently overridden in subclasses.*

If the hash code is the same for unequal elements, it is called a *collision.* If there are many collisions, the insertion and searching time degrades. When there are many elements with the same hash code they cannot be stored in a single array element, which causes the degradation. Instead, they are stored in a linked list data structure similar to Figure 5-2. Basically, when searching for an element in a hash table, the hash code for the key is generated to find the appropriate index into the hash table. If there are multiple elements with the same index in the hash table, a linked list must be traversed to find the element with the specific key.

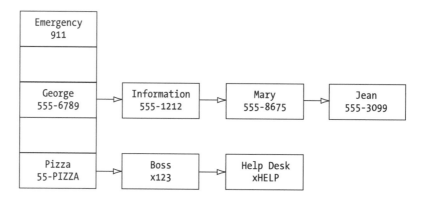

Figure 5-2. A hash table with several collisions.

The process of converting a key (an object) into a hash code is done by the object's hashing algorithm, the hashCode() method of the object in Java. A hashing algorithm must be quick so that the process of finding something is fast. However, a quick algorithm isn't always best because the algorithm needs to spread out the results in order to avoid collisions. To demonstrate, the following example shows a simple hashing algorithm for strings, along with an example of why it is bad. A better example follows.

A simple hashing algorithm for strings adds up the numerical values for the characters of the string. To sum up my first name (John), we would first convert the characters to their integer equivalent:

```
J = 74
o = 111
h = 104
n = 110
```

Then we would add them up:

```
74 + 111 + 104 + 110 = 399
```

Thus, we would store John with an index of 399. Unfortunately, there are several other names that also map to 399: Cary, Cody, and Omar, to name a few. As the word length increases, the likelihood of finding other words with the same sum grows, resulting in too many words for the same index. It is better to spread out the range of possible values.

A slightly more complex means to calculate the hash code is to multiply each character by a power of ten, where the specific power represents the position of the character. For instance, John would be:

$$74*10^3 + 111*10^2 + 104*10^1 + 110*10^0 = 86250$$

And the other three names would translate as follows:

```
Cary: 67*10³ + 97*10² + 114*10¹ + 121*10⁰ = 77961
Cody: 67*10³ + 111*10² + 100*10¹ + 121*10⁰ = 79221
Omar: 79*10³ + 109*10² + 97*10¹ + 114*10⁰ = 90984
```

There is, however, a slight problem with this latter scheme. While the first scheme had too many collisions, this latter scheme has too many holes as the length of the words grows. This brings us to *range conversion*. While the range of possible values generated from all the names in the world is rather large, at any one time you tend not to use them all. For instance, in your phone directory you might have, at most, five hundred people. A simple way to reduce the range would be to take the modulo of each value to use as an index into your data structure:

```
index = largeNumber % arraySize;
```

Research has shown that array sizes for hash tables should be prime numbers. Using a prime number tends to avoid a cluster of resulting indices around the same values, possibly causing several collisions. Therefore, if we pick a prime number 20 to 30% larger than the maximum size to reduce the chance of collision, we should get a nice distribution of elements with minimal collisions. To demonstrate, Figure 5-3 shows range conversion from our large numbers for names into a thirteen-element array. Imagine if we only had ten names in our phone book instead of five hundred.

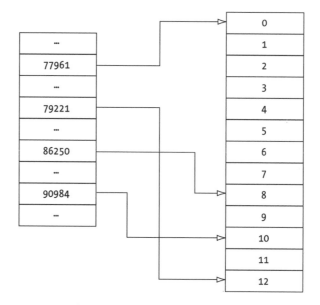

Figure 5-3. Demonstrating how range conversion works.

That's how hash tables work behind the scenes. It's important when working with hash tables to know that they have a certain capacity, and that the hashCode() method for objects stored in the hash table should provide a good distribution. The system-defined classes tend to generate good hash codes already. However, when you create your own classes, you'll need to define your own hash code. We'll look at creating hashing functions more in the "Generating Hash Codes" section of this chapter.

Creating Hash Tables

Creating a Hashtable can be done with one of four constructors; the first three are:

```
public Hashtable()
public Hashtable(int initialCapacity)
public Hashtable(int initialCapacity, float loadFactor)
```

With the first three, unless otherwise specified, the initial capacity of the hash table is 101 for JDK 1.1 and 11 for JDK 1.2 with a load factor of 75%. When the number of elements exceeds the (load factor * the capacity), the hash table will grow by a factor of 2 × capacity + 1.

> **NOTE** *The default growth factor of a* Hashtable *is twice capacity + 1. To keep the hash table growing with roughly prime sizes, you should start the* Hashtable *with a size of 89 instead of the default of 101. This let's the capacity grow to 5759 before it hits a non-prime when resizing. With the default initial size of 101, you'll run into non-primes at nearly all the new sizes starting at 407. Of course, if you know you're going to stuff more than 89 elements into the* Hashtable, *pick a larger initial number, preferably one that appears in the sequence generated from 2n + 1 started at 89: 89, 179, 359, 719, 1439, 2879.*

The final constructor initializes the Hashtable by copying key-value pairs from another key-value pair structure:

```
public Hashtable(Map t)
```

The new hash table is sized to be twice as large as the original structure (or eleven if it is small) with a load factor again of 75%.

> **NOTE** *You'll learn more about the* Map *interface and its implementations in Chapter 10 from Part Two of this book. As Figure 5-1 shows, the* Hashtable *class implements the interface.*

Adding Key-Value Pairs

Once you create a hash table, you can store elements in it. Unlike the `Vector` class from Chapter 3, when you store something in a `Hashtable`, you need to provide both a value and a key to find that value again.

```
public Object put(Object key, Object value)
```

> **NOTE** *In a* `Hashtable`, *neither the key nor the value can be null. Trying to place a null into the* `Hashtable` *will cause a* `NullPointerException` *to be thrown.*

The same value can be stored for multiple keys. However, if you try to `put()` the same key multiple times, the original setting will be replaced. Whenever you set the value for a key in the hash table, the previous setting for the key will be returned. If the key had no prior value, null will be returned.

If you wish to copy all the key-value pairs from one `Hashtable` (or any `Map`) into another `Hashtable`, use the `putAll()` method. If any keys already exist in the hash table, their value will be replaced if they are also found in the passed-in map.

```
public void putAll(Map map)
```

Displaying Hash Table Contents

The `Hashtable` class overrides the `toString()` method of the `Object` class:

```
public String toString()
```

The generated string for a hash table is a comma-delimited list of key-value pairs within braces ({}). For instance, if the key-value pairs within a hash table were key one with value two, key two with value three, key three with value four, and key four with value five, the string returned from a call to the `toString()` method would look like this:

```
{three=four, two=three, four=five, one=two}
```

The listed order does not reflect the order in which the key-value pairs are added to the hash table. Instead, the order reflects the range conversion of the hash codes generated from the keys.

> **NOTE** *Depending upon the capacity of the* Hashtable, *the actual order of key-value pairs may differ. Change the capacity, and you change the order.*

Removing Key-Value Pairs

If you need to remove an element from a hash table, simply call the remove() method with the specific key as its argument:

```
public Object remove(Object key)
```

If the key is present as a key within the hash table, the key-value pair will be removed and the value object will be returned.

To get rid of all key-value pairs from a hash table, call the clear() method instead:

```
public void clear()
```

> **WARNING** *Clearing a hash table does* not *return its internal capacity to the initial capacity. It only nulls out all the entries within the table.*

Sizing Hash Tables

The only control you have over the size of a hash table is when it is created. After creating a hash table, it will grow when necessary based upon its load factor and will increase in capacity at 2n+1. You cannot find out its current capacity. You can only find out the number of key-value pairs within the Hashtable with the help of the size() method:

```
public int size()
public boolean isEmpty()
```

If the size is zero, the isEmpty() method will return true. Otherwise, it returns false.

When the hash table determines that it needs to increase its capacity, the protected rehash() method is called:

```
protected void rehash()
```

This causes a new internal array to be created, inserting into it all the values based upon the range conversion of the hash codes for the new capacity. Unless you subclass Hashtable, you'll never need to call the rehash() method.

> **NOTE** *If you plan to create a hash table with a fixed number of known elements, make the initial capacity equal to the number of elements and make the load factor 1.0f.*

Operating with Hash Tables

Once you've placed elements into a hash table, you can perform many different operations on it. The hash table supports fetching one of the following: a single key, all keys, all values, or all key-value entries. You can also search for a specific key or value within the hash table, among certain other tasks that are Object method specializations.

Fetching Keys and Values

There are several ways to get data out of a Hashtable once you've placed key-value pairs into it. The simplest is to look up the value for a specific key with the get() method:

```
public Object get(Object key)
```

If the key is found for a key-value pair entry within the hash table, its value will be returned. If not found, null is returned.

If, instead of looking up the value for a specific key, you wish to perform some operation on all keys, you can ask for them with the keys() or keySet() methods:

```
public Enumeration keys()
public Set keySet()
```

The keys() method returns the set of keys as an Enumeration. The keySet() method returns the set of keys as a Set object. Which you use depends upon what you wish to do with the keys.

To get the set of all the values in the hash table, you would use either the elements() or the values() method:

```
public Enumeration elements()
public Collection values()
```

The elements() method returns the set of values as an Enumeration. The values() method returns the same data as a Collection. This method returns a Collection instead of a Set because the values may contain duplicates. This is one difference between the two interface definitions you'll learn in Chapters 7 and 8 of this book.

The final manner of getting elements back from a Hashtable is with the entrySet() method:

```
public Set entrySet()
```

This returns each of the key-value pairs together, where the pair is an entry in the returned set.

The entries in the returned Set are of type Map.Entry. While you'll learn more about both in Part Two (Set in Chapter 8 and Map.Entry in Chapter 10), let's examine them by comparing the use of keys() with entrySet() to print out the list of key-value pairs within a Hashtable.

If you wish to print out a listing of key-value pairs with the keys() method, you must perform a look-up for each key returned in the Enumeration:

```
Enumeration enum = hash.keys();
while (enum.hasMoreElements()) {
  String key = (String)enum.nextElement();
  System.out.println(key + " : " + hash.get(key));
}
```

On the other hand, as the following example shows, when working with the Set returned from entrySet(), you already have both the key and value together so you don't need to perform the extra look-up:

```
Set set = hash.entrySet();
Iterator it = set.iterator();
while (it.hasNext()) {
  Map.Entry entry = (Map.Entry)it.next();
  System.out.println(entry.getKey() + " : " + entry.getValue());
}
```

Finding Elements

The Hashtable class contains three methods that let you check to see whether a specific key or a specific value is within the set of entries for the hash table. The simplest of the three is the containsKey() method, which functions like the get() method:

```
public boolean containsKey(Object key)
```

But instead of returning a value for the key, it returns true if the key is present and false if otherwise.

The duplicate pair of methods, contains() and containsValue(), each check to see if a specific value is found within the Hashtable:

```
public boolean contains(Object value)
public boolean containsValue(Object value)
```

Both are functionally equivalent. The duplication is due to the Hashtable implementing the Map interface when reworked into Collections Framework. If possible, their use should be kept to a minimum, as they are very costly to use. While values are normally fetched in a hash table by key, these methods essentially say, "Don't bother using a key to look up the value. Instead, look at all the values and tell me if this specific value is among them." In other words, the system will walk through all the elements of the hash table trying to find one. When the value is not found within the hash table, all entries of the hash table will be traversed. If the value happens to be found, on average, half will be traversed.

Cloning Hash Tables

The Hashtable class provides its own implementation of the clone() method:

```
public Object clone()
```

This functions similarly to passing the hash table to the constructor of a new Hashtable, or creating an empty Hashtable, then calling putAll().

Checking Hash Tables for Equality

The Hashtable class overrides the equals() method from Object to define equality:

```
public boolean equals(Object o)
```

Equality is defined at the Map interface level, not the Hashtable level; so a Hashtable can be equal to any other Map implementation and not just another hash table.

Two maps are defined as equal if both of their entry sets are equal (thisHash.entrySet().equals(map.entrySet()). Two entry sets are equal if their sizes are equal and each set contains every member of the other set. Order is unimportant. Two entries are compared for equality by using their equals()

method. This means that the maps don't have to contain the same contents (instances), only equivalent contents. For instance, if you have two Integer objects, each holding the integer 3, while these are not the same instance, they are equivalent instances.

Hashing Hash Tables

The Hashtable class provides its own hashCode() implementation. The hash code for a Hashtable is the sum of all its elements' hash codes:

```
public int hashCode()
```

Serializing Hash Tables

The Hashtable class implements the Serializable interface. This doesn't mean that all hash tables are automatically serializable. They are only if all the entries, both keys and values, found in the hash table are also serializable. If you try to serialize a hash table with entries that are not serializable, you'll get a NotSerializableException thrown.

Hashtable Immutability

If it occurs that a hash table's contents are initialized to a fixed set of elements, you can make the table read-only to prevent accidental change. The Collections class provides this capability with the public static Map unmodifiableMap(Map map) method:

```
Hashtable h = new Hashtable();
// fill hash table
Map m = Collections.unmodifiableMap(h);
```

Since Hashtable implements the Map interface, you can pass a Hashtable off to the method and get a read-only Map back. You *cannot* cast this Map to a Hashtable. While the code would compile, trying to do this would throw a ClassCastException at runtime.

If you truly need an immutable structure, however, it is better to start out with the HashMap (or TreeMap) from the Collections Framework. If you are making a Hashtable read-only, access will be unnecessarily synchronized.

> **NOTE** *We'll visit the* Map *interface,* HashMap *class, and* TreeMap *class more fully in Chapter 10.*

Generating Hash Codes

While the majority of system classes generate hash codes for you, when creating your own classes it's a good idea to generate hash codes for them, too. In fact, a good rule of thumb is, if you override the equals() method for your class, you must also override the hashCode() method. Whenever two objects are equal, they must return the same hash code.

How do you generate your own hash functions? As shown earlier in the "Understanding Hash Tables" section, you need to come up with a way to combine the different elements of the object into a hash code. In the case of a String, combine the character values. In the case of a general object, combine the hash codes of its subparts. It is important to find a combination that distributes the keys over a large range without clustering them around any single values. It takes practice to get these evenly distributed and has been thoroughly researched in computer science texts. For information beyond basic combinatorics, Robert Uzgalis's online presentation of "Hashing Concepts and the Java Programming Language" at http://www.serve.net/buz/hash.adt/java.000.html offers a great place to start.

Counting Word Occurrences

Listing 5-1 shows the typical demonstrative usage of a Hashtable, which creates a program that counts the number of word occurrences in a file.

Listing 5-1. Counting words with a hash table.

```java
import java.io.*;
import java.util.*;
public class WordCount {
  static final Integer ONE = new Integer(1);
  public static void main (String args[])
      throws IOException {
    Hashtable map = new Hashtable();
    FileReader fr = new FileReader(args[0]);
    BufferedReader br = new BufferedReader(fr);
    String line;
    while ((line = br.readLine()) != null) {
      processLine(line, map);
    }
    Enumeration enum = map.keys();
    while (enum.hasMoreElements()) {
      String key = (String)enum.nextElement();
      System.out.println(key + " : " + map.get(key));
    }
  }
```

```java
static void processLine(String line, Map map) {
  StringTokenizer st = new StringTokenizer(line);
  while (st.hasMoreTokens()) {
    addWord(map, st.nextToken());
  }
}
static void addWord(Map map, String word) {
  Object obj = map.get(word);
  if (obj == null) {
    map.put(word, ONE);
  } else {
    int i = ((Integer)obj).intValue() + 1;
    map.put(word, new Integer(i));
  }
}
}
```

The addWord() method is where the hash table is used. For each word in the file, the hash table checks to see if the word is already in the word list. If it isn't, the word is added with a count of one. Otherwise, the current count is incremented.

If you run the program from Listing 5-1 with itself as input, the output in Listing 5-2 will be produced.

Listing 5-2. The output from running WordCount on itself.

```
br.readLine()) : 1
StringTokenizer : 1
ONE); : 1
void : 3
public : 2
processLine(String : 1
IOException : 1
obj : 1
else : 1
map.get(word); : 1
addWord(Map : 1
throws : 1
(obj : 1
map.get(key)); : 1
(st.hasMoreTokens()) : 1
((Integer)obj).intValue() : 1
import : 2
main : 1
null) : 2
```

```
Hashtable : 1
st.nextToken()); : 1
line; : 1
int : 1
addWord(map, : 1
map : 1
Map : 1
(String : 1
Hashtable(); : 1
line, : 1
!= : 1
} : 9
BufferedReader(fr); : 1
String : 3
{ : 9
Integer(i)); : 1
map, : 1
map) : 1
static : 4
if : 1
i : 1
word) : 1
(String)enum.nextElement(); : 1
br : 1
ONE : 1
map); : 1
new : 6
java.util.*; : 1
key : 1
enum : 1
(enum.hasMoreElements()) : 1
System.out.println(key : 1
processLine(line, : 1
= : 10
BufferedReader : 1
: : 1
Integer : 1
st : 1
1; : 1
Enumeration : 1
Object : 1
final : 1
```

```
+ : 3
== : 1
FileReader : 1
" : 2
StringTokenizer(line); : 1
fr : 1
class : 1
FileReader(args[0]); : 1
((line : 1
Integer(1); : 1
map.put(word, : 2
args[]) : 1
while : 3
map.keys(); : 1
WordCount : 1
java.io.*; : 1
```

If you'd like the word delimiters to be different, you can play with the StringTokenizer constructor call to have different word boundaries. If you'd like the output sorted, you can use a TreeMap instead of a Hashtable. We'll learn more about that in Chapter 10.

UIDefaults Demonstration

There is one Hashtable subclass that is defined with the Swing classes: the UIDefaults class. It provides a hash table for the UIManager to find the look-and-feel-dependent properties for the Swing components. It extends the Hashtable functionality by storing default values in addition to the key-value object pairs. If you search for a key that isn't in the hash table, the set of defaults is also searched. By changing a value in the UIDefaults hash table, you effectively change the properties of the created Swing components. For instance, if you'd like all JButton components to have white text with a red background and a 24-point italic Serif font, add the following to the table:

```
UIManager.put("Button.foreground", Color.white);
UIManager.put("Button.background", Color.red);
Font f = new Font("Serif", Font.ITALIC, 24);
UIManager.put("Button.font", f);
```

Figure 5-4 shows what a bunch of buttons with these defaults would look like. The actual buttons are created simply by calling the constructor: new JButton(label).

Figure 5-4. An example of UIDefaults.

For each entry in the UIDefaults table, there is a string key. The value can be an instance of any type. For a complete list of keys, see Appendix A of my book, *Definitive Guide to Swing for Java 2, Second Edition* (Apress, 2000).

Properties Basics

The Properties class represents yet another specialized Hashtable. Instead of being a collection of key-value pairs of any object, it is customized such that both the keys and the values are only supposed to be strings. However, since this is a subclass of Hashtable, you can call the Hashtable methods directly to store other object types. However, this should be avoided so that the listing, loading, and saving methods work as expected. You'll see more on these capabilities shortly.

> **WARNING**   *Using the* Hashtable *methods to store nonstring objects in a* Properties *table will result in the* store() *method throwing a* ClassCastException *and the* getProperty() *method returning null. The* Properties *class doesn't just call the nonstring objects'* toString() *method to treat them as strings.*

Table 5-3. Summary of the Properties Class

VARIABLE/METHOD NAME	VERSION	DESCRIPTION
Properties()	1.0	Constructs a properties list.
getProperty()	1.0	Retrieves a value for a key in the properties list.
list()	1.0	Lists all the properties and their values.
load()	1.0	Loads the properties list from a stream.
propertyNames()	1.0	Returns a collection of the keys in the properties list.
setProperty()	1.2	Places a key-value pair into the properties list.
store()	1.2	Saves the properties list to a stream.
defaults	1.0	A default set of the property values

You can create properties with or without a set of *default values*. The default values are another set of properties used when you look up values. If you haven't yet stored a value for a key in the new properties list, the value for the key from the defaults set will be returned.

```
public Properties()
public Properties(Properties defaults)
```

Instances of the `Properties` class are both sized and grow like hash tables. If you wish to presize your `Properties` instance, you cannot; there is no way to change the initial capacity or load factor for the hash table used.

Using Properties

The two primary tasks of working with properties are setting and getting. You can also load them from an input stream or save them to an output stream.

Setting and Getting Elements

The `Properties` class has a specialized `setProperty()` method to ensure both the key and the value are strings.

```
public Object setProperty(String key, String value)
```

Keys can consist of any Unicode characters except those listed in Table 5-4, which represent separator characters the `Properties` class uses when its content is written to external storage. Also, keys cannot begin with '#' or '!'—these characters are reserved to represent comment lines in the saved properties files. However, '#' and '!' are valid at other positions.

Table 5-4. Invalid Characters in Keys for Properties

CHARACTER	REPRESENTATION
Equals Sign	=
Colon	:
Space	
Tab	\t
Newline	\n
Return	\r
Formfeed	\f

The `getProperty()` methods are meant to replace the functionality of the `get()` method of `Hashtable` while making sure the value returned is a `String`. Besides doing a direct look-up in the hash table for the properties, there may also be a secondary look-up in the defaults passed to the `Properties` constructor. If that fails and a default value is passed in to the method call, a default setting can be returned from there, too.

```
public String getProperty(String key)
public String getProperty(String key, String defaultValue)
```

If the key is not found and no default value is provided, an empty string is not returned; null is returned instead

Getting a List

Due to the possibility of having a default set of properties, getting a list of all the keys in a property list is a little different than getting the keys of a hash table. You can't just call the keys() method of Hashtable to get all the possible keys. Instead, the Properties class provides its own propertyNames() method, which combines the keys in the properties list with the keys in the defaults properties list passed into the constructor:

```
public Enumeration propertyNames()
```

Of course, if you only want those properties that have been explicitly set, do call the keys() method.

Loading and Saving

Instead of relying on serialization to save a set of Properties, the class provides a pair of loading and saving methods, load() and store():

```
void load(InputStream inStream) throws IOException
void store(OutputStream out, String header) throws IOException
```

The store() method will save the properties file with the header line as a comment, followed by the key-value pairs written out and separated by an equals sign. The load() method will then retrieve what store() saves.

```
# header
key1=value1
key2=value2
key3=value3
```

> **NOTE** *If there is a problem saving or loading the properties list, an* IOException *will be thrown.*

You'll notice that `load()` and `store()` work with `InputStream` and `OutputStream` rather than with `Reader` and `Writer` streams. They automatically encode the streams using ISO 8859-1 character encoding. In order to work properly, these methods do some data conversion. If a key or value is not within the printable set of ASCII characters (32 to 127), the character will be encoded into its Unicode (\uxxxx) representation. Decoding is automatically handled for you, too.

> **TIP** *Be sure to close the output stream after loading and storing the properties. The* `load()` *and* `store()` *methods do not* `close()` *the stream for you.*

While the `load()` method will read in the format that `store()` saves the data in, it also understands several other styles. Many of these conventions exist to simplify reading in some system-generated files. For comments, both the '#' character and the '!' character are supported. For a key-value separator, in addition to the '=' character, the ':' (colon), the space, and the tab are all supported. A newline or formfeed character is valid after a key, but either one means that the key has no value. For instance, the following file initializes six properties:

```
foo:bar
one
two
three=four
five   six seven eight
nine ten
```

If `store()` were used to save the properties, the following would be written out instead:

```
foo=bar
one=
two=
three=four
five=six seven eight
nine=ten
```

> **NOTE** *There is a deprecated* `save()` *method. Use* `store()` *instead as it will throw an exception if there is an error saving the properties;* `save()` *will not.*

Besides loading and saving the property list, you can also just list them to a print stream or print writer. While you can rely on the inherited toString() method from Hashtable, it doesn't present the properties in a friendly format on separate lines. Instead, use the list() method:

```
public void list(PrintStream out)
public void list(PrintWriter out)
```

These will write both the set of properties from the main list and the defaults, with each key-value pair on its own line.

Do not expect to be able to load() in the properties written out with list(). The two methods are not compatible. In fact, if a property value is too long (over forty characters), the displayed value will be chopped down to thirty-seven characters with a trailing set of three periods (. . .).

A common way of calling list() is to pass to it System.out as its argument:

```
props.list(System.out).
```

In either case of using props.list() with a PrintStream or a PrintWriter, output is preceded by the line "— listing properties —". For instance, if we were to list the earlier set of properties shown with the load() method, the following would be displayed:

```
- listing properties -
five=six seven eight
two=
one=
three=four
nine=ten
foo=bar
```

System Properties

All Java programs have a special set of properties called *system properties* that provide information about the environment your program is running in. This information includes things like the vendor and version of the Java runtime, as well as the platform-specific file and line separator. The System class provides several static methods for getting and setting these values, which are listed in Table 5-5.

Table 5-5. Summary of System Properties Methods

VARIABLE/METHOD NAME	VERSION	DESCRIPTION
getProperties()	1.0	Retrieves all the system properties.
getProperty()	1.0	Retrieves a value for a key in the system properties list.
setProperties()	1.0	Replaces the system property list with a new list.
setProperty()	1.2	Places a key-value pair into the system properties list.

You can easily retrieve all the Properties to either work with them as a collection, getProperties(), or to search for individual properties, getProperty(). You can also provide a default value in the event that the system property is not set.

```
public static Properties getProperties()
public static String getProperty(String key)
public static String getProperty(String key, String default)
```

An untrusted applet can only get individual properties, and only a subset at that, as listed in Table 5-6. Their names are fairly self-explanatory.

Table 5-6. Applet-visible System Properties

PROPERTY	EXAMPLE
file.separator	\
java.class.version	47.0
java.specification.name	Java Platform API Specification
java.specification.vendor	Sun Microsystems Inc.
java.specification.version	1.3
java.vendor	Sun Microsystems Inc.
java.vendor.url	http://java.sun.com/
java.version	1.3.0
java.vm.name	Java HotSpot(TM) Client VM
java.vm.specification.name	Java Virtual Machine Specification
java.vm.specification.vendor	Sun Microsystems Inc.
java.vm.specification.version	1.0
java.vm.vendor	Sun Microsystems Inc.
java.vm.version	1.3.0-C
line.separator	\r\n
os.arch	x86
os.name	Windows NT
os.version	4.0
path.separator	;

Notice in Table 5-6 that there is a hierarchy, similar to packages, with names separated by dots. This hierarchy is strictly implicit with no system-defined relationship carried by any two properties that begin with the same prefix. Table 5-6 is not meant to be an exhaustive list of all the available system properties. It is only the list visible to Java applets by the default security manager settings. The most complete list of properties I've seen can be found in *The Java Developers Almanac 2000* by Patrick Chan (Addison-Wesley, 2000).

Many of the properties have to do with specific tasks. For instance, the JDBC driver manager relies on the `jdbc.drivers` property to find the names of the JDBC drivers to use. Or, to make a URL connection through a proxy server, you would set the `http.proxyHost` and `http.proxyPort` system properties. Each of these system properties should be documented along with their related classes.

Aside from getting the values of the different system properties, you can also set them with `setProperty()` or do a complete replacement with the `setProperties()` method:

```
public static String setProperty(String key, String value)
public static void setProperties(Properties props)
```

Normally, you wouldn't do a complete replacement. However, prior to Java 1.2, there was no way to directly set an individual property.

In addition to setting properties in code from a running program, you can also set or replace them from the command line with the –D command-line option to the `java` command. For instance, the following will add the `foo` property to the set of system properties with a value of `bar`.

```
java –Dfoo=bar Program
```

TIP *You can set multiple system properties from the command line using multiple –D settings.*

One last task to mention in dealing with system properties is how to sort the list of keys. Since `Properties` is a type of `Hashtable`, and both implement the `Map` interface, you can convert any `Properties` list into a `TreeMap` to get the key list in sorted order.

Working with Security Providers

The `java.security.Provider` class provides a specialized implementation of the `Properties` class. The key-value pairs represent implementations of crypto algorithms from name to specific class. The `Provider` can also maintain descriptive information about itself, hence the need to subclass.

To demonstrate, let's create a security provider that offers a new type of Message Digest implementation, a *Cyclic Redundancy Check* (CRC):

```
import java.security.Provider;
public class MyProvider extends Provider {
  public MyProvider() {
    super("Zukowski", 1.0,
      "Zukowski Collections Example");
    put("MessageDigest.CRC32", "CRC");
  }
}
```

CRCs are 32-bit hash codes typically used to verify data integrity. They are definitely not meant for security purposes, but they do offer a simple way to demonstrate security providers.

For each key-value pair you put into the hash table, you provide a mapping from security algorithm to class implementation. In this case, we're providing an algorithm implementation named `CRC32` for the `MessageDigest` in the form of the CRC class.

Listing 5-4 shows our implementation. The `CRC32` class found in the `java.util.zip` package really does all the work for us.

Listing 5-4. Our CRC message digest implementation.

```
import java.security.*;
import java.util.zip.CRC32;
public class CRC extends MessageDigest {
  CRC32 crc;
  public CRC() {
    super("CRC");
    crc = new CRC32();
  }
  protected void engineReset() {
    crc.reset();
  }
  protected void engineUpdate(byte input) {
    crc.update(input);
  }
  protected void engineUpdate(byte[] input,
      int offset, int len) {
    crc.update(input, offset, len);
  }
```

```
   protected byte[] engineDigest() {
     long l = crc.getValue();
     byte[] bytes = new byte[4];
     bytes[3] = (byte) ((l & 0xFF000000) > 24);
     bytes[2] = (byte) ((l & 0x00FF0000) > 16);
     bytes[1] = (byte) ((l & 0x0000FF00) > 8);
     bytes[0] = (byte) ((l & 0x000000FF) > 0);
     return bytes;
   }
}
```

The set of available providers is then stored in either the file, /lib/security/java.security, relative to the Java runtime installation directory or added with the Security.addProvider() method in your program. When you then look up a particular algorithm implementation, as in MessageDigest.getInstance("CRC32"), the set of security providers is searched. The first one that provides an implementation of the CRC32 algorithm for message digests is returned. Assuming no others are installed, that would be an instance of our CRC class, which you would then use. Listing 5-5 demonstrates this usage.

Listing 5-5. Testing our CRC message digest implementation.

```
import java.io.*;
import java.security.*;
public class CRCTest {
  static private String hexDigit(byte x) {
    StringBuffer sb = new StringBuffer();
    char c;
    // First nibble
    c = (char) ((x > 4) & 0xf);
    if (c > 9) {
      c = (char) ((c - 10) + 'a');
    } else {
      c = (char) (c + '0');
    }
    sb.append (c);
    // Second nibble
    c = (char) (x & 0xf);
    if (c > 9) {
      c = (char)((c - 10) + 'a');
    } else {
      c = (char)(c + '0');
    }
    sb.append (c);
```

```
      return sb.toString();
  }
  static private byte [] loadByteData (String filename) {
    FileInputStream fis = null;
    try {
      fis = new FileInputStream (filename);
      BufferedInputStream bis = new BufferedInputStream (fis);
      ByteArrayOutputStream baos = new ByteArrayOutputStream();
      int ch;
      while ((ch = bis.read()) != -1) {
        baos.write (ch);
      }
      return baos.toByteArray();
    } catch (IOException e) {
      if (fis != null) {
        try {
          fis.close();
        } catch (IOException ee) {
          // ignore
        }
      }
      return null;
    }
  }
  static private String computeDigest (MessageDigest algorithm, String filename) {
    byte[] content = loadByteData (filename);
    if (content != null) {
      algorithm.reset();
      algorithm.update (content);
      byte digest[] = algorithm.digest();
      StringBuffer hexString = new StringBuffer();
      int digestLength = digest.length;
      for (int i=0;i<digestLength;i++) {
        hexString.append (hexDigit(digest[i]));
        hexString.append (" ");
      }
      return hexString.toString();
    } else {
      return "";
    }
  }
  public static void main (String args[]) {
    MessageDigest algorithm = null;
    Security.addProvider (new MyProvider());
```

```
    try {
      algorithm = MessageDigest.getInstance("CRC32");
    } catch (NoSuchAlgorithmException e) {
      System.err.println ("Invalid algorithm");
      System.exit (-1);
    }
    int argsLength = args.length;
    for (int i=0;i<argsLength;i++) {
      String digest = computeDigest (algorithm, args[i]);
      System.out.println(args[i] + " : " + digest);
    }
  }
}
```

The bulk of the work in the program reads in the input files and formats the output.

When run against itself, the program generates the following output:

```
CRCTest.java : 01 9d da 8d
```

> **NOTE** *If you don't understand the specifics of the Java Security Architecture, the* Securing Java *and* Java 2 Network Security *books are available for free online at* http://www.securingjava.com/ *and* http://www.redbooks.ibm.com/pubs/pdfs/redbooks/sg242109.pdf, *respectively.*

Understanding Resource Bundles

Another type of properties file is meant for internationalization of Java programs. Called *resource bundles,* these files of properties store locale-specific information such as text labels for buttons. The PropertyResourceBundle class is a specific type of resource bundle that relies on the use of properties files. The other type of resource bundle is the ListResourceBundle, which uses a class for storing the key-value pairs. The only magic in working with resource bundles lies in finding the appropriate bundle to get the value out of. Unlike Properties, which have one defaults table to search, there are many levels of variants to search. The ResourceBundle javadoc class documentation describes this searching mechanism at http://java.sun.com/j2se/1.3/docs/api/java/util/ResourceBundle.html.

> **TIP** *For more information about internationalizing your programs with resource bundles, see the Internationalization trail in* The Java Tutorial *at* `http://java.sun.com/docs/books/tutorial/i18n/`.

Summary

This chapter introduced us to the different historical structures Java provides in order to store and work with key-value pairs. While focusing on the workings of the Hashtable, we explored hash codes and hashing in general. We also examined the specific details of using the Java Hashtable class for storing, retrieving, and removing objects, as well as sizing the internal structure of the hash table and checking for equality among many other tasks. Beyond the Hashtable, we saw how Swing uses UIDefaults for storing component properties. Finally, we looked at working with key-value string pairs through the Properties class, as well as the specialized Provider collection for adding security capabilities.

The next chapter introduces us to the BitSet class. You will learn how to use this class as a growable array of booleans.

CHAPTER 6

The BitSet Class

The BitSet class is the least used of the historical collection classes. In this chapter, you'll learn where the class fits in with the remaining collections, as well as how to effectively use the class within your Java programs.

The BitSet class provides a memory-efficient abstraction for a collection of bits. In other words, the class represents a growable, array-like structure of boolean values. In fact, a BitSet can grow without bounds to provide an infinitely large set of indexed boolean values. As shown in Figure 6-1, there isn't anything special about the BitSet class. It is your basic Object subclass, which implements the Cloneable and Serializable interfaces.

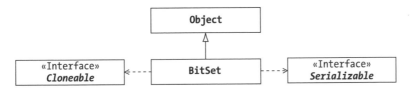

Figure 6-1. The BitSet class hierarchy.

> **NOTE** *In Chapter 8 of this book, you'll learn about the* Set *interface with its* HashSet *and* TreeSet *implementations. As Figure 6-1 shows, the* BitSet *class is* not *another implementation of the* Set *interface.*

BitSet Basics

The BitSet class represents a set of bits where the set grows in size as needed. Each indexed element of the set is a bit with a value of zero or one. A zero setting means the bit is clear (or false if you want to think in terms of boolean values), while a one represents the bit as set. Table 6-1 shows the set of methods provided with the BitSet class.

Table 6-1. Summary of BitSet Class

VARIABLE/METHOD NAME	VERSION	DESCRIPTION
BitSet()	1.0	Creates a bit set with all bits clear.
and()	1.0	Performs a logical AND operation with another bit set.
andNot()	1.2	Performs a logical NOT operation of another bit set, then performs a logical AND operation with this bit set.
clear()	1.0	Clears a specific bit of the set.
clone()	1.0	Copies the bit set.
equals()	1.0	Checks for equality with another object.
get()	1.0	Gets the setting of a specific bit from the set.
hashCode()	1.0	Returns computed hashcode for the bit set.
length()	1.2	Returns the logical size of the set.
or()	1.0	Performs a logical OR operation with another bit set.
set()	1.0	Sets a specific bit of the set.
size()	1.0	Returns the internal space used to represent the bit set.
toString()	1.0	Converts the bit set contents into a string.
xor()	1.0	Performs a logical XOR operation with another bit set.

Creating Bit Sets

There are two ways to create a BitSet. You can either specify an initial bit set size, or not:

```
public BitSet()
public BitSet(int nbits)
```

If you don't specify a size, an internal structure will be created to store sixty-four different bit settings. If you do specify a size, the structure size will be rounded up to the nearest multiple of sixty-four.

> **NOTE** *A* NegativeArraySizeException *will be thrown if the initial size is negative.*

When a bit set is created, all bits in the set are clear, or set to zero. After creating the set, if setting or clearing bits happens at a higher position than the current set size, the set size will grow.

Printing Bit Sets

The BitSet class overrides the toString() method inherited from Object:

```
public String toString()
```

The string generated by calling the toString() method is a comma-delimited list of set bit positions, which is set and is surrounded by curly braces ({ }). For example, if the bits at position 0, 36, and 42 were set, calling toString() would generate the following string: .

```
{0, 36, 42}
```

When a BitSet is first created, the returned string is the empty set:

```
{}
```

Bit Set Operations

Once you've created the bit set, you can work with either individual bits or the set as a whole.

Manipulating Individual Bits

When working with individual bits, you usually need to change or get their setting. There are two methods for changing the setting: set() and clear(). There is one for getting: get(). Each of the methods accepts a position argument to specify the zero-based index of the bit to change.

```
public void set(int position)
public void clear(int position)
public boolean get(int position)
```

If the position specified in the set() method is beyond the size of the bit set, the set grows in increments of sixty-four. Calling clear() with a position beyond the set size does nothing. If the position specified in a call to get() is beyond the set size, false is returned without growing the set. For valid position sizes, true is returned if the position is set (1), or false if clear (0). For all three methods, if the position is negative, an IndexOutOfBoundsException will be thrown.

Manipulating Sets of Bits

There are four methods for performing set-wide operations on the bit set. Each performs a logical operation of the corresponding bits of the two sets:

```
public void and(BitSet set)
public void or(BitSet set)
public void xor(BitSet set)
public void andNot(BitSet set)
```

For the AND operation, each bit in the current bit set will be set (1) if it is already set and if the corresponding bit in the passed-in set is also set. This roughly equates to the following:

```
this[index] &= set[index]
```

For the OR operation, the bit in the current bit set will be set (1) if it is already set or if the corresponding bit in the passed in set is set. This can be expressed as:

```
this[index] |= set[index]
```

For the XOR operation, the bit in the current bit set will be set (1) if it is already set or if the corresponding bit in the passed-in set is set, but not if both bits are set. Or, looked at in another way, the bit is set if it differs from the corresponding bit in the passed-in set and is cleared if it is the same. This can be expressed as:

```
this[index] ^= set[index]
```

For the NAND (not add) operation, the bit in the current bit set will be cleared (0) if the corresponding bit is already set in the passed in set. This roughly equates to the following:

```
this[index] &= ~set[index]
```

To demonstrate these four operations, Table 6-2 shows what happens when you perform the different operations with an original bit set of {1, 2, 3, 4, 5} and a passed in set of {1, 3, 5, 7}.

Table 6-2. Set Manipulation

OPERATION	RESULTS
and()	{1, 3, 5}
or()	{1, 2, 3, 4, 5, 7}
xor()	{2, 4, 7}
andNot()	{2, 4}

If there is a size difference between the two sets, the size of the resulting set depends on the method called. Under no condition will the contents of the passed-in set change in size or content as a result of the method call.

- and(): If the size of the current set is smaller than the passed-in set, the extra bits are ignored. If the size of the current set is larger than the passed-in set, the extra bits are cleared/set to zero.

- or() / xor(): If the size of the current set is smaller than the passed-in set, the size of the current set is increased to match the size of the passed-in set. All new bits are cleared/set to zero before performing the operation.

- andNot(): If the sizes are different in either direction, the extra bits are ignored/unchanged.

> **NOTE** *A* NullPointerException *will be thrown if you pass in a null set to any of these methods.*

Determining Set Size

Think of a BitSet as a dynamically growing array composed of bits, similar to a vector. This dynamically growing structure has two values describing its internal dimensions: a size and a length.

```
public int size()
public int length()
```

The size() method will return the number of bits reserved in the set and grows in increments of sixty-four. Think of this value like the capacity when working with a vector. On the other hand, the length() of a bit set is the last position that is set. Since positions are indexed starting from zero, this equates to the index of the highest set bit plus one.

> **NOTE** *One odd behavior of a bit set's length is that if you clear the highest set bit, the set's length can drop more than one depending upon where the next highest set bit is located.*

Cloning Bit Sets

The BitSet class implements the Cloneable interface, providing you with a clone() method.

```
public Object clone()
```

When you clone() a BitSet, you create another set with the same size and the same bit positions set.

Checking Bit Sets for Equality

The BitSet class overrides the equals() method from Object to define the equality of bit sets.

```
public boolean equals(Object object)
```

Two bit sets are defined as equal if both bit sets have the same set or clear state at every position. In other words, this[index]=object[index] must be true for each index in both sets. When one set is shorter than the other, the remaining elements would need to be clear in the longer set for both sets to be equal.

Hashing Bit Sets

Besides overriding the equals() method of Object, the BitSet class also overrides the hashCode() method. The generated hash code is only based on the position of the set bits:

```
public int hashCode()
```

Using BitSet: an Example

To demonstrate the usage of the BitSet class, Listing 6-1 creates a set of candy where the bit is set if the name has an even number of characters. It then prints out all the odd types of candy and shows the set size and length. Finally, it demonstrates the andNot() method by combining the first set with a second set where the first four elements are all set.

Listing 6-1. Demonstrating the use of BitSet.

```java
import java.util.BitSet;
public class BitOHoney {
 public static void main (String args[]) {
    String names[] = {
       "Hershey's Kisses", "Nestle's Crunch",
       "Snickers", "3 Musketeers",
       "Milky Way", "Twix", "Mr. Goodbar",
       "Crunchie", "Godiva", "Charleston Chew",
       "Cadbury's", "Lindt", "Aero", "Hebert",
       "Toblerone", "Smarties", "LifeSavers",
       "Riesen", "Goobers", "Raisinettes", "Nerds",
       "Tootsie Roll", "Sweet Tarts", "Cotton Candy"};
    BitSet bits = new BitSet();
    for (int i=0, n=names.length; i<n; i++) {
      if ((names[i].length() % 2) == 0) {
        bits.set(i);
      }
    }
    System.out.println(bits);
    System.out.println("Size  : " + bits.size());
    System.out.println("Length: " + bits.length());
    for (int i=0, n=names.length; i<n; i++) {
      if (!bits.get(i)) {
        System.out.println(names[i] + " is odd");
      }
    }
    BitSet bites = new BitSet();
    bites.set(0);
    bites.set(1);
    bites.set(2);
    bites.set(3);
    bites.andNot(bits);
    System.out.println(bites);
  }
}
```

When run, this program produces this output:

```
{0, 2, 3, 5, 7, 8, 12, 13, 15, 16, 17, 21, 23}
Size  : 64
Length: 24
Nestle's Crunch is odd
Milky Way is odd
Mr. Goodbar is odd
Charleston Chew is odd
Cadbury's is odd
Lindt is odd
Toblerone is odd
Goobers is odd
Raisinettes is odd
Nerds is odd
Sweet Tarts is odd
{1}
```

> **TIP** *The 1.1 version of this class was final with many of the operations of the class synchronized (internally). That is no longer the case. You can now subclass* BitSet. *If thread safety is an issue, you'll need to call the necessary methods within a synchronized block. The 1.0 version of the class didn't grow properly under certain conditions.*

Summary

In this chapter, we concluded our look at the historical collection classes by examining the BitSet class. You saw how to perform many operations with the bit set, from working with single bits to combining and comparing multiple bit sets. It is important to remember when working with BitSet that it is only beneficial for large sets of bits. Otherwise, it's just as easy to use a Vector of Boolean objects.

The next chapter begins Part Two in which we'll examine the Collections Framework introduced with the Java 2 release. We'll start by looking at the base Collection and Iterator interfaces of the framework.

Part Two

The Collections
Framework

Collections Introduction

In Part One of this book, we covered the standard Java library support available for working with collections of data in Java 1.0 and Java 1.1. In this part (Part Two), we'll explore the Java Collections Framework added to the core set of Java classes with the release of the Java 2 platform, version 1.2. It is with this framework that Sun finally added standard support for a rich library enabling the manipulation of groups of data. In Part Three, we'll discuss third-party libraries that you can use with Java 1.0 and 1.1 as well as the current releases of Java.

The Java Collections Framework is Sun's simplified solution to providing a framework similar in purpose to the C++ Standard Template Library (STL). While the purpose of the two is the same, to provide a *standard* library for collection classes with their respective languages, the two libraries go about their business in completely different manners. Sun's framework was designed by choice to be small and easy to use and understand, with around twenty-five different classes and interfaces. With STL, you get well over one hundred to work with. While you can definitely do much more out of the box with STL, the learning curve is much greater to become productive. With the Java Collections Framework, it's much simpler to get started and become productive.

In this chapter, I'll provide an overview of the Framework, along with a detailed look into the Collection and Iterator interfaces.

Framework Basics

The Collections Framework consists of three parts: *interfaces, implementations,* and *algorithms.* The interfaces are the abstract data types that the framework supports. The implementations are the concrete versions of these interfaces. The algorithms are the predefined actions that can be defined on either the interfaces or their implementations.

Framework Interfaces

The framework consists of four core interfaces with two specializations for sorting: `Collection`, `List`, `Set`, `Map`, `SortedSet`, and `SortedMap.` Their class hierarchy is shown in Figure 7-1. Getting to know and love these interfaces will help you to fully understand and utilize the framework.

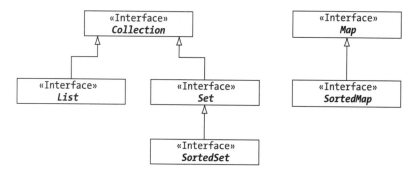

Figure 7-1. The core Collection interface hierarchy.

The base interface of the framework is the `Collection` interface. You can think of a `Collection` as a generic group of data where each data member is called an *element*. The `Collection` may or may not have duplicate elements and it may or may not have ordered elements. The `List` interface is a specialization of the `Collection` interface and is one that defines order for the elements in the collection. There may still be duplicates, but because the collection is ordered, it doesn't matter. The `Set` interface is another specialization of `Collection`. It's a collection of elements without duplicates. If you need an ordered `Set`, go to the `SortedSet` where you can define a sorting order.

The other class hierarchy that is part of the framework has to do with maps. Maps are collections of key-value pairs instead of elements. Because maps have two parts for each element, they are in their own interface hierarchy instead of inheriting from `Collection`. A `Map` is your basic collection of possibly sorted, or possibly not, key-value pairs. To ensure that the keys in the map are sorted, you can use a `SortedMap`.

Framework Implementations

Once you have a grasp of the interfaces that make up the framework, it's time to move on to the concrete implementations of these interfaces. Keeping the two concepts separate and understanding them well allows you to write code like the following:

```
List list = new ...();
```

You can change implementations when business conditions require a change without modifying any of the rest of your code.

Table 7-1 shows the different implementations of the interfaces shown in Figure 7-1. Excluding the historical collections, there are a total of seven different concrete implementations.

Table 7-1. Summary of the Concrete Collection Classes

		IMPLEMENTATIONS			
INTERFACE	HASH TABLE	RESIZABLE ARRAY	BALANCED TREE	LINKED LIST	HISTORICAL
Set	HashSet		TreeSet		
SortedSet			TreeSet		
List		ArrayList		LinkedList	Vector, Stack
Map	HashMap, WeakHashMap		TreeMap		Hashtable, Properties
SortedMap			TreeMap		

> **NOTE** *Notice that most implementations are of the form* ImplementationInterface.

To read (and use) the table, go down the first column until you see the *interface* (type of collection) you wish to use. Once you find the interface, read to the right to find the concrete implementation that most closely matches your specific requirements. For instance, as you'll learn later (and probably should know already), a linked-list-backed collection is great for adding and removing elements from the middle of a collection. If you need this behavior and don't need indexed access, a LinkedList would be a great data structure to pick. On the other hand, if indexed access is your primary concern, an ArrayList is your better bet as it is backed by an array supporting indexed access. If you need both, well, then you either have to create your own implementation to serve that need, or analyze the situation more closely to see which one matches your needs best. In other words, at design time, don't worry about the concrete implementations; just worry about the interfaces.

You'll learn about all the interfaces and their implementations as we travel through Part Two of this book. There are several key concepts to know up front that have to do with the new implementations:

- All implementations are unsynchronized. While you can add synchronized access, you are not forced to be synchronized when you don't need it.

- All implementations offer *fail-fast* iterators. If an underlying collection is modified while you are iterating through its elements, this will be detected upon the next access and cause the iteration to stop immediately by throwing a ConcurrentModificationException.

- All implementations are serializable and cloneable, allowing you to save and copy collections freely.

- All implementations support having null elements. This was not an option with the historical collections.

- The implementations rely on a concept of *optional methods* in interfaces. If an implementation doesn't support an operation, such as adding or removing elements, the implementation throws an UnsupportedOperationException when you call a method that hasn't been fully implemented.

> **NOTE**   *Until the Java programming language supports enumerated types, there is no built-in support for type-safe collections. For more on this topic, see Appendix C.*

Framework Algorithms

The predefined algorithms for supporting the framework are found in the Collections and Arrays classes. The Collections class defines those algorithms that you can perform on the framework interfaces and their concrete implementations. The Arrays class does the same thing but for array-specific algorithms instead. These classes will be discussed in Chapters 12 and 13, respectively.

Collection Interface

As mentioned above, the Collection interface forms the base of the Java Collections Framework. It doesn't really say much about the data it contains, just that it is a group of data to be acted upon collectively. The interface consists of fifteen methods (including two toArray() versions), which are listed in Table 7-2.

Table 7-2. Summary of the Collection Interface

VARIABLE/METHOD NAME	VERSION	DESCRIPTION
add()	1.2	Adds an element to the collection.
addAll()	1.2	Adds a collection of elements to the collection.
clear()	1.2	Clears all elements from the collection.
contains()	1.2	Checks if a collection contains an element.
containsAll()	1.2	Checks if a collection contains a collection of elements.
equals()	1.2	Checks for equality with another object.
hashCode()	1.2	Returns the computed hash code for the collection.
isEmpty()	1.2	Checks if a collection is empty.
iterator()	1.2	Returns an object from the collection that allows all of the collection's elements to be visited.
remove()	1.2	Clears a specific element from collection.
removeAll()	1.2	Clears a collection of elements from the collection.
retainAll()	1.2	Removes all elements from the collection not in another collection.
size()	1.2	Returns the number of elements in the collection.
toArray()	1.2	Returns the elements of a collection as an array.

Think of the methods in eight groups for adding and removing elements and for performing various operations on the collection: fetching, finding, copying, checking size and equality, and hashing. Keep in mind that there are no implementations behind these methods. Collection is just an interface. A description of these operations follows.

> **NOTE** *While not enforceable at the interface level, all concrete implementations of the* Collection *interface should provide both a no-argument constructor and one that accepts a* Collection. *The latter constructor acts as a copy-constructor, effectively copying the elements from one collection to another. You'll notice this done in Chapter 14 when we create custom* Collection *implementations.*

Adding Elements

The Collection interface supports two manners of adding elements: you can either add a single element or a group of elements.

Adding Single Elements

Adding a single element involves calling the add() method:

```
public boolean add(Object element)
```

The add() method takes a single argument, which is the element to be added. At the interface level for Collection, the handling of duplicates and positioning is undefined. Assuming the method doesn't throw an exception, the element is guaranteed to be in the collection after the method returns. If the collection is modified as a result of the call, true is returned. If it isn't modified, false is returned.

As far as exceptions go, an UnsupportedOperationException may be thrown if the add operation isn't supported by the collection, possibly because it was made read-only. You should never get a NullPointerException though, as you can add null to the collection.

Adding Another Collection

You can add a group of elements from another collection with the addAll() method:

```
public boolean addAll(Collection c)
```

Each element in the passed-in collection will be added to the current collection. If the underlying collection changes, true is returned. If no elements are added, false is returned. Again, what happens with duplicates and ordering is unspecified. Here again, if adding elements is unsupported, you'll get an UnsupportedOperationException thrown.

> **WARNING** *Don't try to add a collection to itself. The behavior is undefined. Or, do try if you want to have some fun.*

Removing Elements

The Collection interface supports four different ways to remove elements.

Removing All Elements

The simplest removal method is one that clears out all of the elements with clear():

```
public void clear()
```

While there is no return value, you can still get an UnsupportedOperationException thrown if the collection is read-only.

Removing Single Elements

Instead of clearing out an entire collection, you can remove one element at a time with the remove() method:

```
public boolean remove(Object element)
```

To determine if the element is in the collection, the specific implementation must rely on the element's equals() method for comparison. Because there is no concept of ordering, if the same element is in the collection multiple times, which one is removed is undefined. As long as something is removed, true will be returned as the underlying collection will be modified. And if removal is not supported, you'll get an UnsupportedOperationException thrown.

> **NOTE** *As elements in a generic collection have no position, there is no support for positional removal of elements.*

Removing Another Collection

The third of the removal methods is removeAll():

```
public boolean removeAll(Collection c)
```

The removeAll() method takes a Collection as an argument and removes all instances from the source collection of each element in the collection passed in.

For instance, if the original collection consisted of the following elements:

```
{1, 3, 5, 8, 1, 8, 2, 4, 1, 3, 7, 6}
```

and the collection passed in was:

```
{1, 6}
```

the resultant collection would have every instance of 1 and 6 removed:

```
{3, 5, 8, 8, 2, 4, 3, 7}
```

As with most of the previously shown collection methods, removeAll() returns true if the underlying collection changed, and false or an UnsupportedOperationException, otherwise.

Retaining Another Collection

The retainAll() method works like removeAll(), but in the opposite direction:

```
public boolean retainAll(Collection c)
```

In other words, only those elements within the collection argument are kept in the original collection. Everything else is removed.

Figure 7-2 should help you visualize the difference between removeAll() and retainAll(). The contents of the starting collection are the first five ordinal numbers repeated a second time. The acting collection for removal and retention consists of the elements 2nd, 3rd, and 6th. The 6th element is shown to demonstrate that in neither case will this be added to the original collection.

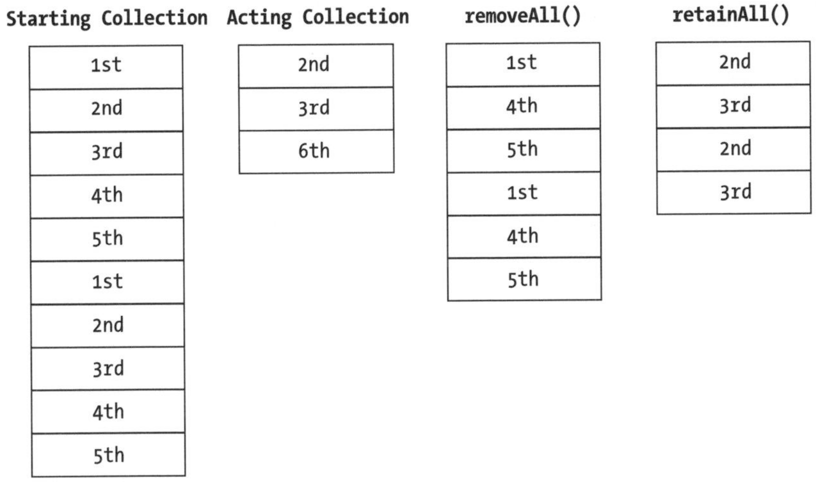

Starting Collection	Acting Collection	removeAll()	retainAll()
1st	2nd	1st	2nd
2nd	3rd	4th	3rd
3rd	6th	5th	2nd
4th		1st	3rd
5th		4th	
1st		5th	
2nd			
3rd			
4th			
5th			

Figure 7-2. The removeAll() method versus the retainAll() method.

Collection Operations

Besides methods for filling a collection, there are several other operations you can perform that deal with the elements. The Collection interface provides support for fetching, finding, and copying, among some other secondary tasks.

Fetching Elements

There is but one sole method to retrieve elements from a collection. By returning an Iterator with the iterator() method, you can step through all the elements:

```
public Iterator iterator()
```

We'll look at the Iterator interface in more depth later in this chapter.

Finding Elements

If, instead of fetching elements in the collection, you only desire to know whether a specific element or set of elements is in the collection, you can find out through this next set of methods.

Checking for Existence

The contains() method reports if a specific element is within the collection:

```
public boolean contains(Object element)
```

If found, contains() returns true, if not, contains() returns false. As with remove(), to determine if an element is in the collection, the element's equals() method is used for comparison.

Checking for Collection Containment

Besides checking to see if a collection contains a single element, you can check to see if a collection contains another whole collection with the containsAll() method:

```
public boolean containsAll(Collection c)
```

This method takes a Collection as its argument and reports if the elements of the passed-in collection are a subset of the current collection. In other words, is each element of the collection argument also an element of the current collection? The current collection can contain other elements, but containsAll() will return false if the passed-in collection contains any elements that are not in the collection to which it is applied.

Checking Size

To find out how many elements are in a collection, use the size() method:

```
public int size()
```

To check for no elements in a collection, the isEmpty() method can be used:

```
public boolean isEmpty()
```

You can think of the isEmpty() method as returning the following value:

```
return (size() == 0);
```

Copying and Cloning Collections

The Collection interface itself is neither Cloneable nor Serializable. You'll find all the system-defined, concrete implementations implementing both interfaces, but at the Collection interface-level, neither is implemented. If you need to make a copy of a collection, your best bet is to just pass the Collection off to the constructor of another collection and you've effectively cloned the collection.

Another manner of copying elements out of a collection is through the toArray() methods:

```
public Object[] toArray()
public Object[] toArray(Object[] a)
```

The first toArray() method will return an Object array containing all the elements in the collection. The position in this array is not meant to imply any meaning from the ordering, it's just that elements in an array need a position. Because this method returns an Object [ ], every time you need to get an element out of the array, you need to cast it to the appropriate type. When all elements of a collection are of the same type, it is easier for you to work with an array of that specific type.

This is where the second version of toArray() comes in handy: Object[] toArray(Object[] a). With this version, the toArray() method consults with the passed-in array to determine the return type (and size). If the passed-in array is large enough to contain all the elements in the collection [collection.size() <= a.length], the elements are placed in the array and returned. If the array is too small, a new array of the same type will be created, sized to the current number of elements in the collection as reported by size(), and used to store all the elements. It is this new array that is returned in this second case, not the original array. If the array passed in is too large, the toArray() method replaces with null the element one beyond the last element copied (a[collection.size()] = null). This may be useful if you know there are no null elements in the collection and don't want to ask the collection its size.

> **WARNING**   *If the elements of the collection are not assignment-compatible with the array type, an* ArrayStoreException *will be thrown.*

When using this version of toArray(), you pass as an argument an array of the appropriate type, such as a String[ ]. You can either let the method size things for you, throwing away your originally created array, or presize the array yourself.

```
// Creating an array to be discarded method:
Collection c = . . .;
String array[] = new String[0];
array = (String[])c.toArray(array);
```

or

```
// Sizing the array yourself.
Collection c = . . .;
String array[] = new String[c.size()];
array = (String[])c.toArray(array);
```

While the latter is the better way, I always think the code line looks weird as compared to calling the no-argument version of the method.

Checking for Equality

The Collection class adds an equals() method to its interface:

```
public boolean equals(Object o)
```

Classes implementing the Collection interface technically don't have to do a thing because the Object class, which all classes extend from, defines a public equals() method. However, the equals() method is part of the interface to make sure you define equality when creating your own collections. Some, like List and Set, require that collections of a certain type are only equal to other collections of the same type.

Hashing Collections

Besides overriding the equals() method of Object, the Collection interface also defines a hashCode() method:

```
public int hashCode()
```

Again, there is no requirement that you must provide a hashCode() method. However, as with noncollection classes, if two instances are equal(), then the generated hash codes must be the same. Usually, combining the hash codes from the elements of the collection will generate the hash code.

Iterator Interface

We've seen the Iterator interface a few times already, with vectors in Chapter 3, and briefly above. This interface is the Collections Framework equivalent to the Enumeration interface in the historical classes, offering a standard way to step through all the elements in a collection. As Figure 7-3 shows, it has one subinterface and, more importantly, does not extend from the Enumeration interface.

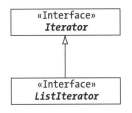

Figure 7-3. The Iterator interface hierarchy.

> **NOTE** *We'll explore the* ListIterator *interface in Chapter 9.*

As Table 7-3 shows, there are only three methods in the interface.

Table 7-3. Summary of the Iterator Interface

VARIABLE/METHOD NAME	VERSION	DESCRIPTION
hasNext()	1.2	Checks for more elements in the iterator.
next()	1.2	Fetches the next element of the iterator.
remove()	1.2	Removes an element from the iterator.

Using an Iterator

Compared to an Enumeration, hasNext() is equivalent to hasMoreElements() and next() equates to nextElement(). The basic usage flow follows. As with Enumeration, there is no implied element order, everything in the collection will be visited if you walk through the entire iterator:

```
Collection c = . . .
Iterator i = c.iterator();
while (i.hasNext()) {
  process(i.next());
}
```

> **NOTE** *If* next() *is called after* hasNext() *returns false, a* NoSuchElementException *will be thrown. Also note that if you know how many elements are supposed to be in the collection, you don't have to call* hasNext() *between calls to* next().

The remove() method is unique to Iterator and without an equivalent in Enumeration. When remove() is called, it will remove from the source collection the last item retrieved from next(), if supported by the underlying collection. If not supported, an UnsupportedOperationException is thrown. If remove() is called twice in succession without a call to next() in between, an IllegalStateException is thrown. It's also possible to get a ConcurrentModificationException thrown if someone else is modifying the collection while you're iterating through it with next() or remove(). Using the remove() method to eliminate elements from the source collection is the only safe way to update a collection while iterating through the elements. You should not try to remove elements from the original collection directly.

Filtering Iterator

Have you ever wanted to work with an Enumeration (and now Iterator) but work only with those elements that passed a preliminary test case? Let's create our own custom Iterator that accepts a *predicate*, a method that returns true or false and does this filtering for us.

Our Predicate interface will have one method, boolean predicate(Object element), where the object passed into the method will be each element from the iterator to be tested:

```
interface Predicate {
  boolean predicate(Object element);
}
```

Then, we need to create an Iterator implementation that, given an Iterator and a Predicate, will have next() return only those items that pass the predicate test and have hasNext() detect when there is a next. For simplicity's sake, we won't support remove() and just throw an UnsupportedOperationException when called—the next() method has to detect if next() is called multiple times in succession without a hasNext() call in between. This is perfectly valid for an iterator, we just need to be sure our implementation deals with it. All of this is done in the PredicateIterator implementation shown in Listing 7-1.

Listing 7-1. Our custom `PredicateIterator`.

```java
import java.util.*;
class PredicateIterator implements Iterator {
  Iterator iter;
  Predicate pred;
  Object next;
  boolean doneNext = false;
  public PredicateIterator(Iterator iter, Predicate pred) {
    this.iter = iter;
    this.pred = pred;
  }
  public void remove() {
    throw new UnsupportedOperationException();
  }
  public boolean hasNext() {
    doneNext = true;
    boolean hasNext;
    while (hasNext = iter.hasNext()) {
      next = iter.next();
      if (pred.predicate(next)) {
        break;
      }
    }
    return hasNext;
  }
  public Object next() {
    if (!doneNext) {
      boolean has = hasNext();
      if (!has) {
        throw new NoSuchElementException();
      }
    }
    doneNext = false;
    return next;
  }
}
```

Listing 7-2 tests our `PredicateIterator` by creating a simple predicate test of strings starting with "Hi" and using command-line arguments as the collection.

Listing 7-2. Testing our PredicateIterator.

```
import java.util.*;
public class PredTest {
  static Predicate pred = new Predicate() {
    public boolean predicate(Object o) {
      return o.toString().startsWith("Hi");
    }
  };
  public static void main (String args[]) {
    List list = Arrays.asList(args);
    Iterator i1 = list.iterator();
    Iterator i = new PredicateIterator(i1, pred);
    while (i.hasNext()) {
      System.out.println(i.next());
    }
  }
}
```

Those elements that pass the predicate are simply printed out.

If you run this program with the command, java ProdTest One Two Hi Three Four High Six Seven Higher, your results will be:

```
Hi
High
Higher
```

> **NOTE** *The base* Iterator *returned from the list collection we are using detects concurrent modifications, so we don't have to add code to detect concurrent modifications to our decorated iterator.*

Collection Exceptions

The ConcurrentModificationException and UnsupportedOperationException are two exceptions that are unique (so far) to the Collections Framework. They provide support for the fail-safe behavior of collections and for the decorator-like capabilities offered by many of the collection interface wrappers.

ConcurrentModificationException

The ConcurrentModificationException has to do with the fail-fast nature of the
collection iterators. If an underlying collection is modified outside the remove()
method of the Iterator while you are iterating through its elements, this will be
detected upon the next access and a ConcurrentModificationException will be
thrown, thereby causing the iteration to stop.

To demonstrate, the following program causes a
ConcurrentModificationException to be thrown. It starts by walking through the
elements of an Iterator but adds an element after printing the first one. As this
modifies the underlying collection, the iterator is immediately invalidated such
that the second call to next() fails miserably (however, hasNext() still succeeds):

```
import java.util.*;
public class FailExample {
  public static void main (String args[]) {
    List list = new ArrayList(Arrays.asList(args));
    Iterator i = list.iterator();
    while (i.hasNext()) {
      System.out.println(i.next());
      list.add("Add");
    }
  }
}
```

Running the program with at least two elements on the command line will
produce similar results:

```
One
Exception in thread "main" java.util.ConcurrentModificationException
        at java.util.AbstractList$Itr.checkForComodification(AbstractList _
.java:445)
        at java.util.AbstractList$Itr.next(AbstractList.java:418)
        at FailExample.main(FailExample.java:8)
```

As java.util.ConcurrentModificationException is a runtime exception, you
don't have to place all your iterating code in a try-catch block.

The modification methods of the Collection interface are as follows:

* add()

* addAll()

* clear()

* remove()

* removeAll()

* retainAll()

Other classes and interfaces can add to this set, such as the set() method of the List interface, or the addFirst(), addLast(), removeFirst(), and removeLast() methods of the LinkedList class. Basically, any method apart from the iterator's remove() method that can cause the underlying collection to change should cause a ConcurrentModificationException to be thrown when iterating through the modified collection.

While you won't normally create these exceptions yourself, there are two constructors:

```
public ConcurrentModificationException()
public ConcurrentModificationException(String message)
```

UnsupportedOperationException

Located in the java.lang package, the UnsupportedOperationException is thrown when you try to call a collections-related method on an instance of a collection's interface that doesn't provide a complete implementation of that interface. Unlike adapter classes, where empty stubs are valid, the collections classes have several capabilities that are optional, like adding elements to a collection. If a collection is a fixed-size or read-only collection, you can't add or remove elements from it. Trying to perform such an operation causes this exception to be thrown.

For instance, since Arrays.asList() returns a fixed-length collection, you can't add anything to it without causing the exception to be thrown:

```
List list = Arrays.asList(args);
list.add("Add");   // Throws UnsupportedOperationException
```

Like ConcurrentModificationException, you won't normally create this run-time exception yourself. However, there are two constructors here, too:

```
public UnsupportedOperationException()
public UnsupportedOperationException(String message)
```

Summary

In this chapter, you were introduced to the capabilities of the Java Collections Framework and we examined two of its key interfaces: Collection and Iterator. You saw how you can add a decorator around an Iterator and learned about the collection-specific exceptions: ConcurrentModificationException and UnsupportedOperationException.

You'll learn about the Set interface in the next chapter, as well as the hash-table-based HashSet and the balanced, tree-based TreeSet. You'll see how these can be used to maintain duplicate-free collections.

Sets

The Set interface is the first type of Collection we'll discuss. This interface represents a group of elements without duplicates. There is nothing in the interface definition that forces the group to not have duplicates; it is the actual implementations that enforce this part of the definition. The elements of the group have no perceived order, though specific implementations of the interface may place an order on those items.

Figure 8-1 shows the class hierarchy diagram for the Set interface, along with the base abstract implementation, the concrete implementation classes, and other interfaces implemented by these classes.

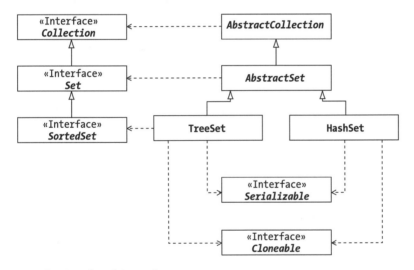

Figure 8-1. The Set class hierarchy.

Set Basics

In Java, a set represents a collection of unique elements. Not only must these elements be unique, but while they are in the set, each element must not be modified. While there is no programmatic restriction preventing you from modifying elements in a set, if an element were to change, it could become forever lost in the set.

While not immediately obvious in Table 8-1, the Set interface definition is the same as the Collection interface definition shown in Chapter 7.

Table 8-1. Summary of Interface Set

VARIABLE/METHOD NAME	VERSION	DESCRIPTION
add()	1.2	Adds an element to the set.
addAll()	1.2	Adds a collection of elements to the set.
clear()	1.2	Clears all elements from the set.
contains()	1.2	Checks if the set contains an element
containsAll()	1.2	Checks if the set contains a collection of elements.
equals()	1.2	Checks for equality with another object.
hashCode()	1.2	Returns a computed hash code for the set.
isEmpty()	1.2	Checks if the set is empty.
iterator()	1.2	Returns an object from the set that allows all of the set's elements to be visited.
remove()	1.2	Clears a specific element from the set.
removeAll()	1.2	Clears a collection of elements from the set.
retainAll()	1.2	Removes all elements from the set not in another collection.
size()	1.2	Returns the number of elements in the set.
toArray()	1.2	Returns the elements of the set as an array.

The Collection Framework provides two concrete set implementations: HashSet and TreeSet. The HashSet represents a set backed by a hash table providing constant lookup-time access to unordered elements. On the other hand, the TreeSet maintains its elements in an ordered fashion within a balanced tree. Since the Set interface is identical to the Collection interface, we'll immediately jump into the concrete implementations.

HashSet Class

The Collection Framework introduces the HashSet collection. This implementation is backed by a hash table (HashMap, actually) for storing unique elements. The backing hash table ensures that duplicate elements are avoided as each element is stored and retrieved through its hash code, providing constant retrieval time.

> **NOTE** *For more on hash codes, see Chapter 5. The* HashMap *is the framework's replacement to the historical* Hashtable *class. It, too, provides storage for key-value pairs.* HashSet *just stores a dummy 'present' object as the value for every key.*

Most of the `HashSet` functionality is provided through the `AbstractCollection` and `AbstractSet` superclasses, which `HashSet` shares with `TreeSet`. As Table 8-2 shows, the `HashSet` class only needs to provide constructors and customize eight of its methods.

Table 8-2. Summary of the HashSet Class

VARIABLE/METHOD NAME	VERSION	DESCRIPTION
HashSet()	1.2	Constructs a hash set.
add()	1.2	Adds an element to the set.
clear()	1.2	Removes all elements from the set.
clone()	1.2	Creates a clone of the set.
contains ()	1.2	Checks if an object is in the set.
isEmpty()	1.2	Checks if the set has any elements.
iterator()	1.2	Returns an object from the set that allows all of the set's elements to be visited.
remove()	1.2	Removes an element from the set.
size()	1.2	Returns the number of elements in the set.

While only eight methods are shown here, we should look at all those defined within the `Set` interface. These methods can, again, like `Collection`, be broken down into eight groups with `HashSet` adding a ninth for its constructors. The methods of the eight groups allow you to add and remove elements as well as perform operations on the set as a whole.

Creating a HashSet

The `HashSet` class provides four constructors broken into two sets. The first three constructors create empty sets of varying sizes:

```
public HashSet()
public HashSet(int initialCapacity)
public HashSet(int initialCapacity, int loadFactor)
```

If unspecified, the initial set size for storing elements will be the default size of a `HashMap`, which happens to be eleven or 101, depending upon what Java version you are using. When the set capacity reaches full and a new element is added, the internal structure will double in size before adding the new element (and copying in the old elements). If you don't like the 75%-full aspect, you can provide the constructor with a custom load factor.

> **TIP**   *When creating any collection, it is always best to have the local vari-*
> *able be of the interface type, as in* Set set = new HashSet(). *That way, if*
> *you later decide to change the set to a* TreeSet *or some other set implemen-*
> *tation, you won't have to change any code as you'll only be using the meth-*
> *ods of the* Set *interface.*

The fourth constructor acts as a copy constructor, copying the elements from one set into the newly created set:

```
public HashSet(Collection col)
```

You cannot provide a custom initial capacity or load factor. Instead, the internal map will be sized at twice the size of the collection, or eleven if the collection is small (five or less elements), keeping the default load factor of 75%.

> **NOTE**   *If the original collection had duplicates, only one of the duplicates*
> *will be in the final created set.*

An easy way to initialize a set without manually adding each element is to create an array of the elements, create a List from that array with Arrays.asList(), then call this constructor with the list as the collection:

```
String elements[] = {"Irish Setter", "Poodle", "English Setter",
    "Gordon Setter", "Pug"};
Set set = new HashSet(Arrays.asList(elements));
```

Adding Elements

When you need to add elements to a set, you can either add a single element or a group of elements.

Adding Single Elements

To add a single element, call the add() method:

```
public boolean add(Object element)
```

The add() method takes a single argument of the element to add. If the element is not in the set, it is added and true is returned. If the element happens to be in the set already, because element.equals(oldElement) returns true (for some element in the set), then the new element replaces the old element in the collection and false is returned. If the old element has no other references, it becomes eligible for garbage collection. See Figure 8-2 to help you visualize this replacement scenario.

```
// Create two equal objects
StringBuffer stringBufferA = new StringBuffer("Irish Setter");
StringBuffer stringBufferB = new StringBuffer("Irish Setter");

Set set = new HashSet();

boolean returnValue = set.add(stringBufferA);
// returnValue is true



returnValue = set.add(stringBufferB);
// returnValue is false
```

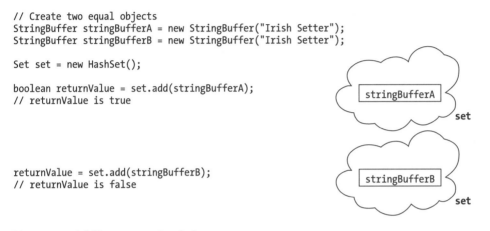

Figure 8-2. Adding a contained element to a set.

If you are working with a set that was made to be read-only, or if adding elements is not supported, then an UnsupportedOperationException will be thrown.

> **TIP** *If you need to modify an element in a set, you should remove it, modify it, and then re-add it. If you don't, you can consider the object lost as there is no way of finding the object without manually digging through all the objects in the set. This is true when the change affects the results of* hashCode(). *If the change doesn't affect the method results, the change can be made. However, you should then question why the* hashCode() *results didn't change.*

Adding Another Collection

You can add a group of elements from another collection to the set with the addAll() method:

```
public boolean addAll(Collection c)
```

Each element in the collection passed in will be added to the current set via the equivalent of calling the add() method on each element. If the underlying set changes, true is returned. If no elements are added, false is returned. As with add(), if equal elements are in both sets, true is returned with the new element replacing the old element in the set.

An UnsupportedOperationException will be thrown when working with a set that doesn't support adding elements.

Removing Elements

You can remove elements from a set in four different ways.

Removing All Elements

The simplest removal method, clear(), clears all of the elements from the set:

```
public void clear()
```

While there is no return value, you can still get an UnsupportedOperationException thrown when working with a read-only set.

Removing Single Elements

Use the remove() method if you wish to remove a single element at a time:

```
public boolean remove(Object element)
```

Determining whether the element is in the set is done via the equals() method of the element. If the element is found, the element is removed from the set and true is returned. If not found, false is returned. If removal is not supported, you'll get an UnsupportedOperationException thrown whether the element is present or not.

Removing Another Collection

The third way to remove elements is with removeAll():

```
public boolean removeAll(Collection c)
```

The removeAll() method takes a Collection as an argument and removes from the set all instances of each element in the collection passed in. The Collection passed in can be a Set or some other Collection implementation. For instance, if the original set consisted of the following elements:

```
{"Irish Setter", "Poodle", "English Setter", "Gordon Setter", "Pug"}
```

and the collection passed in was

```
{"Poodle", "Pug", "Poodle", "Pug", "Poodle", "Pug", "Pug", "Pug"}
```

the resulting set would have every instance of "Poodle" and "Pug" removed. Since a set cannot have duplicates, it would remove one for each:

```
{"Irish Setter", "English Setter", "Gordon Setter"}
```

As with most of the previously shown set methods, removeAll() returns true if the underlying set changed, and false or an UnsupportedOperationException, otherwise. And again, the equals() method is used to check for element equality.

Retaining Another Collection

The retainAll() method works like removeAll(), but in the opposite direction:

```
public boolean retainAll(Collection c)
```

In other words, only those elements within the collection argument are kept in the original set. Everything else is removed, instead.

Figure 8-3 should help you visualize the difference between removeAll() and retainAll(). The contents of the starting set are the five dogs listed previously (Irish Setter, Poodle, English Setter, Gordon Setter, Pug). The acting collection consists of the elements Pug, Poodle, and Samoyed. The Samoyed element is shown to demonstrate that in neither case will this be added to the original collection. Remember that sets are unordered, so the resultant set may not keep the elements in the original order.

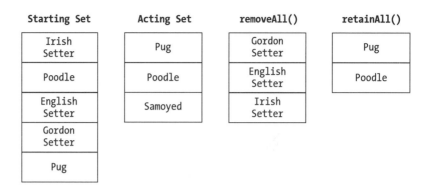

Figure 8-3. The removeAll() method versus the retainAll() method.

Set Operations

Besides methods for filling a set, there are several other operations you can per-form, all of which deal with the elements. You'll find support for fetching, finding, and copying elements, among some other secondary tasks.

Fetching Elements

To work with all of the elements of the set, you can call the iterator() method to get an Iterator:

```
public Iterator iterator()
```

Since the elements of a hash set are unordered, the order of the elements returned has nothing to do with the order in which they were added or any kind of sort order. And as the capacity of the hash set changes, the elements may be reordered. In other words, don't rely on the element order returned to be consis-tent between calls.

Working with an Iterator returned from a Set is no different than every other Iterator:

```
String elements[] = {"Irish Setter", "Poodle", "English Setter",
    "Gordon Setter", "Pug"};
Set set = new HashSet(Arrays.asList(elements));
Iterator iter = set.iterator();
while (iter.hasNext()) {
  System.out.println(iter.next());
}
```

Running this will result in output similar to the following; remember that order doesn't matter as long as each element in the set is displayed:

```
Gordon Setter
Poodle
English Setter
Pug
Irish Setter
```

Finding Elements

If, instead of fetching elements in the set, you desire to know only whether a specific element or set of elements is in the set, this next set of methods provides discovery capabilities about the set.

Checking for Existence

The contains() method reports if a specific element is within the set:

```
public boolean contains(Object element)
```

If found, contains() returns true; if not, false. As with remove(), equality checking is done through the element's equals() method.

Checking for Set Containment

Besides checking to see if a set contains a single element, the containsAll() method allows you to check if a set contains another whole collection:

```
public boolean containsAll(Collection c)
```

This method takes a Collection as its argument and reports if the elements of the passed-in collection are a subset of the current set. In other words, is each element of the collection also an element of the current collection? The current set can contain other elements but the passed-in collection cannot or containsAll() will return false. If an element is in the passed-in collection multiple times, it only needs to be in the source set once to be successful.

Checking Size

To find out how many elements are in a set, use the `size()` method:

```
public int size()
```

To combine the process of getting the size and checking for no elements in the set, use the `isEmpty()` method instead:

```
public boolean isEmpty()
```

You can think of the `isEmpty()` method as returning the following value, however, the use of `isEmpty()` is faster:

```
return (size() == 0);
```

Copying and Cloning Sets

There are many ways to duplicate a `HashSet`. You can clone it, serialize it, copy it, or simply call the previously shown copy constructor.

Hash sets are `Cloneable` and have a public `clone()` method:

```
public Object clone()
```

Calling the `clone()` method of a `HashSet` creates a shallow copy of that `HashSet`. In other words, the elements of the set aren't duplicated. Initially, both sets will refer to the same elements. However, adding or removing elements in one has no effect on the other. Changes to the attributes of a common element will be reflected in both sets. And while changes to a single element will be reflected in both collections, changing elements while they are in the set should be avoided. If you do, and an individual element's hash code is changed, the set no longer knows of the existence of the element in the set except through its iterator.

Calling `clone()` can be a little ugly if you only have a reference to the interface. You must call the `clone()` method of a concrete class, not an interface. Calling it on an interface is effectively like calling it on `Object` and the `clone()` method of `Object` is protected. Thus, you must cast both the method call and the return value of the method call like so:

```
Set set = . . .
Set set2 = ((Set)((HashSet)set).clone());
```

Besides implementing `Cloneable`, `HashSet` implements the empty `Serializable` interface. If, and only if, all of the elements of a `HashSet` are `Serializable` can you save the `HashSet` to an `ObjectOutputStream` and later read it in to an `ObjectInputStream`. The following demonstrates this:

```
FileOutputStream fos = new FileOutputStream("set.ser");
ObjectOutputStream oos = new ObjectOutputStream(fos);
oos.writeObject(set);
oos.close();
FileInputStream fis = new FileInputStream("set.ser");
ObjectInputStream ois = new ObjectInputStream(fis);
Set anotherSet = (Set)ois.readObject();
ois.close();
System.out.println(set3);
```

This is also helpful for passing sets across an `HttpServletResponse` through a servlet, across a URL connection, or some other socket connection.

Another manner of copying elements out of a set is through the `toArray()` methods:

```
public Object[] toArray()
public Object[] toArray(Object[] a)
```

The first `toArray()` method will return an `Object` array containing all the elements in the collection. The position of an element in the array is not meant to imply any position for that element inside the set. It just so happens that elements in an array need an index.

Because this method returns an `Object` [ ], every time you need to get an element out of the array, you need to cast it to the appropriate type. When all elements of a collection are of the same type, it is easier for you to work with an array of that specific type.

As with the generic `Collection` interface definition, this is where the second version of `toArray()` comes in handy: `Object[] toArray(Object[] a)`. With this version, the `toArray()` method consults with the passed-in array to determine the return type (and size). If the passed-in array is large enough to contain all the elements in the collection [`set.size() <= a.length`], the elements are placed in the array and returned. If the array is too small, a new array of the same type will be created, sized to the current number of elements in the set as reported by `size()`, and used to store all the elements. It is this new array that is returned in the second case, not the original. If the array passed in is too large, the element located at the index in the array one position after the last item from the set will be set to null (`a[collection.size()] = null`). This may be useful if you know there are no null elements in the set and don't want to ask the set its size.

> **WARNING** *If the elements of the collection are not assignment-compatible with the array type, an* ArrayStoreException *will be thrown.*

Checking for Equality

The HashSet class defines equality through its equals() method:

```
public boolean equals(Object o)
```

A HashSet is equal to another object if the other object implements the Set interface, has the same size(), and contains all the same elements.

Calling the equals() method on a HashSet effectively calls the equals() method on each element within the set—or at least until one reports that there is no equivalent element in the passed-in set.

Hashing Collections

The HashSet class overrides the hashCode() method to define an appropriate hash code for the set:

```
public int hashCode()
```

The hashCode() method works such that no matter what internal order the hash set elements are in, the same hashCode() must be returned. In other words, it sums up the hash codes of all the elements.

> **PERFORMANCE NOTE** *Starting with Java 1.3, hash codes for Strings are now cached. Previously, they were recomputed each time they were needed.*

TreeSet Class

The other concrete Set implementation is the TreeSet. The TreeSet class works exactly the same as the HashSet class with one notable exception: instead of keeping its elements unordered, a TreeSet keeps its elements ordered internally. Not only are the elements ordered, but the tree is balanced. More specifically, it's a red-black tree. Having a balanced tree guarantees a quick o(log n) search time at the cost of a more time-intensive insertion (and deletion). Of course, elements added to the tree must be orderable.

> **NOTE** *Red-black tree rules refresher:*
> 1. *Every node in the tree is either black or red.*
> 2. *The root is always black.*
> 3. *If a node is red, its children must be black.*
> 4. *Every path from the root to a leaf (or null child) must contain the same number of black nodes.*

Because TreeSet implements the SortedSet interface as well as the Set interface, understanding TreeSet is a little more involved than HashSet. Table 8-3 lists the methods you'll need to know to use TreeSet.

Table 8-3. Summary of the TreeSet Class

VARIABLE/METHOD NAME	VERSION	DESCRIPTION
TreeSet()	1.2	Constructs a tree set.
add()	1.2	Adds an element to the set.
addAll()	1.2	Adds a collection of elements to the set.
clear()	1.2	Removes all elements from the set.
clone()	1.2	Creates a clone of the set.
comparator()	1.2	Retrieves a comparator for the set.
contains ()	1.2	Checks to see if an object is in the set.
first()	1.2	Retrieves the first element of the set.
headSet()	1.2	Retrieves a subset at the beginning of the entire set.
isEmpty()	1.2	Checks if the set has any elements.
iterator()	1.2	Returns an object from the set that allows all of the set's elements to be visited.
last()	1.2	Retrieves the last element of the set.
remove()	1.2	Removes an element from the set.
size()	1.2	Returns the number of elements in the set.
subSet()	1.2	Retrieves a subset of the entire set.
tailSet()	1.2	Retrieves a subset at the end of the entire set.

As the behavior of most of the TreeSet methods duplicates that of HashSet, we'll only look at those methods that are new or specialized to TreeSet. These new methods happen to be those implemented for the SortedSet interface.

> **NOTE** *In addition to their coverage here, the* SortedSet *interface and sorting support in general will be examined in more depth in Chapter 11.*

Creating a TreeSet

The TreeSet class provides four constructors broken into two sets. The first two constructors create empty tree sets:

```
public TreeSet()
public TreeSet(Comparator comp)
```

In order to maintain an ordering, elements added to a tree set must provide some way for the tree to order them. If the elements implement the Comparable interface, the first constructor is sufficient. If, however, the objects aren't comparable or you don't like the default ordering provided, you can pass along a custom Comparator to the constructor that will be used to keep elements ordered. Once the TreeSet is created, you cannot change the comparator.

> **NOTE** *Similar to the* HashSet *relying on a* HashMap *for the internal storage, the* TreeSet *relies on a* TreeMap *internally.*

The second two constructors are copy constructors, copying all elements from one collection into another:

```
public TreeSet(Collection col)
public TreeSet(SortedSet set)
```

If the other collection is a SortedSet, the TreeSet is able to perform some optimizations while adding elements. It also retains the original set's comparator.

> **TIP** *If you find yourself needing to add many elements to a* TreeSet, *it is frequently quicker to copy the set to another collection, add the elements, and then create a new* TreeSet *from the modified collection. This avoids forcing the* TreeSet *to keep the set sorted after each insert.*

Adding Elements

To add a single element, call the add() method:

```
public boolean add(Object element)
```

The add() method for TreeSet is not that different from the add() method for HashSet. The key difference is that the element to add must implement the Comparable interface or the TreeSet constructor must have been passed a Comparator. If both of these are not true then a ClassCastException will be thrown. Not only must the single element be comparable, but each element must be comparable to every other element in the set. In other words, you can't have something like a Date and a Long in the same TreeSet without writing your own Comparator.

Comparing

The comparator() method allows you to get the current Comparator for the tree:

```
public Comparator comparator()
```

While this method isn't frequently called directly, if you're interested in finding out what comparator a TreeSet is using, you can ask, and then possibly create another tree with the same comparator. The method returns null if the natural ordering of the set elements is used.

Here's a demonstration of creating a tree with a Comparator, filling the tree, and getting that comparator:

```java
import java.util.*;
public class Comp {
  public static void main (String args[]) throws Exception {
    String elements[] = {"Irish Setter", "Poodle", "English Setter",
      "Gordon Setter", "Pug"};
    Set set = new TreeSet(Collections.reverseOrder());
    for (int i=0, n=elements.length; i<n; i++) {
      set.add(elements[i]);
    }
    System.out.println(set);
    System.out.println(((TreeSet)set).comparator());
  }
}
```

Retrieving the Ends

You can use the first() and last() methods of TreeSet to get the elements at the ends of the tree:

```
public Object first()
public Object last()
```

The ends of the tree are defined by element comparing. Given that elements are added in order, either natural or otherwise, the end points naturally fall out of that. The first() element is the one that is ordered first in the set, while last() is last. A NoSuchElementException will be thrown by either method if there are no elements in the set.

> **NOTE** *There is no method to ask for the current tree root. Given all the rotations necessary to maintain a red-black tree, and the fact that the root is bound to change with the next set of additions, there is no way to ask for the root, nor is there much value in having one.*

Fetching Elements

The other way to fetch elements from a TreeSet is with the iterator() method:

```
public Iterator iterator()
```

Since the elements of a tree set are ordered, the order of the elements returned will be the order in which they are in the tree.

If we change our earlier example to use a TreeSet instead of a HashSet:

```
String elements[] = {"Irish Setter", "Poodle", "English Setter",
    "Gordon Setter", "Pug"};
Set set = new TreeSet(Arrays.asList(elements));
Iterator iter = set.iterator();
while (iter.hasNext()) {
  System.out.println(iter.next());
}
```

. . . you'll notice the order printed is now alphabetical, which is the natural ordering of strings.

```
English Setter
Gordon Setter
Irish Setter
Poodle
Pug
```

Working with Subsets

Since a TreeSet is ordered, a subset of the tree set is also ordered. As such, the
TreeSet class provides several methods for working with these subsets. The two
that are simplest to explain are headset() and tailSet():

```
public SortedSet headSet(Object toElement)
public SortedSet tailSet(Object fromElement)
```

The third method subSet() provides the end points:

```
public SortedSet subSet(Object fromElement, Object toElement)
```

All of these methods will give you a view into the underlying tree such that
changes to that view are reflected in the set from which the view came from. In
other words, if you remove something from the subset, it's gone. In addition, if
you try to add something to the subtree, it must "fit" within your view of the tree.
And if you add something to the original view, the subset will be altered, too.

One end point for the headSet() and tailSet() is easy. For the headSet(), the
first element will always be the first() element. Similarly, for the tailSet(), the
last element will be the last() element. These are always included in their respective subsets.

As far as the other element specifying the range goes, the fromElement will be
in the subset while the toElement will not:

```
fromElement <= set view < toElement
```

If you want the toElement to be in the subset, you must pass in the next node
of the tree, or at least a value that is just beyond the element. In the case of string
nodes, this would be adding something to the end to ensure that your node is
there:

```
SortedSet headSet = set.headSet(toElement+"\0");
```

If you don't want the `fromElement` to be in the subset, you must do the same thing on the other side:

```
SortedSet tailSet = set.tailSet(fromElement+"\0");
```

To get a set that includes both ends, use:

```
SortedSet bothEnds = set.subSet(fromElement, toElement+"\0");
```

Or, for a set that includes neither end, use:

```
SortedSet neitherEnd = set.subSet(fromElement+"\0", toElement);
```

To demonstrate with our earlier five-dog set (Irish Setter, Poodle, English Setter, Gordon Setter, Pug):

- tailSet("Irish Setter")

  [Irish Setter, Poodle, Pug]

- headSet("Irish Setter")

  [English Setter, Gordon Setter]

- headSet("Irish Setter\0")

  [English Setter, Gordon Setter, Irish Setter]

- tailSet("Irish Setter\0")

  [Poodle, Pug]

- subSet("Irish Setter", "Poodle\0")

  [Irish Setter, Poodle]

- subSet("Irish Setter", "Irish Setter\0")

  [Irish Setter]

- subSet("Irish Setter", "Irish Setter")

  [ ]

While displaying elements in an easily sorted manner is nice, if you don't need the behavior, the cost to add elements and search for them is not worth it.

Summary

This chapter introduced you to the Set interface and its concrete implementation classes, HashSet and TreeSet. The two implementations offer either quick insertion/search times or ordered access, respectively. Which you choose depends upon your specific needs. Both allow you to maintain groups of unique items, and neither replaces an historical collection.

In the next chapter, you'll learn about the List interface and its implementations: the array-backed ArrayList and the linked list-backed LinkedList classes. You'll also see how the ListIterator interface extends the basic capabilities of the Iterator interface. Using these new interfaces and classes, you'll see how to effectively work in Java with sequences of elements.

CHAPTER 9

Lists

While the Set interface is the simplest of the collection types (as it doesn't add any behavior to the Collection interface), you're more likely to use the List interface and its implementations: ArrayList and LinkedList. Beyond the basic collection capabilities, the List interface adds positional access to a collection so its elements have some kind of sequential order. Thus, when retrieving elements out of a list, instead of using an Iterator to visit each element, you can fetch a ListIterator to take advantage of that positioning in order to move in both directions.

The class hierarchy diagram for the List interface, its abstract and concrete implementations, and its related interfaces are shown in Figure 9-1.

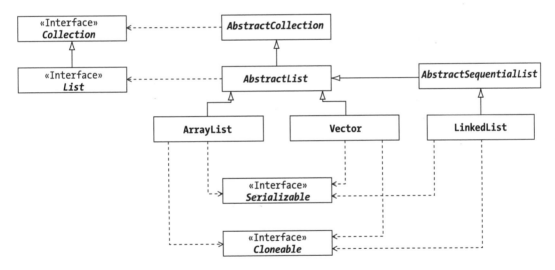

Figure 9-1. The List class hierarchy.

List Basics

Originally demonstrated with the historical Vector class in Chapter 3, lists in Java permit ordered access of their elements. They can have duplicates and because their lookup key is the position and not some hash code, every element can be modified while they remain in the list.

Table 9-1 lists the methods of the List interface. Added to those in the Collection interface are methods supporting element access by position or order.

Table 9-1. Summary of the List Interface

VARIABLE/METHOD NAME	VERSION	DESCRIPTION
add()	1.2	Adds an element to the list.
addAll()	1.2	Adds a collection of elements to the list.
clear()	1.2	Clears all elements from the list.
contains()	1.2	Checks to see if an object is a value within the list.
containsAll()	1.2	Checks if the list contains a collection of elements.
equals()	1.2	Checks for equality with another object.
get()	1.2	Returns an element at a specific position.
hashCode()	1.2	Computes hash code for the list.
indexOf()	1.2	Searches for an element within the list.
isEmpty()	1.0	Checks if the list has any elements.
iterator()	1.2	Returns an object from the list that allows all of the list's elements to be visited.
lastIndexOf()	1.2	Searches from the end of the list for an element.
listIterator()	1.2	Returns an object from the list that allows all of the list's elements to be visited sequentially.
remove()	1.2	Clears a specific element from the list.
removeAll()	1.2	Clears a collection of elements from the list.
retainAll()	1.2	Removes all elements from the list not in another collection.
set()	1.2	Changes an element at a specific position within the list.
size()	1.2	Returns the number of elements in the list.
subList()	1.2	Returns a portion of the list.
toArray()	1.2	Returns the elements of the list as array.

You'll find three concrete list implementations in the Collections Framework: Vector, ArrayList, and LinkedList. The Vector class from the historical group has been reworked into the framework and was discussed in Chapter 3. ArrayList is the replacement for Vector in the new framework. It represents an unsynchronized vector where the backing store is a dynamically growable array. On the other hand is LinkedList, which, as its name implies, is backed by the familiar linked list data structure.

> **NOTE**   *There is no predefined sorted List implementation (TreeList). If you need to maintain the elements in a sorted manner, consider either maintaining your elements in a different collection or sorting the elements after you are done inserting (into another collection type). You can manually keep the elements in a LinkedList in a sorted manner. However, insertion becomes a very costly operation, as you must manually traverse the list before each insertion.*

What's New

Looking quickly at the list doesn't reveal what's added to the List interface as compared to the Collection interface it extends. Table 9-2 highlights those new methods. You'll find some repeated methods from the Collection interface. When also found in the Collection interface, the List version includes an additional argument to specify position.

Table 9-2. Methods Added to List Interface

VARIABLE/METHOD NAME	VERSION	DESCRIPTION
add()	1.2	Adds an element to the list at a specific index.
addAll()	1.2	Inserts a collection of elements to the list starting at a specific position.
get()	1.2	Returns an element at a specific position.
indexOf()	1.2	Searches for an element within the list.
lastIndexOf()	1.2	Searches from the end of the list for an element.
listIterator()	1.2	Returns an object from the list that allows all of the list's elements to be visited sequentially.
remove()	1.2	Clears a specific element from the list.
set()	1.2	Changes the element at a specific position within the list.
subList()	1.2	Returns a portion of the list.

We'll examine all of the methods of List in detail as we look at the specific implementations.

Usage Issues

When using the List interface, one of the first problems or at least questions you may run across is the name conflict with the java.awt.List class. How can you use both classes in the same program? Or, at a minimum, how can you import both packages into the same program when you need to use only one of the two classes?

- **Solution 1—*Fully qualify everything:***

  The simplest way to use both classes in the same program is to always fully qualify all class names.

  ```java
  java.util.List list = new ArrayList();
  java.awt.List listComp = new java.awt.List();
  ```

This gets tedious fast but is less of an issue if you are using the Swing component set and don't ever need to use the `List` component from the Abstract Window Toolkit (AWT).

- **Solution 2—*Only import needed classes:***

  Instead of using wildcard imports, you can import only those classes you need.

  ```
  import java.awt.Graphics;
  import java.util.List;
  ```

  This gets into religious programming issues almost as bad as where to put the {}'s on code lines! Personally, I avoid this, as I don't like having a full page of just import lines. If you are using an IDE tool that automatically inserts these, this may be less of an issue.

- **Solution 3—*Double import the specific class you need:***

  Nowadays, with Swing around, you don't use `java.awt.List` any more. If that's the case, just import both packages with a wildcard and import `java.util.List` manually.

  ```
  import java.awt.*;
  import java.util.*;
  import java.util.List;
  ```

  The compiler is smart enough to realize that, if you have `List list;`, you must mean the class that you specifically imported and not the `java.awt.List` class, even though the `java.awt` package was imported first.

> **NOTE** *Regarding Solution 3, this behavior is mandated by Section 7.5 of the Java Language Specification.*

ArrayList Class

The `ArrayList` class is the Collection Framework's replacement for the `Vector` class. Functionally equivalent, their primary difference is that `ArrayList` usage is not synchronized by default, whereas `Vector` is. Both maintain their collection of data in an ordered fashion within an array as their backing store.

> **NOTE** *To clarify terminology,* ordered *means the elements are held according to the positional index inserted, while* sorted *refers to the comparison of element values for ordering.*

The array provides quick, random access to elements at a cost of slower insertion and deletion of those elements not at the end of the list. If you need to frequently add and delete elements from the middle of the list, consider using a LinkedList (described later in this chapter).

ArrayList shares some similarities with HashSet and TreeSet and provides some behavior that is not the same. The base implementation class is similar to HashSet and TreeSet—both extend from the AbstractCollection superclass. However, instead of further extending from AbstractSet, ArrayList extends from AbstractList. Unlike the sets, ArrayList supports storing duplicate elements. While much of the ArrayList behavior is inherited from AbstractList, the class still needs to customize the majority of its behavior. Table 9-3 lists the constructors and methods that ArrayList overrides.

Table 9-3. Summary of the ArrayList Class

VARIABLE/METHOD NAME	VERSION	DESCRIPTION
ArrayList()	1.2	Constructs an empty list backed by an array.
add()	1.2	Adds an element to the list.
addAll()	1.2	Adds a collection of elements to the list.
clear()	1.2	Clears all elements from the list.
clone()	1.2	Creates a clone of the list.
contains()	1.2	Checks to see if an object is a value within the list.
ensureCapacity()	1.2	Ensures capacity of internal buffer is at least a certain size.
get()	1.2	Returns an element at a specific position.
indexOf()	1.2	Searches for an element within the list.
isEmpty()	1.2	Checks if list has any elements.
lastIndexOf()	1.2	Searches from end of list for an element.
remove()	1.2	Clears a specific element from the list.
removeRange()	1.2	Clears a range of elements from the list.
set()	1.2	Changes an element at a specific position within the list.
size()	1.2	Returns the number of elements in the list.
toArray()	1.2	Returns elements of the list as an array.
trimToSize()	1.2	Trims capacity of internal buffer to actual size.

While Table 9-3 lists (only) sixteen methods, there are actually nineteen versions including overloaded varieties. Add in the eleven inherited methods (excluding the Object-specific ones that are not overridden) and there is much you can do with a List. We'll look at their usage in groups.

Creating an ArrayList

You can use one of three constructors to create an ArrayList. For the first two constructors, an empty array list is created. The initial capacity is ten unless explicitly specified by using the second constructor. When that space becomes too small, the list will increase by approximately half.

```
public ArrayList()
public ArrayList (int initialCapacity)
```

> **NOTE** *Unlike* Vector, *you cannot specify a capacity increment. For Sun's reference implementation, the formula to increase capacity is* newCapacity = (oldCapacity * 3)/2 + 1. *If you happen to call the constructor with a negative initial capacity, an* IllegalArgumentException *will be thrown.*

The final constructor is the copy constructor, creating a new ArrayList from another collection:

```
public ArrayList(Collection col)
```

You cannot provide a custom initial capacity. Instead, the internal array will be sized at 10% larger than the collection size. Also, since lists support duplicates, duplicate elements are retained.

One example of creating an ArrayList from a list is worth noting. You can create a List from an array with Arrays.asList(). This is fine if you only want a list that cannot grow. However, if you want to be able to add or remove elements from the list, you must pass that newly created list into a constructor of a concrete collection:

```
String elements[] = {"Schindler's List", "Waiting List", "Shopping List",
  "Wine List"};
List list = new ArrayList(Arrays.asList(elements));
```

Adding Elements

You can add either a single element or a group of elements to the list.

Adding Single Elements

Add a single element to the list by calling the add() method:

```
public boolean add(Object element)
public boolean add(int index, Object element)
```

There are two varieties of the add() method. When called with only an element argument, the element is added to the end of the list. When add() is called with both element and index arguments, the element is added at the specific index and any elements after it are pushed forward in the list. Figure 9-2 should help you visualize this. The program used to add the elements follows.

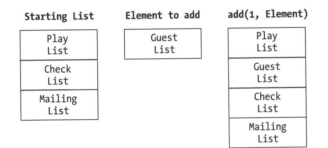

Figure 9-2. Adding elements in the middle of a List.

```
// Create/fill collection
List list = new ArrayList();
list.add("Play List");
list.add("Check List");
list.add("Mailing List");
// Add in middle
list.add(1, "Guest List");
```

> **NOTE** *Like arrays, the index used by a* List *starts at zero.*

Since all lists are ordered, the elements are held in the order in which they are added. That is so, unless you explicitly specify the position to add the element, as in `list.add(1, "Guest List")`.

If you are working with a read-only list or one that doesn't support the adding of elements, an `UnsupportedOperationException` will be thrown. To create a read-only list, use the `unmodifiableList()` method of the `Collections` class described in the "Read-Only Collections" section of Chapter 12.

If the internal data structure is too small to handle storing the new element, the internal data structure will automatically grow. If you try to add the element at a position beyond the end of the list (or before the beginning), an `IndexOutOfBoundsException` will be thrown.

Adding Another Collection

You can add a group of elements to a list from another collection with the `addAll()` method:

```
public boolean addAll(Collection c)
public boolean addAll(int index, Collection c)
```

Each element in the collection passed in will be added to the current list via the equivalent of calling the `add()` method on each element. If an index is passed to the method call, elements are added starting at that position, moving existing elements down to fit in the new elements. Otherwise, they are added to the end. The elements are added in the order in which the collection's iterator returns them.

> **NOTE** *Calling* `addAll()` *is efficient in that it will only move the elements of the original list once when adding in the middle of the list.*

If the underlying list changes, true is returned. If no elements are added, false is returned. The only way for false to be returned is if the collection passed in is empty.

If adding elements to the list is not supported, an `UnsupportedOperationException` will be thrown.

Getting an Element

The ArrayList class supports retrieval of a single element by index with get():

```
public Object get(int index)
```

To get the object at a specific position, just call get():

```
Object obj = list.get(5);
```

If you call get() with an index outside the valid range of elements, an IndexOutOfBoundsException is thrown.

Removing Elements

Like sets, lists support removal in four different ways.

Removing All Elements

The simplest removal method, clear(), is one that clears all of the elements from the list:

```
public void clear()
```

There is no return value. However, you can still get an UnsupportedOperationException thrown if the list is read-only.

Removing Single Elements

Use the remove() method if you wish to remove a single element at a time:

```
public boolean remove(Object element)
public Object remove(int index)
```

You can remove a single element by position or by checking for equality. When passing in an element, the equals() method is used to check for equality. As List supports duplicates, the first element in the list that matches the element will be removed.

The value returned depends on which version of remove() you use. When passing in an object, remove() returns true if the object was found and removed from the list, otherwise, false is returned. For the version accepting an index argument, the object removed from the specified position is returned.

Certain removal-failure cases result in an exception being thrown. If removal is not supported, you'll get an `UnsupportedOperationException` thrown whether the element is present or not. If the index passed in is outside the valid range of elements, an `IndexOutOfBoundsException` is thrown.

Removing Another Collection

The third way to remove elements is with `removeAll()`:

```
public boolean removeAll(Collection c)
```

The `removeAll()` method takes a `Collection` as an argument and removes from the list all instances of each element in the collection passed in. If an element from the passed-in collection is in the list multiple times, all instances are removed.

For instance, if the original list consisted of the following elements:

```
{"Access List", "Name List", "Class List", "Name List", "Dean's List"}
```

and the collection passed in was:

```
{"Name List", "Dean's List"}
```

the resulting list would have every instance of "Name List" and "Dean's List" removed:

```
{"Access List", "Class List"}
```

As with most of the previously shown set methods, `removeAll()` returns true if the underlying set changes and false or an `UnsupportedOperationException`, otherwise. Not surprisingly, the `equals()` method is used to check for element equality.

Retaining Another Collection

The `retainAll()` method works like `removeAll()` but in the opposite direction:

```
public boolean retainAll(Collection c)
```

In other words, only those elements within the collection argument are kept in the original set. Everything else is removed, instead.

Figure 9-3 should help you visualize the difference between `removeAll()` and `retainAll()`. The contents of the starting list are the four lists mentioned previously (Access List, Name List, Class List, Dean's List). The acting collection consists of the elements: Name List, Dean's List, and Word List. The Word List element is included in the acting collection to demonstrate that in neither case will this be added to the original collection.

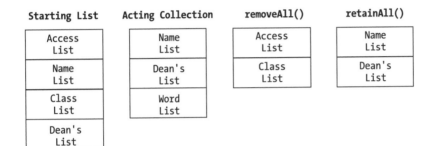

Figure 9-3. The removeAll() method versus the retainAll() method.

Removing Ranges

The `removeRange()` method is a protected support method used by `ArrayList`. Unless you subclass `ArrayList`, you'll never use it directly:

```
protected void removeRange(int fromIndex, int toIndex)
```

The indices passed into the method represent the starting index and the index beyond the last element to remove. That means that if `fromIndex` is equal to `toIndex`, nothing will be removed. Also, calling `removeRange()` with an index beyond the ends of the list results in an `ArrayIndexOutOfBoundsException` thrown.

Elements are removed by shifting the remaining elements to fill the space of the removed elements, thus decreasing the size of the list.

List Operations

Lists support several operations that have to do with working with the elements in the collection. There is support for fetching, finding, and copying elements, among some other secondary tasks.

Fetching Elements

To work with all elements of the list, you can call the iterator() method to get an Iterator or the listIterator() method to get a ListIterator:

```
public Iterator iterator()
public ListIterator listIterator()
public ListIterator listIterator(int index)
```

Since the elements of a list are ordered, calling iterator() or listIterator() with no arguments returns the same collection of ordered elements. The only difference is the set of methods you can use with the returned iterator. The second version of listIterator() allows you to get an iterator starting with any position within the list.

Using an iterator returned from a List is like using any other iterator. The only difference is that the order of the elements in the list is preserved:

```
List list = Arrays.asList(new String[] {"Hit List", "To Do List", "Price List",
  "Top Ten List"});
Iterator iter = list.iterator();
while (iter.hasNext()) {
  System.out.println(iter.next());
}
```

Running this will result in the following output:

```
Hit List
To Do List
Price List
Top Ten List
```

ListIterator will be discussed in further detail later in this chapter.

Finding Elements

Besides fetching elements of the list, you can check to see if the list contains a single element or collection of elements.

Checking for Existence

Use the `contains()` method to check if a specific element is part of the list:

```
public boolean contains(Object element)
```

If found, `contains()` returns true, if not, false. As with `remove()`, equality checking is done through the `equals()` method of the element.

Checking for Position

If, instead of seeing only whether an element is in the list, you want to know where in the list it's located, that's where the `indexOf()` and `lastIndexOf()` methods come in:

```
public int indexOf(Object element)
public int lastIndexOf(Object element)
```

Starting at the beginning or end, you can find out where in the vector the next instance of a specific element is located. Unlike `Vector`, there is no way to start at a position other than the beginning or end.

Both `indexOf()` and `lastIndexOf()` use `equals()` to check for equality and return –1 if the element is not found. Also, the found position is reported from the beginning of the list, not relative to the position searched from.

If you're interested in finding all of the positions for a single element in an `ArrayList`, you're out of luck. You'll need to convert the list to a `Vector` and use the versions of `indexOf()` or `lastIndexOf()` that support a starting position other than the end.

Checking for List Containment

In addition to checking whether the list includes a specific element, you can check to see if the list contains a whole collection of other elements with the `containsAll()` method:

```
public boolean containsAll(Collection c)
```

This method takes a `Collection` as its argument and reports if the elements of the passed-in collection are a subset of the current list. In other words, is each element of the collection also an element of the list? The current list can contain other elements but the passed-in collection cannot or `containsAll()` will return false. If an element is in the passed-in collection multiple times, it only needs to be in the source list once to be successful.

Replacing Elements

You can replace elements in a list with the `set()` method:

```
public Object set(int index, Object element)
```

Use the `set()` method when you need to replace the element at a specific position in the list. The object being replaced is returned by the `set()` method. If the index happens to be invalid, an `IndexOutOfBoundsException` is thrown.

Checking Size

To find out how many elements are in a list, use its `size()` method:

```
public int size()
```

`ArrayList` also has an `isEmpty()` method to get the size and to check to see if no elements are in the list:

```
public boolean isEmpty()
```

Checking Capacity

Similar to a `Vector`, an `ArrayList` has a capacity as well as a size. The *capacity* represents the size of the internal backing store, or the number of elements the array list can hold before the internal data structure needs to be resized. Minimizing excess memory usage by the backing store preserves memory but causes a higher insertion-time price when that capacity is exceeded. Working with capacity properly can improve performance immensely without wasting too much memory.

Use the `ensureCapacity()` method to check that the internal data structure has enough capacity before adding elements:

```
public void ensureCapacity(int minimumCapacity)
```

While you don't have to call `ensureCapacity()` yourself, if you plan on inserting a considerable number of elements, it is best to make sure that all of the elements will fit before even adding the first. This will reduce the number of resizes necessary for the internal data structure.

After adding all of the elements you need to add to a list, call the `trimToSize()` method:

```
public void trimToSize()
```

The `trimToSize()` method makes sure that there is no unused space in the internal data structure. Basically, the capacity of the internal data structure is reduced (by creating a new array) if the size is less than the capacity.

Copying and Cloning Lists

`ArrayList` supports the standard mechanisms for duplication. You can clone them, serialize them, copy them, or simply call the standard copy constructor.

The `ArrayList` class is `Cloneable` and has a public `clone()` method:

```
public Object clone()
```

When you call the `clone()` method of an `ArrayList`, a shallow copy of the list is created. The new list refers to the same set of elements as the original. It does not duplicate those elements, too.

Since `clone()` is a method of the `ArrayList` class and not the `List` (or `Collection`) interface, you must call `clone()` on a reference to the class, not the interface:

```
List list = ...
List list2 = ((List)((ArrayList)list).clone());
```

In addition to implementing the `Cloneable` interface, `ArrayList` implements the empty `Serializable` interface. If all of the elements of an `ArrayList` are `Serializable`, you can then serialize the list to an `ObjectOutputStream` and later read it back from an `ObjectInputStream`. The following demonstrates this:

```
FileOutputStream fos = new FileOutputStream("list.ser");
ObjectOutputStream oos = new ObjectOutputStream(fos);
oos.writeObject(list);
oos.close();
FileInputStream fis = new FileInputStream("list.ser");
ObjectInputStream ois = new ObjectInputStream(fis);
List anotherList = (List)ois.readObject();
ois.close();
System.out.println(anotherList);
```

Among other uses, `ArrayList`'s serializability is useful when saving information between session requests in a servlet.

ArrayList also supports the standard toArray() methods from Collection for copying elements out of a list into an array:

```
public Object[] toArray()
public Object[] toArray(Object[] a)
```

The first toArray() method returns an Object array containing all the elements in the list. The position of list elements is preserved in the object array. The second version allows you to get an array of a specific type, Object or otherwise. This would allow you to avoid casting whenever you need to get an element out of the array.

> **WARNING**   *If the elements of the list are not assignment-compatible with the array type, an* ArrayStoreException *will be thrown.*

Checking for Equality

The ArrayList class gets its equals() method from the AbstractList class:

```
public boolean equals(Object o)
```

An ArrayList is equal to another object if the other object implements the List interface, has the same size(), and contains the same elements in the same positions.

The equals() method of the elements is used to check if two elements at the same position are equivalent.

Hashing Lists

Like equals(), ArrayList gets its hashCode() method from AbstractList:

```
public int hashCode()
```

The hashCode() for a list is defined in the List interface javadoc:

```
hashCode = 1;
Iterator i = list.iterator();
while (i.hasNext()) {
  Object obj = i.next();
  hashCode = 31*hashCode + (obj==null ? 0 : obj.hashCode());
}
```

AbstractList implements the method as such.

LinkedList Class

The final concrete List implementation provided with the Collection Framework is the LinkedList. The LinkedList class is a doubly linked list, which internally maintains references to the previous and next element at each node in the list. As Table 9-4 shows, LinkedList has the previously introduced List interface methods as well as a special set for working from the ends of the list.

Table 9-4. Summary of the LinkedList Class

VARIABLE/METHOD NAME	VERSION	DESCRIPTION
LinkedList()	1.2	Constructs an empty list backed by a linked list.
add()	1.2	Adds an element to the list.
addAll()	1.2	Adds a collection of elements to the list.
addFirst()	1.2	Adds an element to beginning of the list.
addLast()	1.2	Adds an element to end of the list.
clear()	1.2	Clears all elements from the list.
clone()	1.2	Creates a clone of the list.
contains()	1.2	Checks to see if an object is a value within the list.
get()	1.2	Returns an element at a specific position.
getFirst()	1.2	Returns the first element in a list.
getLast()	1.2	Returns the last element in a list.
indexOf()	1.2	Searches for an element within the list.
lastIndexOf()	1.2	Searches from end of the list for an element.
listIterator()	1.2	Returns an object from the list that allows all of the list's elements to be visited sequentially.
remove()	1.2	Clears a specific element from the list.
removeFirst()	1.2	Removes the first element from the list.
removeLast()	1.2	Removes the last element from the list.
set()	1.2	Changes an element at a specific position within the list.
size()	1.2	Returns the number of elements in the list.
toArray()	1.2	Returns the elements of the list as an array.

As the behavior of most of the LinkedList methods duplicates that of ArrayList, we'll look only at those that are new or specialized to LinkedList.

Creating a LinkedList

There are two constructors for LinkedList: one for creating an empty list, and the other, the standard copy constructor:

```
public LinkedList()
public LinkedList(Collection col)
```

Adding Elements

To add a single element, call the add() method:

```
public boolean add(Object element)
public boolean add(int index, Object element)
```

The two basic varieties of add() are the same as ArrayList and add the element to the end of the list unless an index is specified.

You can also treat the linked list as a stack or queue and add elements at the head or tail with addFirst() and addLast(), respectively:

```
public boolean addFirst(Object element)
public boolean addLast(Object element)
```

The addLast() method is functionally equivalent to simply calling add(), with no index.

If you are using a list that doesn't support adding elements, an UnsupportedOperationException gets thrown when any of these methods are called.

Retrieving the Ends

You can use the getFirst() and getLast() methods of LinkedList to get the elements at the ends of the list:

```
public Object getFirst()
public Object getLast()
```

Both methods only *retrieve* the element at the end—they don't remove it. A NoSuchElementException will be thrown by either method if there are no elements in the list.

Removing Elements

LinkedList provides the removeFirst() and removeLast() methods to remove the elements at the ends of the list:

```
public Object removeFirst()
public Object removeLast()
```

While both a stack and a queue usually remove elements from the beginning of a data structure, the `removeLast()` method is provided in case you choose to work with the linked list in reverse order.

Using a list that doesn't support element removal results in an `UnsupportedOperationException` when any of the removal methods are called. Also, calling either method with no elements in the list results in a `NoSuchElementException`.

LinkedList Example

To demonstrate the use of a `LinkedList`, let's create a thread pool. If you aren't familiar with a *thread pool*, it's a collection of threads that sit around waiting for work to be done. Instead of creating a thread when you need work to be done, the creation process happens once and then you reuse the existing threads. You can also limit the number of threads created, preserving system resources.

The pool will maintain a list of `TaskThread` instances that sit around waiting for jobs to be done. Let's look at this class first in Listing 9-1. Basically, the constructor maintains a reference to the thread pool while the thread's `run()` method sits in an infinite loop. The mechanism to get the next job blocks so that the threads aren't sitting around in a busy-wait loop.

Listing 9-1. Defining a thread for a thread pool.

```java
public class TaskThread extends Thread {
  private ThreadPool pool;

  public TaskThread(ThreadPool thePool) {
    pool = thePool;
  }

  public void run() {
    while (true) {
      // blocks until job
      Runnable job = pool.getNext();
      try {
        job.run();
      } catch (Exception e) {
        // Ignore exceptions thrown from jobs
        System.err.println("Job exception: " + e);
      }
    }
  }
}
```

The actual ThreadPool class shown in Listing 9-2 is rather simple. When the pool is created, we create all the runnable threads. These are maintained in a LinkedList. We treat the list as a queue, adding at the end and removing at the beginning. When a new job comes in, we add it to the list. When a thread requests a job, we get it from the list. Appropriate synchronization is done to block threads while the list is empty:

Listing 9-2. Defining the thread pool.

```java
import java.util.*;

public class ThreadPool {
  private LinkedList tasks = new LinkedList();

  public ThreadPool(int size) {
    for (int i=0; i<size; i++) {
      Thread thread = new TaskThread(this);
      thread.start();
    }
  }

  public void run(Runnable task) {
    synchronized (tasks) {
      tasks.addLast(task);
      tasks.notify();
    }
  }

  public Runnable getNext() {
    Runnable returnVal = null;
    synchronized (tasks) {
      while (tasks.isEmpty()) {
        try {
          tasks.wait();
        } catch (InterruptedException ex) {
          System.err.println("Interrupted");
        }
      }
      returnVal = (Runnable)tasks.removeFirst();
    }
    return returnVal;
  }
```

The test program is included as part of the pool class. It creates a pool of two threads to do work and five jobs that just print a message twenty-five times each:

```java
public static void main (String args[]) {
  final String message[] = {"Reference List", "Christmas List",
    "Wish List", "Priority List", "'A' List"};
  ThreadPool pool = new ThreadPool(message.length/2);
  for (int i=0, n=message.length; i<n; i++) {
    final int innerI = i;
    Runnable runner = new Runnable() {
      public void run() {
        for (int j=0; j<25; j++) {
          System.out.println("j: " + j + ": " + message[innerI]);
        }
      }
    };
    pool.run(runner);
  }
}
```

When you run the program you'll notice that, at most, two threads are running, and as each task finishes, the thread grabs another waiting task from the pool. Part of the output follows:

```
. . .
j: 20: Reference List
j: 21: Reference List
j: 22: Reference List
j: 23: Reference List
j: 24: Reference List
j: 0: Wish List
j: 1: Wish List
j: 2: Wish List
j: 3: Wish List
j: 4: Wish List
j: 5: Wish List
j: 6: Wish List
j: 7: Wish List
j: 0: Priority List
j: 1: Priority List
j: 2: Priority List
. . .
```

The main ThreadPool class can be improved in many ways. For instance, you can use lazy initialization to create the threads in the pool, waiting until they are first needed before taking the creation hit. You can also add support for priorities to the queue. Right now, jobs are handled in the order in which they come in. A priority queue implementation is shown in the "Creating Advanced Collections" section of Chapter 16. You can use that as your data structure instead of the LinkedList to manage tasks.

ListIterator

The ListIterator is an extension to the Iterator. Because lists are ordered and support positional access, you can use a ListIterator for bidirectional access through the elements of a list. The methods that support this are found in Table 9-5.

Table 9-5. Summary of the ListIterator Interface

VARIABLE/METHOD NAME	VERSION	DESCRIPTION
add()	1.2	Adds an element to the list.
hasNext()	1.2	Checks in the forward direction for more elements in the iterator.
hasPrevious()	1.2	Checks in the reverse direction for more elements in the iterator.
next()	1.2	Fetches the next element of the iterator.
nextIndex()	1.2	Returns the index of the next element of the iterator.
previous()	1.2	Fetches the previous element of the iterator.
previousIndex()	1.2	Returns the index of the previous element of the iterator.
remove()	1.2	Removes an element from the iterator.
set()	1.2	Changes the element at a specific position within the list.

While Iterator is very simple to use, there are many different ways to use ListIterator.

- **Like an Iterator:**

    Since ListIterator extends from Iterator, you can use hasNext() and next() to scroll forward through the list:

    ```
    ListIterator iter = list.listIterator();
    while (iter.hasNext()) {
    ```

```
System.out.println(iter.next());
}
```

- **In reverse order:**

  The hasPrevious() and previous() methods function similarly to hasNext() and next(), taking you in the reverse direction. You just need to start at the end:

  ```
  ListIterator iter = list.listIterator(list.size());
  while (iter.hasPrevious()) {
    System.out.println(iter.previous());
  }
  ```

- **In both directions:**

  You can intermix next() and previous() calls to alternate directions.

- **To modify the list:**

  While Iterator only supports remove(), ListIterator adds set() and add() to the table.

For the last two cases, it is important to understand the concept of cursor position within the iterator. The cursor position is not pointing at an element but is instead positioned between elements (or at an end of the list). It is from this cursor position that all of the operations of the ListIterator are performed. For instance, if you have a six-element list, there will be seven cursor positions as shown in Figure 9-4.

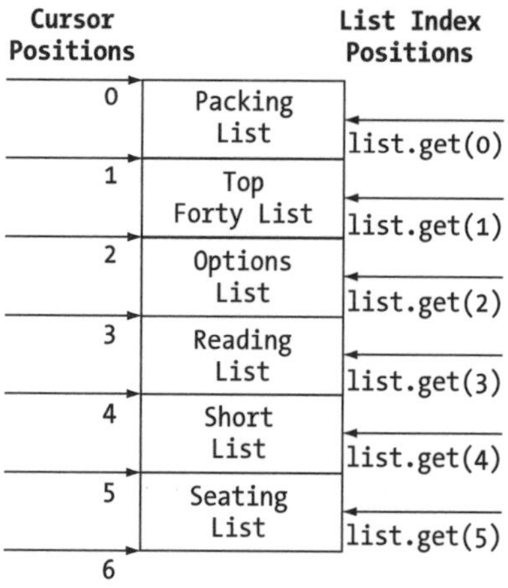

Figure 9-4. Understanding ListIterator cursor positions.

Using the next() and previous() methods allows you to move the cursor:

```
public Object next()
public Object previous()
```

Using the nextIndex() and previousIndex() methods allows you to find out the index of the elements around the current cursor position:

```
public int nextIndex()
public int previousIndex()
```

You can then use the index returned to fetch the element from the list if you don't like next() and previous(). Both methods return –1 if you are at a list end without an element in the appropriate direction: at the end for nextIndex() or at the beginning for previousIndex().

Instead of checking for –1 at the ends, you can use hasNext() and hasPrevious() to detect end cases:

```
public boolean hasNext()
public boolean hasPrevious()
```

Both return true if there are additional elements in the given direction, or false, if not.

The remaining three methods allow you to modify the list that the iterator came from: add(), remove(), and set().

```
public void add(Object element)
public void remove()
public void set(Object element)
```

Noticeably absent from all three methods is an index. Which element is affected by each call? The add() method inserts the new element before the implicit cursor no matter which direction you are traversing through the list. On the other hand, the remove() and set() methods affect the element last returned by next() or previous().

All three operations are optional and would throw an UnsupportedOperationException if attempted on a list that didn't support the operations. It is also possible to get an IllegalStateException thrown if you try to set() or remove() an element after remove() or add() has been called.

To demonstrate using the list from Figure 9-4 as a guide, imagine starting at cursor position 3. Here, next() would return "Reading List" and previous() would return "Options List." Assuming the last iterator method called was next(), you can change the "Reading List" to an "Endangered Species List" with a call to set("Endangered Species List"). Or you can remove it with a call to remove(). If you were to call add("Best Sellers List"), this element would be inserted between "Reading List" and "Options List" no matter which direction you were traversing through the list. When you add() an element, the previous and next indices get incremented so the next() element would remain the same: "Reading List."

Summary

In this chapter, we explored the many facets of the List interface and its two new concrete implementations: ArrayList and LinkedList. With ArrayList, you have quick, random access, while LinkedList provides quick insertions and deletions at positions other than the end. Which of the two you use depends upon your specific needs but you'll use both frequently instead of the historical Vector class to maintain ordered lists of elements. You also learned how to take advantage of the ListIterator interface to traverse a list bidirectionally (instead of just forward as with an Iterator).

The next chapter introduces the Map interface with its HashMap and TreeMap implementations. You'll learn to use these classes to maintain key-value pairs, either unordered or ordered. You'll also learn about the WeakHashMap and how you can use it effectively to maintain a weakly referenced map.

CHAPTER 10

Maps

The Map interface of the Collections Framework replaces the historical Dictionary class. While Dictionary was a class, and an abstract one at that, it was entirely full of abstract methods and should have been an interface. Its replacement truly is just an interface. The interface defines the basic support for storing key-value pairs in collections where each key can map to, at most, one value.

While Map is part of the framework, it does not extend from the Collection interface. Instead, it is the root of its own hierarchy. There are four concrete implementations of the Map interface: HashMap, WeakHashMap, TreeMap, and the historical Hashtable. In addition, the elements of the map are defined to be of type Map.Entry. To help you see how the Map interface interconnects with the other aspects of the Collections Framework, Figure 10-1 shows its abstract and concrete implementations as well as its related interfaces.

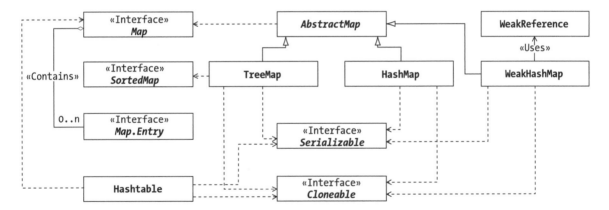

Figure 10-1. The Map class hierarchy.

> **NOTE** *The* WeakHashMap *relies on weakly reachable keys through the* WeakReference *class. We'll discuss this in more depth in the "WeakHashMap" section later in this chapter.*

Map Basics

Ever need to look up a name in a phone book or a definition in a dictionary? This is the basic operation of a map: given some key, a name or word, the map finds out what value is associated with that key. While nowadays people have many phone numbers (with cell phones and whatnot), and words can have multiple definitions, the concept is what is important—given some key, the map finds its value. If it isn't in the phone book or dictionary, it has no value.

You'll find the Map interface methods listed in Table 10-1. Remember that Map doesn't extend from Collection, so this is everything . . . there are no additional inherited methods.

Table 10-1. Summary of the Map Interface

VARIABLE/METHOD NAME	VERSION	DESCRIPTION
clear()	1.2	Removes all the elements from the map.
containsKey()	1.2	Checks to see if an object is a key for the map.
containsValue()	1.2	Checks to see if an object is a value within the map.
entrySet()	1.2	Returns the set of key-value pairs in the map.
equals()	1.2	Checks for equality with another object.
get()	1.2	Retrieves a value for a key in the map.
hashCode()	1.2	Computes a hash code for the map.
isEmpty()	1.2	Checks if hash map has any elements.
keySet()	1.2	Retrieves a collection of the keys of the map.
put()	1.2	Places a key-value pair into the map.
putAll()	1.2	Places a collection of key-value pairs into the map.
remove()	1.2	Removes an element from the map.
size()	1.2	Returns the number of elements in the map.
values()	1.2	Retrieves a collection of the values of the map.

The four concrete map implementations found in the framework are Hashtable, HashMap, WeakHashMap, and TreeMap. The historical Hashtable class has been reworked into the framework and was discussed in Chapter 5. HashMap, which represents an unsynchronized hash table, replaces Hashtable in the new framework. The second new map is a WeakHashMap. It is identical to a HashMap but relies on weak references for its keys. The third and final new map is the TreeMap, which maintains the map entries sorted by key in a balanced, red-black tree.

> **WARNING** *If you use a* Hashtable *as a map, remember to not call the legacy methods.*

Map.Entry Interface

Elements of a map are of type Map.Entry, an inner interface of the Map interface. Each key-value pair is an instance of this interface. As a user of a map, you never create an instance; instead, the concrete maps have package-private classes that implement the interface. When you get the entrySet() for a map, the method returns all the key-value pairs for the entries in the map as a set of Map.Entry elements.

Table 10-2 reflects the methods of the Map.Entry interface that you can use to work with each entry.

Table 10-2. Summary of the Map.Entry Interface

VARIABLE/METHOD NAME	VERSION	DESCRIPTION
equals()	1.2	Checks for equality with another object.
getKey()	1.2	Retrieves the key for a map entry.
getValue()	1.2	Retrieves the value for a map entry.
hashCode()	1.2	Computes the hash code for a map entry.
setValue()	1.2	Changes the value for a map entry.

The equals() and hashCode() methods override the Object behavior to ensure that two equal entries, possibly from different maps, have the same hash code:

```
public boolean equals(Object element)
public int hashCode()
```

They take special care to deal with the possibility of having null keys and values.

You can access the key or value of the entry with the getKey() and getValue() methods, respectively:

```
public Object getKey()
public Object getValue()
```

> **NOTE** *Since maps support null keys and values, either* getKey() *or* getValue() *could return null.*

The final method of the interface is the setValue() method, which allows you to replace the value for the key associated with the entry:

```
public Object setValue(Object newValue)
```

The value originally associated with the key is returned from the setValue() method. If the map you are working with is read-only, you'll get an UnsupportedOperationException thrown. There is no setKey() method because changing the key would require the removal of the entry and addition of a new entry—a set of operations you can't do from the interface.

The nice thing about getting the set of map entries is that you don't have to do a lookup for each key if you need to get each value, too. For instance, the following allows you to print the value of each system property using map entries:

```
Properties props = System.getProperties();
Iterator iter = props.entrySet().iterator();
while (iter.hasNext()) {
  Map.Entry entry = (Map.Entry)iter.next();
  System.out.println(entry.getKey() + " -- " + entry.getValue());
}
```

Now, compare that to the code necessary to do the same thing with the older Enumeration and Properties methods:

```
Properties props = System.getProperties();
Enumeration enum = props.propertyNames();
while (enum.hasMoreElements()) {
  String key = (String)enum.nextElement();
  System.out.println(key + " -- " + props.getProperty(key));
}
```

While this code may look simpler, the call to getProperty() for each key adds up to make the operation more costly. For the Iterator version, the Map.Entry already has the property value and doesn't require an extra lookup.

> **NOTE** *Remember that the historical* Properties *class extends from* Hashtable *and* Hashtable *was reworked to support the* Map *interface.*

HashMap Class

The HashMap is the most commonly used implementation of the Map interface. It provides a basic key-value map where the elements are unordered. If you need to maintain map keys in an ordered fashion, that's where the TreeMap comes in handy, which will be explored later in this chapter.

The basics of the HashMap come from the AbstractMap. Table 10-3 lists its constructors and the methods it overrides.

Table 10-3. Summary of the HashMap Class

VARIABLE/METHOD NAME	VERSION	DESCRIPTION
HashMap()	1.2	Constructs an empty hash map.
clear()	1.2	Removes all the elements from the hash map.
clone()	1.2	Creates a clone of the hash map.
containsKey()	1.2	Checks to see if an object is a key for the hash map.
containsValue()	1.2	Checks to see if an object is a value within the hash map.
entrySet()	1.2	Returns a set of key-value pairs in the hash map.
get()	1.2	Retrieves the value for a key in the hash map.
isEmpty()	1.2	Checks if hash map has any elements.
keySet()	1.2	Retrieves a collection of the keys of the hash map.
put()	1.2	Places a key-value pair into the hash map.
putAll()	1.2	Places a collection of key-value pairs into the hash map.
remove()	1.2	Removes an element from the hash map.
size()	1.2	Returns the number of elements in the hash map.
values()	1.2	Retrieves a collection of the values of the hash map.

Basically, all of the methods of the Map interface defined in the AbstractMap class are overridden, adding in a method from Object, too. Unlike some concrete collections, the HashMap class adds no new methods beyond the Map interface.

Creating a HashMap

There are four constructors for creating a HashMap. The first three constructors permit creation of an empty HashMap:

```
public HashMap()
public HashMap(int initialCapacity)
public HashMap(int initialCapacity, float loadFactor)
```

Unless specified otherwise, the initial capacity of the internal data structure is 101 or 11, depending upon which version of Java you are using. For the 1.2 release, it is 101, and for 1.3, it is 11. Unless specified otherwise, the default load factor is 75%. When the number of elements in the map exceeds the (`load factor * the capacity`), the map grows by a factor of $2 \times$ capacity + 1.

> **TIP** *As explained in the "Creating Hash Tables" section of Chapter 5, a better initial capacity is 89. This will keep the table growing with roughly prime sizes to around 3000 elements. Also, the default initial size is not part of the class definition so it is possible that a third-party implementation doesn't use 11 or 101 as the default initial size.*

The fourth and final constructor is the standard copy constructor, which creates a new `HashMap` from another map:

```
public HashMap(Map map)
```

This final constructor doesn't permit a custom capacity or load factor. Instead, the internal structure will be sized at twice the map size, or 11, whichever is greater, with a default load factor of 75%. The default size of 11 *is* part of the class definition here.

Adding Key-Value Pairs

Now that you've created the `HashMap`, you can add key-value pairs to it. The mechanism to add a pair is the `put()` method:

```
public Object put(Object key, Object value)
```

Unlike a `Hashtable`, both the key and the value for a `HashMap` can be null. If the key happens to already be in the map, the old value is replaced and returned. Otherwise, null is returned. The map uses the key's hash code to determine where to store the key-value pair internally. For a full explanation of the use of hash codes, see the "Understanding Hash Tables" section in Chapter 5.

To copy all the key-value pairs from one `Map` into another, use the `putAll()` method:

```
public void putAll(Map map)
```

The value is replaced for every key in the passed-in map that already exists in the `HashMap`.

Displaying Contents

You'll find the toString() method of Object overridden in HashMap:

```
public String toString()
```

Similar to the other collection classes, the returned string will be a comma-delimited list of the collection elements within braces ({ }). For the hash map, each key-value element is displayed separated by an equal sign. For instance, if the map contained the original thirteen colonies of the United States and their current capital, the returned string might look something like the following:

```
{South Carolina=Columbia, North Carolina=Raleigh, Georgia=Atlanta,
Massachusetts=Boston, Delaware=Dover, New York=Albany,
Pennsylvania=Harrisburg, New Jersey=Trenton, Rhode Island=Providence,
Maryland=Annapolis, Virginia=Richmond, Connecticut=Hartford,
New Hampshire=Concord}
```

The listed order does not reflect the order in which the elements are added to the hash map. Instead, the order reflects the range conversion of the hash codes generated from the keys.

> **NOTE** *Keep in mind that the order of the elements within a* HashMap *could be different. Had the map capacity been different, the actual key-value pair order would have been different, too.*

Removing Key-Value Pairs

When you need to remove an element from a hash map, call the remove() method with the key as its argument:

```
public Object remove(Object key)
```

If the key is present as a key within the hash table, the key-value pair will be removed and the value object will be returned. If the object is not present in the map, null will be returned.

> **WARNING** *Since null is valid for the value associated with a key, you cannot rely on the return value to determine if the key was originally present.*

Removal of all elements from a map is done through the clear() method:

```
public void clear()
```

> **WARNING**   *Removing all elements from a map does not return the space used by the internal data structure. The capacity of the structure remains the same. Only the entries of the structure are nulled out.*

Sizing Hash Maps

When you create a hash map, you can size the internal data structure it uses. Once it is created, you no longer have direct control. Only when the number of elements within the map exceeds the capacity × the load factor will the capacity increase at 2n + 1. In fact, you cannot find out its current capacity—you can only find out the number of key-value pairs within the HashMap with the help of the size() method, and if it is empty, with isEmpty():

```
public int size()
public boolean isEmpty()
```

When the size is zero, isEmpty() returns true. Otherwise, it returns false. Using isEmpty() to check for emptiness is more efficient than manually comparing the size() to zero yourself.

When the hash map determines that it needs to increase its capacity, the private rehash() method is called. This causes a new internal data structure to be created, inserting into it all of the values based upon the range conversion of hash codes for the keys based on the new capacity.

Map Operations

Maps provide several operations for working with the elements of the collection. The hash map supports fetching one of the following: a single key, all keys, all values, or all key-value pairs. You can also search for a specific key or value within the hash table, among other tasks that are specializations of Object methods.

Fetching Keys and Values

The HashMap supports several mechanisms to retrieve keys and values out of the map—thankfully, not as many as Hashtable. The simplest is to find a value based upon a specific key with the get() method:

```
public Object get(Object key)
```

If the key is not found within the map, null is returned. Otherwise, the current value for the key within the map is returned.

> **NOTE** *Remember that keys can have null values in a* HashMap *so* get() *can return null if the key was present but has a null value.*

Since objects are stored (and searched for) by the hash code of the key, you shouldn't modify the attributes of a key object after it has been placed in a HashMap (or any map). If the hash code for an element changes after it is in a map, the only way you'll be able to find the object is to iterate through all the elements. The get() method will no longer function properly.

Instead of looking up the value for individual keys, you can get the set of all keys with the keySet() method:

```
public Set keySet()
```

The keySet() method returns the set of keys as a Set object.

To get the set of all the values in the hash map, call the values() method:

```
public Collection values()
```

The values() method returns a set of all values in the map as a Collection. Because values can have duplicates, you get a Collection back instead of a Set. This means that if the same value is in the map multiple times, it will be in the collection of values multiple times as well.

To get a set of Map.Entry elements back from a HashMap, use the entrySet() method:

```
public Set entrySet()
```

Each element of the Set returned is of type Map.Entry. When you need to work with the key-value pairs together, this is the best of all of the mechanisms.

Finding Elements

There are two ways to check if something is in a hash map. The `containsKey()` method allows you to check for the existence of a key within the map, and the `containsValue()` method allows you to check for a value within the map:

```
public boolean containsKey(Object key)
public boolean containsValue(Object value)
```

The `containsKey()` method is like the `get()` method but instead of returning to you the value at the key, you get back a boolean value stating whether or not the key is present. If found, you get true; false, otherwise. If your map supports null values associated with keys, you would need to use `containsKey()` to find out if a key is in a map, and not just `get()` to get the value as `get()` could return null if the key was found or not.

The `containsValue()` method checks for the existence of a specific value within the `HashMap`. The `containsValue()` method is very inefficient as it must basically do a table scan to check for existence since values are stored by key. If you frequently find yourself checking for values within a map, you're probably better off maintaining two maps, one for each direction. The `containsValue()` method is especially inefficient if you are frequently searching for values *not* in the map. To find nothing in the hash map requires checking every element of the map.

Cloning Hash Map

The `HashMap` class provides its own implementation of the `clone()` method:

```
public Object clone()
```

This functions similarly to passing the hash map to the copy constructor of a `HashMap` or to creating an empty `HashMap` and calling `putAll()`.

Checking Hash Maps for Equality

You'll find the `equals()` method to define equality from `Object` overridden in the `AbstractMap` class:

```
public boolean equals(Object o)
```

Two maps are defined as equal if both of their entry sets are equal (`thisHash.entrySet().equals(map.entrySet())`). Two entry sets are equal if their sizes are equal and each set contains every member of the other set. Order is unimportant. Two entries are compared for equality by using their equals() method. This means that the maps don't have to contain the same instances, only equivalent instances.

Hashing Hash Maps

The AbstractMap class provides the hashCode() implementation for HashMap. The hash code for a HashMap is the sum of all of its elements' hash codes:

```
public int hashCode()
```

Serializing Hash Maps

HashMap implements the Serializable interface. However, in order for a HashMap to be serializable, all the keys and values of the map must also be serializable. If they are not and you try to serialize the map, you'll get a NotSerializableException thrown.

WeakHashMap Class

The WeakHashMap functions identically to the HashMap with one very important exception: if the Java memory manager no longer has a strong reference to the object specified as a key, then the entry in the map will be removed. If you are not familiar with strong and weak references, see the "Understanding Weak References" section, which follows. The methods that support WeakHashMap are found in Table 10-4.

Table 10-4. Summary of the WeakHashMap Class

VARIABLE/METHOD NAME	VERSION	DESCRIPTION
WeakHashMap()	1.2/1.3	Creates an empty weak hash map.
clear()	1.2	Removes all elements from the hash map.
containsKey()	1.2	Checks to see if an object is a key for the hash map.
entrySet()	1.2	Returns a set of key-value pairs in the hash map.
get()	1.2	Retrieves a value for a key in the hash map.
isEmpty()	1.2	Checks if the hash map has any elements.
put()	1.2	Places a key-value pair into the hash map.
remove()	1.2	Removes an element from the hash map.
size()	1.2	Returns the number of elements in the hash map.

The methods for WeakHashMap are essentially the same as HashMap, the only difference being with the constructors.

Creating a WeakHashMap

The four constructors of WeakHashMap are the same as HashMap:

```
public WeakHashMap()
public WeakHashMap(int initialCapacity)
public WeakHashMap(int initialCapacity, float loadFactor)
public WeakHashMap(Map map)
```

The final copy constructor was missing from the Java 1.2 release and was added with the 1.3 release.

To fully understand the use of WeakHashMap, it is necessary to understand the different types of Reference objects that Java supports.

Understanding Weak References

You'll find the Reference class in the java.lang.ref package. It defines the concept of *reference objects*. Instead of providing variables that directly reference your memory, you create a reference object that indirectly holds a reference to the object. The reference objects are then maintained in a reference queue (ReferenceQueue), which monitors the references for reachability by the garbage collector.

There are four types of references to objects. Direct references like you normally use, as in Integer i = new Integer(13), are called *strong references* and have no special class. The remaining three are *soft references* (SoftReference), *weak references* (WeakReference), and *phantom references* (PhantomReference). Their class hierarchy is shown in Figure 10-2.

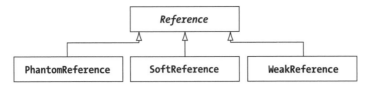

Figure 10-2. The Reference class hierarchy.

Soft references are like a cache. When memory is low, the garbage collector can arbitrarily free up soft references if there are no strong references to the object. If you are using soft references, the garbage collector is required to free them all before throwing an OutOfMemoryException.

Weak references are weaker than soft references. If the only references to an object are weak references, the garbage collector can reclaim the object's memory at any time—it doesn't have to wait until the system runs out of memory. Usually, it will be freed the next time the garbage collector runs.

Phantom references are special. They allow you to be notified before the garbage collector performs finalization and frees the object. Think of it as a mechanism to perform cleanup.

> **NOTE** *Reference objects are a little more involved then this. However, the description provided here should be sufficient to understand* WeakHashMap. *For more information, visit the javadoc for the* java.lang.ref *package at* http://java.sun.com/j2se/1.3/docs/api/java/lang/ref /package-summary.html.

Using a WeakHashMap

Before showing a long example, let's look at a simple example. Listing 10-1 creates a WeakHashMap with a new String object in it. (You must make a new String for the key or else the reference to the string-constant pool will never go away.) It then creates a second thread that watches the map and reports if the map is empty. When the map is empty, the thread ends. The program ends when the secondary thread ends. Since the strong reference to the key added to the map is gone as soon as the put() call returns, the reference is eligible for garbage collection, meaning its weak reference in the map is, too.

Listing 10-1. Demonstrating the WeakHashMap.

```java
import java.util.*;
public class Weak {
  private static Map map;
  public static void main (String args[]) {
    map = new WeakHashMap();
    map.put(new String("Maine"), "Augusta");
    Runnable runner = new Runnable() {
      public void run() {
        while (map.containsKey("Maine")) {
          try {
            Thread.sleep(500);
          } catch (InterruptedException ignored) {
          }
          System.out.println("Thread waiting");
          System.gc();
        }
      }
    };
    Thread t = new Thread(runner);
    t.start();
    System.out.println("Main waiting");
    try {
      t.join();
    } catch (InterruptedException ignored) {
    }
  }
}
```

If you do not include the call to System.gc(), the system may never run the garbage collector as not much memory is used by the program. For a more active program, the call would be unnecessary.

WeakHashMap Example

For a longer and more useful example, let's look at a very good use of WeakHashMap objects: to maintain the list of listeners associated with a data model, or component. This is a good use of WeakHashMap because it stops the listeners from being the only thing preventing an object from being garbage collected. If you don't remember to remove the listener, or think that because your method returned, the object will be automatically garbage collected, it won't—the listener reference is a strong reference.

> **NOTE** *There are times when using a WeakHashMap to manage listeners is not perfect. For instance, if you create an anonymous class in the call to addXXXListener(), a WeakHashMap could immediately throw the listener away as there are no strong references.*

To demonstrate, Listing 10-2 delves into Swing and creates a `ListModel` that relies on a `WeakHashMap` for the storage of the `ListDataListener` objects. Much of the code makes the model try to mimic the `DefaultListModel` class, although the data is stored in an `ArrayList` instead of a `Vector`. Besides the declaration at the top, you really can't tell that the listener list was maintained in a `WeakHashMap`. The most interesting methods that access the map elements are towards the bottom of the class definition.

Listing 10-2. Using a WeakHashMap to maintain a listener list.

```
import java.io.Serializable;
import java.util.*;
import java.lang.ref.*;
import javax.swing.*;
import javax.swing.event.*;

public class WeakListModel implements ListModel, Serializable {

  private final Object present = new Object();
  private Map listenerList = Collections.synchronizedMap(new WeakHashMap());
  private ArrayList delegate = new ArrayList();

  public int getSize() {
    return delegate.size();
  }

  public Object getElementAt(int index) {
    return delegate.get(index);
  }

  public void trimToSize() {
    delegate.trimToSize();
  }

  public void ensureCapacity(int minCapacity) {
    delegate.ensureCapacity(minCapacity);
  }
```

```java
public int size() {
  return delegate.size();
}

public boolean isEmpty() {
  return delegate.isEmpty();
}

public Enumeration elements() {
  return Collections.enumeration(delegate);
}

public boolean contains(Object elem) {
  return delegate.contains(elem);
}

public int indexOf(Object elem) {
  return delegate.indexOf(elem);
}

public int lastIndexOf(Object elem) {
  return delegate.lastIndexOf(elem);
}

public Object elementAt(int index) {
  return delegate.get(index);
}

public Object firstElement() {
  return delegate.get(0);
}

public Object lastElement() {
  return delegate.get(delegate.size()-1);
}

public void setElementAt(Object obj, int index) {
  delegate.set(index, obj);
  fireContentsChanged(this, index, index);
}

public void removeElementAt(int index) {
  delegate.remove(index);
  fireIntervalRemoved(this, index, index);
}
```

```
public void insertElementAt(Object obj, int index) {
  delegate.add(index, obj);
  fireIntervalAdded(this, index, index);
}

public void addElement(Object obj) {
  int index = delegate.size();
  delegate.add(obj);
  fireIntervalAdded(this, index, index);
}

public boolean removeElement(Object obj) {
  int index = indexOf(obj);
  boolean rv = delegate.remove(obj);
  if (index >= 0) {
    fireIntervalRemoved(this, index, index);
  }
  return rv;
}

public void removeAllElements() {
  int index1 = delegate.size()-1;
  delegate.clear();
  if (index1 >= 0) {
    fireIntervalRemoved(this, 0, index1);
  }
}

public String toString() {
  return delegate.toString();
}

public synchronized void addListDataListener(ListDataListener l) {
  listenerList.put(l, present);
}

public synchronized void removeListDataListener(ListDataListener l) {
  listenerList.remove(l);
}

protected synchronized void fireContentsChanged(
    Object source, int index0, int index1) {
  ListDataEvent e = null;
```

```
                    Set set = new HashSet(listenerList.keySet());
                    Iterator iter = set.iterator();

                    while (iter.hasNext()) {
                      if (e == null) {
                        e = new ListDataEvent(
                          source, ListDataEvent.CONTENTS_CHANGED, index0, index1);
                      }
                      ListDataListener ldl = (ListDataListener)iter.next();
                      ldl.contentsChanged(e);
                    }
                  }

                  protected synchronized void fireIntervalAdded(
                      Object source, int index0, int index1) {
                    ListDataEvent e = null;

                    Set set = new HashSet(listenerList.keySet());
                    Iterator iter = set.iterator();

                    while (iter.hasNext()) {
                      if (e == null) {
                        e = new ListDataEvent(
                          source, ListDataEvent.INTERVAL_ADDED, index0, index1);
                      }
                      ListDataListener ldl = (ListDataListener)iter.next();
                      ldl.intervalAdded(e);
                    }
                  }

                  protected synchronized void fireIntervalRemoved(
                      Object source, int index0, int index1) {
                    ListDataEvent e = null;

                    Set set = new HashSet(listenerList.keySet());
                    Iterator iter = set.iterator();

                    while (iter.hasNext()) {
                      if (e == null) {
                        e = new ListDataEvent(
                          source, ListDataEvent.INTERVAL_REMOVED, index0, index1);
                      }
```

```
        ListDataListener ldl = (ListDataListener)iter.next();
        ldl.intervalRemoved(e);
      }
    }

  public EventListener[] getListeners(Class listenerType) {
    Set set = listenerList.keySet();
    return (EventListener[])set.toArray(new EventListener[0]);
  }
}
```

> **NOTE** *This code may seem overly synchronized but it is necessary because the weak references can be removed from the map at any time. Making a copy of the map and using the copy won't help, as you'll then have two places from which the references could be dropped. Also, when notifying the listener list, a new set is created instead of using the* `listenerList.keySet()`, *so that if a listener tries to remove itself from the listener list, the original set is still notified.*

To demonstrate the program, Listing 10-3 creates a `WeakListModel` and modifies the data in the model. The strong reference to the listener is lost in the middle of the run, thus the listener should not be notified anymore, even though you don't explicitly remove the reference.

Listing 10-3. Testing our new `WeakListModel`.

```
import javax.swing.*;
import javax.swing.event.*;

public class TestListModel {
  public static void main (String args[]) {
    ListDataListener ldl = new ListDataListener() {
      public void intervalAdded(ListDataEvent e) {
        System.out.println("Added: " + e);
      }
      public void intervalRemoved(ListDataEvent e) {
        System.out.println("Removed: " + e);
      }
      public void contentsChanged(ListDataEvent e) {
        System.out.println("Changed: " + e);
      }
    };
```

```
        WeakListModel model = new WeakListModel();
        model.addListDataListener(ldl);
        model.addElement("New Jersey");
        model.addElement("Massachusetts");
        model.addElement("Maryland");
        model.removeElement("New Jersey");
        ldl = null;
        System.gc();
        model.addElement("New Jersey");
        System.out.println(model);
    }
}
```

When the test program is executed, the following is output:

```
Added: javax.swing.event.ListDataEvent[source=[New Jersey]]
Added: javax.swing.event.ListDataEvent[source=[New Jersey, Massachusetts]]
Added: javax.swing.event.ListDataEvent[source=[New Jersey, Massachusetts,
  Maryland]]
Removed: javax.swing.event.ListDataEvent[source=[Massachusetts, Maryland]]
[Massachusetts, Maryland, New Jersey]
```

Notice that the listener does not respond to the final "add" call, even though New Jersey is in the final dump of the model.

TreeMap Class

The final Map implementation is the TreeMap. A TreeMap is a map that maintains its keys ordered within a balanced, red-black tree. As Table 10-5 shows, TreeMap has the previously introduced Map interface methods, as well as those that come from the SortedMap interface.

Table 10-5. Summary of the TreeMap Class

VARIABLE/METHOD NAME	VERSION	DESCRIPTION
TreeMap()	1.2	Constructs an empty tree map.
clear()	1.2	Removes all the elements from the tree map.
clone()	1.2	Creates a clone of the tree map.
comparator()	1.2	Retrieves the comparator for the map.
containsKey()	1.2	Checks to see if an object is a key for the tree map.
containsValue()	1.2	Checks to see if an object is a value within the tree map.
entrySet()	1.2	Returns a set of key-value pairs in the tree map.
firstKey()	1.2	Retrieves the first key of the map.
get()	1.2	Retrieves a value for a key in the tree map.
headMap()	1.2	Retrieves the sub map at the beginning of the entire map.
keySet()	1.2	Retrieves a collection of keys from the tree map.
lastKey()	1.2	Retrieves the last key of the map.
put()	1.2	Places a key-value pair into the tree map.
putAll()	1.2	Places a collection of key-value pairs into the tree map.
remove()	1.2	Removes an element from the tree map.
size()	1.2	Returns the number of elements in the tree map.
subMap()	1.2	Retrieves a sub map of the entire map.
tailMap()	1.2	Retrieves a sub map at the end of the entire map.
values()	1.2	Retrieves a collection of values from the tree map.

Since TreeMap behaves so much like HashMap, we'll focus our attention only on the new behavior introduced with TreeMap.

Creating a TreeMap

There are four constructors for TreeMap. The basic two are present: one, the no argument version, creates an empty list, and the other, the standard copy constructor.

```
public TreeMap()
public TreeMap(Map map)
```

Sorted maps require two additional constructors; one accepts a Comparator to define a custom sort order, and the other accepts a SortedMap for an optimized copy constructor:

```
public TreeMap(Comparator comp)
public TreeMap(SortedMap map)
```

Elements in a TreeMap are sorted by their natural ordering—they must implement Comparable—unless a Comparator is provided. If a SortedMap is provided, the new TreeMap retains its Comparator.

Viewing Sub Maps

Since a TreeMap is sorted, you can work with subsets of the map with the help of the headMap(), tailMap(), and subMap() methods:

```
SortedSet headMap(Object toKey)
SortedSet tailMap(Object fromKey)
SortedSet subMap(Object fromKey, Object toKey)
```

To specify the range, one end point for headMap() and tailMap() should be fairly self-explanatory: the first and last key, respectively. For the other end point, if fromKey is in the map, it will be in the sub map, and if toKey is in the map, it will *not* be in the sub map.

```
fromKey <= map keys < toKey
```

If you want toKey to be in the sub map, you must pass in something that is beyond it. If the element is a string, this can be done by appending something to the element:

```
Map headMap = map.headMap(toKey+"\0");
```

Working with End Points

The firstKey() and lastKey() methods of TreeMap let you quickly access the keys at the end of the map:

```
Object firstKey()
Object lastKey()
```

If you need to traverse a map backwards, just keep getting the last key and the head map before it:

```
if (!map.isEmpty()) {
  Object last = map.lastKey();
  boolean first = true;
  do {
    if (!first) {
      System.out.print(", ");
    }
    System.out.print(last);
    last=map.headMap(last).lastKey();
    first=false;
  } while (last != map.firstKey());
  System.out.println();
}
```

> **NOTE** *Traversing a tree backwards in this manner is inefficient and not recommended. However, if it is more difficult to come up with a comparator to reverse the elements, then this trick will work.*

Sharing Comparators

The final method of the interface is the `comparator()` method:

```
Comparator comparator()
```

If the natural ordering of the elements is used, null will be returned.

> **NOTE** *See the "Understanding Comparator" section of Chapter 11 for more information on comparators.*

Map Usage

To demonstrate the usage of `HashMap` and `TreeMap`, Listing 10-4 revises the word count program from Chapter 5 to use these newer classes of the Collection Framework. Besides just replacing the `Hashtable` with a `HashMap`, this program shows how easy it is to sort the words with the `TreeMap`.

Listing 10-4. Counting words with a hash map.

```java
import java.io.*;
import java.util.*;

public class WordCount {
  static final Integer ONE = new Integer(1);

  public static void main (String args[])
      throws IOException {

    HashMap map = new HashMap();
    FileReader fr = new FileReader(args[0]);
    BufferedReader br = new BufferedReader(fr);
    String line;
    while ((line = br.readLine()) != null) {
      processLine(line, map);
    }
    printMap(map);
    System.out.println("—");
    printMap(new TreeMap(map));
  }
  static void printMap(Map map) {
    Iterator itor = map.entrySet().iterator();
    while (itor.hasNext()) {
      Map.Entry entry = (Map.Entry)itor.next();
      System.out.println(entry.getKey() + " : " + entry.getValue());
    }
  }
  static void processLine(String line, Map map) {
    StringTokenizer st = new StringTokenizer(line);
    while (st.hasMoreTokens()) {
      addWord(map, st.nextToken());
    }
  }
  static void addWord(Map map, String word) {
    Object obj = map.get(word);
    if (obj == null) {
      map.put(word, ONE);
    } else {
      int i = ((Integer)obj).intValue() + 1;
      map.put(word, new Integer(i));
    }
  }
}
```

When executed on itself, the sorted version of the output looks like the following:

```
!= : 1
" : 2
((Integer)obj).intValue() : 1
((line : 1
(Map.Entry)itor.next(); : 1
(String : 1
(itor.hasNext()) : 1
(obj : 1
(st.hasMoreTokens()) : 1
+ : 3
1; : 1
: : 1
= : 10
== : 1
BufferedReader : 1
BufferedReader(fr); : 1
FileReader : 1
FileReader(args[0]); : 1
HashMap : 1
HashMap(); : 1
IOException : 1
Integer : 1
Integer(1); : 1
Integer(i)); : 1
Iterator : 1
Map : 1
Map.Entry : 1
ONE : 1
ONE); : 1
Object : 1
String : 2
StringTokenizer : 1
StringTokenizer(line); : 1
System.out.println("—"); : 1
System.out.println(entry.getKey() : 1
TreeMap(map)); : 1
WordCount : 1
addWord(Map : 1
addWord(map, : 1
args[]) : 1
br : 1
```

```
       br.readLine()) : 1
       class : 1
       else : 1
       entry : 1
       entry.getValue()); : 1
       final : 1
       fr : 1
       i : 1
       if : 1
       import : 2
       int : 1
       itor : 1
       java.io.*; : 1
       java.util.*; : 1
       line, : 1
       line; : 1
       main : 1
       map : 1
       map) : 2
       map); : 1
       map, : 1
       map.entrySet().iterator(); : 1
       map.get(word); : 1
       map.put(word, : 2
       new : 6
       null) : 2
       obj : 1
       printMap(Map : 1
       printMap(map); : 1
       printMap(new : 1
       processLine(String : 1
       processLine(line, : 1
       public : 2
       st : 1
       st.nextToken()); : 1
       static : 5
       throws : 1
       void : 4
       while : 3
       word) : 1
       { : 10
       } : 10
```

> **TIP**   *If you only need to display the final output sorted, it is much more efficient to wait until all of the elements are added to the map before sorting. That way, you don't have to keep the tree sorted as each element is added.*

Summary

In this chapter, we explored how the Collections Framework provides support for maintaining key-value pairs through the Map interface and its three new concrete implementations: HashMap, WeakHashMap, and TreeMap. You learned about HashMap, the most commonly used implementation, as the replacement for Hashtable to store key-value pairs in an unordered map. You learned about the different operations you can perform upon a map, HashMap or otherwise. In the explanation of WeakHashMap, we took a detour to better understand how weak references can be used as keys to build upon the basic HashMap and how you can better maintain a list of event listeners. The final implementation, TreeMap, provides a map whose keys are maintained in a sorted order.

The next chapter explores how the Collections Framework supports maintaining elements in a sorted order through the Comparator and Comparable interfaces used within a SortedSet and SortedMap. We'll also revisit the TreeSet and TreeMap classes.

Sorting

In earlier chapters, we looked at the usage of the TreeSet and TreeMap classes with respect to their lives as a set and map, respectively. In this chapter, we'll examine the underlying support these classes use to sort their elements. For TreeSet, there is the SortedSet interface, which defines how to maintain the elements of the set in an ordered fashion. For TreeMap there is the SortedMap interface, which defines the mechanism for maintaining the map's keys in an ordered manner. Both SortedSet and SortedMap rely on the underlying elements to be comparable, either by implementing the Comparable interface directly or by providing a custom Comparator. It is these last two interfaces that we'll look at first.

Comparable Basics

System-defined classes that have a natural ordering implement the Comparable interface as of Java 1.2. Previously, there was no system-defined concept of ordering, just as there was no Collections Framework. Internally, the ordering is done through the compareTo() method of each implementation, which is the sole method of the interface as shown in Table 11-1.

Table 11-1. Summary of the Comparable Interface

VARIABLE/METHOD NAME	VERSION	DESCRIPTION
compareTo()	1.2	Checks for ordering with another object.

System-Defined Comparable Classes

There are fourteen system classes that have a natural ordering and implement the interface. These are listed in Table 11-2, which shows how the elements of each class are ordered.

Table 11-2. Comparable Implementers

CLASS NAME	ORDERING
BigDecimal	Numerical (signed)
BigInteger	Numerical (signed)
Byte	Numerical (signed)
Character	Numerical (unsigned)
CollationKey	Alphabetical, by locale
Date	Chronological
Double	Numerical (signed)
File	Alphabetical of path
Float	Numerical (signed)
Integer	Numerical (signed)
Long	Numerical (signed)
ObjectStreamField	Alphabetical of type string
Short	Numerical (signed)
String	Alphabetical

In a perfect world, the only elements you would place in a sorted set or map would be instances of these classes and you would like the natural order provided by these classes. If that were all you ever needed to do, you wouldn't need to know anything else about the Comparable interface.

Understanding Comparable

Assuming you'd like to know more about Comparable, here's how a properly written compareTo() method works:

```
public int compareTo(Object obj)
```

- **Elements must be mutually comparable**.

  You can only compare like elements. If you try to compare two elements that are not *mutually comparable*, a ClassCastException will be thrown. Quite simply, two elements are mutually comparable if they can be compared to one another. With respect to collection usage, this basically means don't try to add elements of type Date and File to a TreeSet—they aren't mutually comparable. In most cases, the two objects must be of the same type (or a subtype) to be mutually comparable. For instance, you can't compare a Double to a Float or any other numeric type.

- **The return value states the relative position to the natural ordering.**

  The compareTo() method can return one of three values. It will return a negative number if the current object comes before the object compared to. It will return a positive number if the current object comes after the object compared to. Finally, it will return zero if the two objects are equal. The magnitudes of the positive/negative numbers returned have no significance.

- **The natural ordering *should be* consistent with equals().**

  If two elements are equal as defined by the object's equals() method, then compareTo() should return zero. This rule is a *should* rule, not a *must* rule. If the class is not consistent, the javadoc associated to the class should include a note that reflects this, such as:

  Note: This class has a natural ordering that is inconsistent with equals.

> **NOTE** *If you implement* Comparable *for your custom class and it is not consistent with* equals(), *it won't work properly within a* SortedSet *or* SortedMap.

- **Never call the method directly**

  The mechanisms within the Collections Framework call the compareTo() method for you when necessary. It is not your responsibility to call the method.

Using Comparable

To demonstrate the use of Comparable, let's create a class that implements the interface. Imagine having an employee object that should be sorted by department and name. This basically involves daisy-chaining the compareTo() calls for each field in the class. As soon as one call returns a non-zero value, return that value. Otherwise, keep comparing fields. For equals(), you'll need to "and" (&&) the results of checking equality for all of the fields in the class. And for good measure, throw in the toString() and hashCode() methods.

The source code for just such a class is shown in Listing 11-1.

Listing 11-1. Creating a Comparable object.

```java
import java.util.*;

public class Employee implements Comparable {
  String department, name;

  public Employee(String department, String name) {
    this.department = department;
    this.name = name;
  }

  public String getDepartment() {
    return department;
  }

  public String getName() {
    return name;
  }

  public String toString() {
    return "[dept=" + department +
      ",name=" + name + "]";
  }

  public int compareTo(Object obj) {
    Employee emp = (Employee)obj;
    int deptComp = department.compareTo(emp.getDepartment());

    return ((deptComp == 0) ?
      name.compareTo(emp.getName()) :
      deptComp);
  }

  public boolean equals(Object obj) {
    if (!(obj instanceof Employee)) {
      return false;
    }
    Employee emp = (Employee)obj;
    return department.equals(emp.getDepartment()) &&
           name.equals(emp.getName());
  }
```

```
public int hashCode() {
    return 31*department.hashCode() + name.hashCode();
  }
}
```

> **TIP** *When defining the* compareTo() *method, be sure not to overload the method by declaring it as having an argument of the specific object type you want to compare to. It won't be called naturally as it isn't part of the* Comparable *interface.*

Listing 11-2 demonstrates the usage of the comparable employee by creating a company with a bunch of employees. For simplicity's sake, names are held as one field of the form "Lastname, Firstname" to ensure that they are ordered properly in one field.

Listing 11-2. Testing our Comparable object.

```
import java.util.*;

public class Company {
  public static void main (String args[]) {
    Employee emps[] = {
      new Employee("Finance", "Degree, Debbie"),
      new Employee("Finance", "Grade, Geri"),
      new Employee("Finance", "Extent, Ester"),
      new Employee("Engineering", "Measure, Mary"),
      new Employee("Engineering", "Amount, Anastasia"),
      new Employee("Engineering", "Ratio, Ringo"),
      new Employee("Sales", "Stint, Sarah"),
      new Employee("Sales", "Pitch, Paula"),
      new Employee("Support", "Rate, Rhoda"),
    };
    Set set = new TreeSet(Arrays.asList(emps));
    System.out.println(set);
  }
}
```

Running the program displays the sorted company roster on one really long line. Notice how the elements are sorted by department first and name second.

```
[[dept=Engineering,name=Amount, Anastasia], [dept=Engineering,name=Measure,
Mary], [dept=Engineering,name=Ratio, Ringo], [dept=Finance,name=Degree,
Debbie], [dept=Finance,name=Extent, Ester], [dept=Finance,name=Grade, Geri],
[dept=Sales,name=Pitch, Paula], [dept=Sales,name=Stint, Sarah],
[dept=Support,name=Rate, Rhoda]]
```

Comparator Basics

While Comparable objects are able to compare multiple instances of themselves, a Comparator is a class that can compare two other objects. When you don't like the natural ordering of a class or your class doesn't implement Comparable, you can provide a custom ordering by creating a class that implements Comparator. Table 11-3 lists the methods of the Comparator interface.

Table 11-3. Summary of the Comparator Interface

VARIABLE/METHOD NAME	VERSION	DESCRIPTION
compare()	1.2	Checks for ordering between two elements.
equals()	1.2	Checks for equality with another Comparator.

Understanding Comparator

Of the two methods in the interface, you actually only have to implement one.

The compare() method functions similarly to the compareTo() method, however, both objects to compare must be passed in as arguments:

```
public int compare(Object obj1, Object obj2)
```

The equals() method has nothing to do with comparing elements for sorting. It is meant to compare the Comparator to another Comparator:

```
public boolean equals(Object obj)
```

As this method is already implemented in the Object class, your Comparator does not have to override the behavior. However, if you wish to provide a way for different comparators to be equal, override the method. It's possible that different implementations impose the same order on elements, but in different manners.

There is one predefined Comparator already implemented for you. If you wish to sort elements in their reverse natural order, you can get the reverseOrder() comparator from the Collections class.

For instance, if our company set were sorted using the reverse comparator, the output would be as follows:

```
[[dept=Support,name=Rate, Rhoda], [dept=Sales,name=Stint, Sarah],
[dept=Sales,name=Pitch, Paula], [dept=Finance,name=Grade, Geri],
[dept=Finance,name=Extent, Ester], [dept=Finance,name=Degree, Debbie],
[dept=Engineering,name=Ratio, Ringo], [dept=Engineering,name=Measure, Mary],
[dept=Engineering,name=Amount, Anastasia]]
```

The set was created with the following code to Listing 11-2:

```
Set set = new TreeSet(Collections.reverseOrder());
set2.addAll(Arrays.asList(emps));
```

When creating a TreeSet with a custom Comparator, you can't use the copy constructor. You must manually add each element to the set.

Using Comparator

To demonstrate writing a custom Comparator, imagine a new manager coming into the previous company who likes to see employee names first and their department last. While the reverse order Comparator was able to reverse the natural order, it can't reverse the sort order of the internal fields. For this to be done, you must create your own Comparator. Listing 11-3 shows one such comparator.

Listing 11-3. Writing Your own Comparator.
```
import java.util.*;

public class EmpComparator implements Comparator {
  public int compare(Object obj1, Object obj2) {
    Employee emp1 = (Employee)obj1;
    Employee emp2 = (Employee)obj2;

    int nameComp = emp1.getName().compareTo(emp2.getName());

    return ((nameComp == 0) ?
      emp1.getDepartment().compareTo(emp2.getDepartment()) :
      nameComp);
  }
}
```

Now, when you use this comparator, the order of the elements would be as follows:

```
[[dept=Engineering,name=Amount, Anastasia], [dept=Finance,name=Degree,
Debbie], [dept=Finance,name=Extent, Ester], [dept=Finance,name=Grade, Geri],
[dept=Engineering,name=Measure, Mary], [dept=Sales,name=Pitch, Paula],
[dept=Support,name=Rate, Rhoda], [dept=Engineering,name=Ratio, Ringo],
[dept=Sales,name=Stint, Sarah]]
```

This is basically all there is to say with regards to comparators and comparables. The key thing to remember when writing your own is to make sure that you don't accidentally use a non-unique sort field, like a date, when you are using the Comparator with a SortedSet or SortedMap. If you do, only one of the elements will be added to the collection.

Imagine adding a start date to the Employee class. If multiple employees started on the same date, their setting would be the same. Now imagine creating a Comparator that allowed you to sort a group of employees on their start date. When comparing employees with the same start date, compare() would produce a zero, meaning they are equal, and the second employee (and beyond) would not be added to the set or tree. If you run across this behavioral problem, you'll need to add a secondary field to the comparison to ensure instances where equals() returns false results in compareTo() returning a non-zero value.

If you did have a misbehaving comparator, you could still use it to sort a List with Collections.sort(List, Comparator) and an array of Object elements with Arrays.sort(Object[], Comparator). These methods are described in Chapters 12 and 13, respectively.

SortedSet

The basis of maintaining order within the elements of a set is defined in the SortedSet interface. While set elements by definition have no order, those concrete sets that also implement the SortedSet interface actually do keep their elements ordered. As far as those concrete implementations provided with the Collections Framework, only TreeSet implements the interface. This is shown in Figure 11-1.

The SortedSet interface has only six methods, which are listed in Table 11-4.

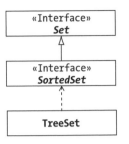

Figure 11-1. Class hierarchy of the SortedSet interface.

Table 11-4. Summary of the SortedSet *Interface*

VARIABLE/METHOD NAME	VERSION	DESCRIPTION
comparator()	1.2	Retrieves the comparator for the set.
first()	1.2	Retrieves the first element of the set.
headSet()	1.2	Retrieves a sub set from the beginning of the entire set.
last()	1.2	Retrieves the last element of the set.
subSet()	1.2	Retrieves a sub set of the entire set.
tailSet()	1.2	Retrieves a sub set from the end of the entire set.

Understanding SortedSet

The six methods of SortedSet can be broken up into three groupings: for viewing subsets, for working from endpoints, and for sharing comparators. In addition, there is some special behavior necessary to create concrete implementations.

Viewing Subsets

Because the elements of a sorted set are ordered, you can get a subset of those elements. The headSet(), tailSet(), and subSet() allow you to acquire the subset to work with:

```
SortedSet headSet(Object toElement)
SortedSet tailSet(Object fromElement)
SortedSet subSet(Object fromElement, Object toElement)
```

When you grab the subset, any changes you make to the subset will be reflected in the underlying set. Assuming your set supports removals, any removal of elements will be done from both. As far as additions are concerned, you can only add elements to the part of the set you are working with, if, of course, the set supports additions. If you try to add an element that goes beyond the range provided, an `IllegalArugmentException` will be thrown.

To specify the range (as mentioned in the description of `TreeSet` in Chapter 8), one end point for the `headSet()` and `tailSet()` is easy—it will be the first and last element respectively. As far as the other end point goes, the from-element will be in the subset while the to-element will not:

```
fromElement <= set view < toElement
```

In order for the `toElement` to be in the created subset, you must pass in something that is beyond it. In the case of a the element being a string, this can be done by appending something to the element:

```
Set headSet = set.headSet(toElement+"\0");
```

For the `fromElement` not to be in the subset, you must do the same thing from the other side:

```
Set tailSet = set.tailSet(fromElement+"\0");
```

If you wish to specify both ends and you want both to be included in the subset, use `subSet()` with appropriate arguments:

```
Set bothEnds = set.subSet(fromElement, toElement+"\0");
```

And finally, for neither end to be included in your subset, reverse the appending:

```
Set neitherEnd = set.subSet(fromElement+"\0", toElement);
```

Working with Endpoints

The `first()` and `last()` methods provide easy access to the ends of the set.

```
Object first()
Object last()
```

Unlike regular sets, since the elements of sorted sets are ordered, you can find out which element is first and last. These two methods just make it easier so you don't have to iterate through them all to get the last one.

If you need to visit each element of a set you can get its iterator with
iterator(). As previously mentioned, for a SortedSet, this will return the elements
in the order they are maintained within the set. If, however, you wish to visit the
elements in reverse order, you might think you need to either create a second set
with a new Comparator or copy the elements out to an array and traverse the array
backwards. While both of those will probably be faster, neither is absolutely necessary. As shown in Listing 11-4, you can actually combine the usage of the headSet()
and last() methods to slowly iterate backwards through a sorted set.

Listing 11-4. Looping through a sorted set backwards.

```
try {
  Object last = set.last();
  boolean first = true;
  while (true) {
    if (!first) {
      System.out.print(", ");
    }
    System.out.println(last);
    last=set.headSet(last).last();
  }
} catch (NoSuchElementException e) {
  System.out.println();
}
```

A more probable reason to use the first() and last() methods is for getting
the head and tail elements of a (sub)set, possibly for removal.

Sharing Comparators

The final method of the interface is the comparator() method:

```
Comparator comparator()
```

The comparator() method is provided so you can share comparators across
sorted sets. If the natural ordering of the elements is used, null will be returned.

Creating Implementations

When creating concrete implementations of SortedSet, you should provide two
additional constructors besides the no argument version and the copy constructor to accept a generic Collection. The first additional constructor would accept a

custom `Comparator`, and the second, a `SortedSet`. In the case of the `SortedSet` constructor, the new set would use the same `Comparator` as the sorted set passed to it, creating a second set with the elements in the same order.

When creating new sorted sets from old sorted sets, you must be sure that the declaration type of the set passed into the constructor is correct. For instance, in the following example, the custom comparator will not be associated with the second set:

```
Set set1 = new TreeSet(new MyComparator());
Set set2 = new TreeSet(set1);
```

Because the declaration type of `set1` is `Set`, the standard copy constructor will be called. If you wish to have the `SortedSet` version of the constructor called, you must be sure that either `set1` is declared to be of type `SortedSet` or that you cast the variable type in the constructor call:

```
Set set3 = new TreeSet((SortedSet)set1);
```

Besides the constructor differences in implementing `SortedSet`, there are two other differences reflected by the behavior of methods inherited from the `Set` interface. Because the elements in a `SortedSet` have an order, the elements returned by the `iterator()` for the set honor that order. In addition, when copying elements into an array with `toArray()`, these elements retain the order from the sorted set, too.

Using TreeSet

The `TreeSet` class is the only implementation of `SortedSet` in the Collections Framework. It basically maintains its elements in a balanced, red-black tree. For more information on its usage, see the "TreeSet Class" section in Chapter 8.

SortedMap

The `SortedMap` interface defines the basis for keeping the keys in a map sorted. There is only one concrete implementation found in the Collections Framework, the `TreeMap` class. This relationship is shown in Figure 11-2.

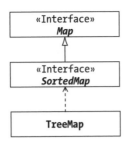

Figure 11-2. Class hierarchy of the SortedMap interface.

Similar to the SortedSet interface, the SortedMap interface offers six new methods to those offered by its parent interface. These are listed in Table 11-5.

Table 11-5. Summary of the SortedMap *Interface*

VARIABLE/METHOD NAME	VERSION	DESCRIPTION
comparator()	1.2	Retrieves the comparator from the map.
firstKey()	1.2	Retrieves the first key from the map.
headMap()	1.2	Retrieves a sub map from the beginning of the entire map.
lastKey()	1.2	Retrieves the last key from the map.
subMap()	1.2	Retrieves a sub map of the entire map.
tailMap()	1.2	Retrieves a sub map from the end of the entire map.

Understanding SortedMap

The six methods of SortedMap can be broken into the same three groupings as SortedSet. The method sets are for viewing sub maps, working from endpoints, and sharing comparators. In addition, there is some special behavior necessary to create concrete implementations.

Viewing Sub Maps

The headMap(), tailMap(), and subMap() methods offer the ability to work with ordered subsets of the original maps:

```
SortedSet headMap(Object toKey)
SortedSet tailMap(Object fromKey)
SortedSet subMap(Object fromKey, Object toKey)
```

The method for specifying keys is identical to that of specifying endpoint elements for a sorted set. By default, the fromKey is included in the sub map and the toKey is not. You must perform additional work if you don't want the fromKey or do want the toKey.

Working with Endpoints

The first() and last() methods of TreeMap allow you quick access to the keys at the end of the map:

```
Object first()
Object last()
```

As with a sorted set, you can use the last() and tailMap() methods to traverse the keys of a map backwards.

Sharing Comparators

The comparator() method allows you to find out what, if any, comparator is associated with the sorted map:

```
Comparator comparator()
```

When the natural ordering is used to order the keys associated with a map, null will be returned from calls to comparator().

Creating Implementations

Similar to implementing SortedSet, concrete implementations of SortedMap should provide two additional constructors besides the no argument version and the copy constructor. The first new one would accept a custom Comparator, and the second, a SortedMap. In the case of the SortedMap constructor, the new map would use the same Comparator as the sorted map passed to it, creating a second map with the keys in the same order.

When working with a SortedMap, there are two differences reflected by the methods inherited from Map. Because the keys in a SortedMap have an order, the keys and values returned by the keySet(), values(), and entrySet() methods for the map honor that order. Values are returned in the sort order of the keys. In all three cases, the collections returned do not implement the SortedSet interface;

they are just ordered. In addition, when copying elements into an array with
`toArray()`, these elements will retain the key order in the sorted map.

Using TreeMap

The only implementation of the `SortedMap` interface found in the Collections
Framework is `TreeMap`. Like `TreeSet`, it maintains its key-value pairs in a balanced,
red-black tree. Actually, `TreeSet` uses a `TreeMap` under the covers. For more information on how to use a `TreeMap`, see the "TreeMap Class" section in Chapter 10.

Summary

This chapter explored the depths of working with sorted collections. We looked at
how the collections support the ordering of objects through the `Comparable` and
`Comparator` interfaces. We also examined the collection interfaces which define
the basis for collections that keep their elements ordered: `SortedSet` and
`SortedMap`. Once these four interfaces are understood, you'll be able to utilize the
`TreeSet` and `TreeMap` implementations to the fullest.

   In the next chapter you'll learn about the special collection support offered by
the `Collections` class. The `Collections` class offers many extensions to the basic
collection implementations to support the creation of thread-safe and synchronized collections and operations like searching as well as ordering collection
elements.

CHAPTER 12

Special Collections Support

The Collections class is one of two special classes in the framework that consists solely of static methods and objects for working with specific instances of collections. (The Arrays class described in Chapter 13 is the other.)

When looking at this class, it might help to think of the three variables and twenty-six methods in five groups. The three variables and a trio of methods make up one group of defining, prebuilt collections. Then there is the set of wrapped collection methods that offer read-only and synchronized access to the different collections. The third set supports sorting collections. The fourth goes hand-in-hand with sorting—this set is for searching collections. The final set is for a series of generic operations on lists. All of these variables and methods are listed in Table 12-1.

Table 12-1. Summary of the Collections Class

VARIABLE/METHOD NAME	VERSION	DESCRIPTION
EMPTY_LIST	1.2	Represents an empty immutable list.
EMPTY_MAP	1.3	Represents an empty immutable map.
EMPTY_SET	1.2	Represents an empty immutable set.
binarySearch()	1.2	Searches for element in list with binary search.
copy()	1.2	Copies elements between two lists.
enumeration()	1.2	Converts a collection to an enumeration.
fill()	1.2	Fills a list with a single element.
max()	1.2	Searches for maximum value within the collection.
min()	1.2	Searches for minimum value within the collection.
nCopies()	1.2	Creates an immutable list with multiple copies of an element.
reverse()	1.2	Reverses elements within list.
reverseOrder()	1.2	Returns compartor for reversing order of comparable elements.
shuffle()	1.2	Randomly reorders elements in list.

Table 12-1. Continued

VARIABLE/METHOD NAME	VERSION	DESCRIPTION
singleton()	1.2	Returns an immutable set of one element.
singletonList()	1.3	Returns an immutable list of one element.
singletonMap()	1.3	Returns an immutable map of one element.
sort()	1.2	Reorders the elements in a list.
synchronizedCollection()	1.2	Creates a thread-safe collection.
synchronizedList()	1.2	Creates a thread-safe list.
synchronizedMap()	1.2	Creates a thread-safe map.
synchronizedSet()	1.2	Creates a thread-safe set.
synchronizedSortedMap()	1.2	Creates a thread-safe sorted map.
synchronizedSortedSet()	1.2	Creates a thread-safe sorted set.
unmodifiableCollection()	1.2	Creates a read-only collection.
unmodifiableList()	1.2	Creates a read-only list.
unmodifiableMap()	1.2	Creates a read-only map.
unmodifiableSet()	1.2	Creates a read-only set.
unmodifiableSortedMap()	1.2	Creates a read-only sorted map.
unmodifiableSortedSet()	1.2	Creates a read-only sorted set.

> **NOTE** *The* enumeration() *method will be described in Chapter 15.*

Prebuilt Collections

The Collections class comes with six prebuilt collections. Half of them are empty, while the other half have a single element in them.

Empty Collections

The Collections class provides three constants to represent empty collections:

```
public static final List EMPTY_LIST
public static final Map EMPTY_MAP
public static final Set EMPTY_SET
```

These are useful when methods require a collection argument but you have nothing to put in it, and when you want to ensure that it remains empty.

Think of each of these implementations as having called the default constructor for one of the concrete collection implementations, and then having called the appropriate `unmodifiableXXX()` method to ensure the collection doesn't change. You'll learn more about the `unmodifiableXXX()` methods shortly in the "Read-Only Collections" section. For instance, the following would act similar to the `EMPTY_LIST` defined above:

```
List emptyList = Collections.unmodifiableList(new LinkedList());
```

There are two benefits to using the constants over creating the implementations yourself. The key difference is that the implementations behind the constants have been optimized with the knowledge that they are empty. Creating the implementations yourself and making them unmodifiable requires the creation of necessary internal data structures, even though they will never be used. A secondary benefit of using the empty collection constants is that you can share the same empty implementation with anyone else without having to create extra object instances.

> **NOTE**   *One nice thing about working with the* `EMPTY_MAP` *implementation is that even the collections that the map methods return are of the* `EMPTY_SET` *variety (*`entrySet()`, `keySet()`, *and* `values()`*).*

Singleton Collections

There exists a trio of methods for creating single-element collections, which act similar to the specialized methods for creating empty collections:

```
public static List singletonList(Object element)
public static Set singleton(Object element)
public static Map singletonMap(Object key, Object value)
```

> **NOTE**   *Both* `singletonList()` *and* `singletonMap()` *were added with the 1.3 release of the Java 2 platform.*

These are useful when you have a single element and when a method you need to call requires a collection, not an element.

Like the empty collections, an attempt to modify the collection causes an `UnsupportedOperationException` to be thrown. When trying to add a single element or check for its pre-existence in a collection, there is no difference in calling

methods like add(elementOfSingletonCollection) versus
addAll(singletonCollection), or contains(elementOfSingletonCollection)
versus containsAll(singletonCollection).

There is, however, a big difference between
remove(elementOfSingletonCollection) and removeAll(singletonCollection).
With remove(elementOfSingletonCollection), only the first instance of the element is removed from the collection. However, with
removeAll(singletonCollection), all instances of the element will be removed.
Figure 12-1 should help you visualize this difference.

Original List (list)

One	Two	Three	One	Two	Three

List.remove("One");

Two	Three	One	Two	Three

list.removeAll(Collections.singleton("One"));

Two	Three	Two	Three

Figure 12-1. The remove(element) versus the removeAll(singletonCollection).

Wrapped Collections

The Collections class provides two sets of wrapper methods that decorate the
underlying collections. The first set of wrappers allows you to create an unmodifiable or *read-only* collection. The second set allows you to create a synchronized or
thread-safe collection.

Read-Only Collections

When working with collections, there are times when you need, or at least prefer,
unmodifiable access to your collection instance. This may be because you are finished adding and removing elements from the collection but you still need to use
the collection, or because you need to pass your collection to someone you don't
necessarily know. Or perhaps you know them, but you don't want them to change
anything. To ensure that your collections will not be modified, the Collections
class provides a set of six methods to create read-only instances—one for each
Collection, List, Map, Set, SortedMap, and SortedSet interface:

```
public static Collection unmodifiableCollection(Collection c)
public static List unmodifiableList(List l)
public static Map unmodifiableMap(Map m)
public static Set unmodifiableSet(Set s)
public static SortedMap unmodifiableSortedMap(SortedMap m)
public static SortedSet unmodifiableSortedSet(SortedSet s)
```

These methods work like the Decorator pattern by wrapping additional functionality around an underlying collection. This time, however, the decorated implementations remove functionality instead of adding capabilities. If you try to modify the collection directly or try to modify the collection through an acquired iterator, the underlying collection will remain unchanged and an UnsupportedOperationException will be thrown.

To use these factory methods, simply create the collection:

```
Set simpsons = new HashSet();
```

Fill it up:

```
simpsons.add("Bart");
simpsons.add("Hugo");
simpsons.add("Lisa");
simpsons.add("Marge");
simpsons.add("Homer");
simpsons.add("Maggie");
simpsons.add("Roy");
```

And then pass off the protected collection to a third party:

```
public Set getFamily() {
  return Collections.unmodifiableSet(simpsons);
}
```

Alternatively, keep it to yourself by dropping any reference to the modifiable collection:

```
simpsons = Collections.unmodifiableSet(simpsons);
```

That's really all there is to making and using a read-only collection. Since UnsupportedOperationException is a RuntimeException, you don't even have to use the collection in a try-catch block.

> **NOTE** *Once you've wrapped access to a concrete collection implementa-*
> *tion, you can no longer call any methods of the specific implementation.*
> *You are limited to accessing the collection from the specific interface meth-*
> *ods only.*

Thread-Safe Collections

Similar to read-only collections, thread-safe collections are factory decorators
that wrap instances of the six core interfaces into thread-safe versions:

```
public static Collection synchronizedCollection(Collection c)
public static List synchronizedList(List l)
public static Map synchronizedMap(Map m)
public static Set synchronizedSet(Set s)
public static SortedMap synchronizedSortedMap(SortedMap m)
public static SortedSet synchronizedSortedSet(SortedSet s)
```

Remember, none of the new collection implementations are thread-safe.
While all of the historical collection classes are thread-safe out of the box, even if
you don't need thread safety with the older implementations, you are still forced
to be synchronized. If you do need thread safety, the new collections framework
implementations allow you to call one of these methods to create a thread-
safe implementation:

```
Map map = Collections.synchronizedMap(new HashMap(89));
```

> **WARNING** *Do not keep a reference to the unsynchronized backing collec-*
> *tion lying around. If you do, you've essentially bypassed the thread safety*
> *added by the creation of the synchronized version.*

To extend this synchronized access one step further, when iterating over a
synchronized collection you must manually synchronize this access, as shown
here:

```
simpsons = Collections.synchronizedSet(simpsons);
synchronized(simpsons) {
  Iterator iter = simpsons.iterator();
  while (iter.hasNext()) {
    System.out.println(iter.next());
  }
}
```

The iterator itself is not synchronized and iterating through a collection requires multiple calls back into the collection. If you don't synchronize the getting and use of your iterator, your iteration through the collection will not be atomic and the underlying collection may change.

In case you want to iterate through the elements or values of a Map, remember to synchronize on the Map and not on the Set returned from the entrySet() and keySet() methods, nor on the Collection returned from values(). This ensures synchronization on the same object as the synchronized map, as shown here:

```
Map map = Collections.synchronizedMap(new HashMap(89));
Set set = map.entrySet();
synchronized(map) {
  Iterator iter = set.iterator();
  while (iter.hasNext()) {
    System.out.println(iter.next());
  }
}
```

> **TIP** *If you can avoid it, don't waste CPU cycles by converting an historical collection like a* Vector *into a thread-safe* List. *It's already thread-safe. While the code will still work, it will require an extra level of indirection for all method calls to ensure thread safety.*

Sorting

While Chapter 11 described the high-level support for sorting in the Collections Framework, the Collections class offers a little more. And while two of the three methods could be moved directly into one class, List, all are better served by keeping all the collection utility routines in a central location, the Collections class.

Sorting Lists

The sort() routine allows you to sort in place the elements of the List:

```
public static void sort(List list)
public static void sort(List list, Comparator comp)
```

If the elements within the List implement the Comparable interface, you can call the one-argument version of the method. If you don't like the order that the Comparable implementation provides, or if the elements don't implement Comparable, you can provide your own Comparator to take its place and call the two-argument version of sort().

To demonstrate, Listing 12-1 takes the command-line argument array passed into main(), converts it to a List (with a method you'll learn about in Chapter 15), and then sorts and prints out the elements.

Listing 12-1. Sorting a List.
```java
import java.util.*;
public class SortTest {
  public static void main(String args[]) throws Exception {
    List list = Arrays.asList(args);
    Collections.sort(list);
    for (int i=0, n=list.size(); i<n; i++) {
      if (i != 0) System.out.print(", ");
      System.out.print(list.get(i));
    }
    System.out.println();
  }
}
```

If the program in Listing 12-1 is executed with the command java SortTest Bart Hugo Lisa Marge Homer Maggie Roy, you'll get the following results:

```
Bart, Homer, Hugo, Lisa, Maggie, Marge, Roy
```

The sort() method will be revisited later in the chapter with the rest of the generic List operations.

Reversing Order

The reverseOrder() method of Collections doesn't actually take a collections argument. Instead of taking one as its argument, what is returned by this method can be used anywhere a Comparator can be used:

```
public static Comparator reverseOrder()
```

This `Comparator` would be used to sort the elements of any collection that accepts a `Comparator` into its reverse natural ordering. The reverse comparator requires that the underlying elements implement the `Comparable` interface. If not, when you sort the collection with the reverse comparator, a `ClassCastException` will be thrown.

To demonstrate, if you were to change the `Collections.sort(list);` line in Listing 12-1 to this single line:

```
Collections.sort(list, Collections.reverseOrder());
```

you would get the following results when the program is run with the same command line arguments:

```
Roy, Marge, Maggie, Lisa, Hugo, Homer, Bart
```

Searching

The `Collections` class provides a sextet of methods for searching for elements in a collection. The two `binarySearch()` methods work with a `List`, while the four `min()` and `max()` methods work with any `Collection`.

Binary Searching

If you have a `List` whose elements are sorted, perhaps by `Collections.sort()`, you can use the `binarySearch()` method of `Collections` to locate an element in the `List`:

```
public static int binarySearch(List list, Object key)
public static int binarySearch(List list, Object key, Comparator comp)
```

While you can use the `contains()` method of `List` to check for an element, the performance of the two can be drastically different. On average, `contains()` will search through half the elements in a `List` before finding; though if not present, `contains()` must search through everything. With `binarySearch()`, that number can be reduced to log(n) for lists that support random access, like `ArrayList`, and n*log(n) for those that support sequential access. However, if `binarySearch()` is called on a subclass of `AbstractSequentialList`, like `LinkedList`, then the performance grows linearly.

> **NOTE** *Of course, if your list is unsorted, you either must use* `List.contains()`, *or make a copy of the list, sort the copy, and use* `binarySearch()` *on the copy. See the description of the* `copy()` *method of* `Collections` *later in the chapter to see how to make a copy of a* `List`.

When called, binarySearch() can return one of two types of values. If the element is found in the list, the index into the list is returned. However, if the element is not found, the returned value can be used to determine where in the list to insert the element in order to have a larger sorted list with the new element present. To find the insertion point, negate the number and subtract one:

```
index = -returnedValue -1;
```

Listing 12-2 demonstrates how to use binarySearch() to locate elements and how to insert an element into a sorted list when that search key is not found.

Listing 12-2. Sorting, searching, and inserting into a sorted list.

```java
import java.util.*;
public class SearchTest {
  public static void main(String args[]) {
    String simpsons[] = {"Bart", "Hugo", "Lisa", "Marge",
                         "Homer", "Maggie", "Roy"};

    // Convert to list
    List list = new ArrayList(Arrays.asList(simpsons));

    // Ensure list sorted
    Collections.sort(list);
    System.out.println("Sorted list: [length: " + list.size() + "]");
    System.out.println(list);

    // Search for element in list
    int index = Collections.binarySearch(list, "Maggie");
    System.out.println("Found Maggie @ " + index);

    // Search for element not in list
    index = Collections.binarySearch(list, "Jimbo Jones");
    System.out.println("Didn't find Jimbo Jones @ " + index);

    // Insert
    int newIndex = -index - 1;
    list.add(newIndex, "Jimbo Jones");
```

```
    System.out.println("With Jimbo Jones added: [length: " + list.size() + "]");
    System.out.println(list);
  }
}
```

The program takes the Simpson family from the earlier examples and places them in a List for sorting, searching, and inserting. When this program is executed, you'll get the following output:

```
Sorted list: [length: 7]
[Bart, Homer, Hugo, Lisa, Maggie, Marge, Roy]
Found Maggie @ 4
Didn't find Jimbo Jones @ -4
With Jimbo Jones added: [length: 8]
[Bart, Homer, Hugo, Jimbo Jones, Lisa, Maggie, Marge, Roy]
```

Notice how easily the List remains sorted by using the return value from binarySearch() to insert Jimbo Jones into the family while still keeping the list sorted.

> **NOTE** *If you use binarySearch() to search for an element that is in the list multiple times, which of the multiple objects that is returned remains undefined.*

Finding Extremes

The Collections class provides min() and max() methods to find elements at the lowest and highest extremes:

```
public static Object min(Collection col)
public static Object min(Collection col, Comparator comp)
public static Object max(Collection col)
public static Object max(Collection col, Comparator comp)
```

As both of these methods are passed a Collection, there is no presorting involved. If the collection consists of elements that implement the Comparable interface, you can call the one-argument version of each, passing in just the collection. If, however, you don't like the natural ordering of the elements or they don't implement Comparable, you must call the two-argument versions and pass in your own Comparator. Listing 12-3 demonstrates this.

Listing 12-3. Demonstrating the use of min() and max().

```java
import java.util.*;
public class MinMaxTest {
  public static void main(String args[]) {
    String simpsons[] = {"Bart", "Hugo", "Lisa", "Marge",
                          "Homer", "Maggie", "Roy"};
    List list = Arrays.asList(simpsons);

    // Min should be Bart
    System.out.println(Collections.min(list));
    // Max should be Roy
    System.out.println(Collections.max(list));

    Comparator comp = Collections.reverseOrder();

    // Reversed Min should be Roy
    System.out.println(Collections.min(list, comp));
    // Reversed Max should be Bart
    System.out.println(Collections.max(list, comp));
  }
}
```

> **NOTE**   *If the collection is empty,* NoSuchElementException *is thrown when* min() *or* max() *are called.*

Generic List Operations

The Collections class provides a series of routines to perform generic operations on a List. You can copy elements from one list to another. You can fill or create a list with a single element repeated. In addition, you can order the elements in the list in reverse order, random order, or sorted order.

Copying Lists

The copy() method lets you copy elements from one List into another:

```java
public static void copy(List dest, List src)
```

> **TIP**   *The argument order for* copy() *is the reverse of the* System.arraycopy() *method where the source list is first and the destination second.*

When copying elements, you must create the destination list before making the copy. If the list doesn't exist yet, don't use copy(). Instead, call the List constructor that takes another List as its argument. In the event that the destination list is too small, an IndexOutOfBoundsException is thrown. If the destination list is larger than the source list, those elements beyond the end of the source list will not be changed.

The following demonstrates the use of copy():

```
List wineMakers = Arrays.asList(new String[] {"Ugolin", "Cesar"});
List barFlies = Arrays.asList(new String[] {"Barney", "Carl", "Lenny"});
Collections.copy(barFlies, wineMakers); // works
Collections.copy(wineMakers, barFlies); // IndexOutOfBoundsException thrown
```

Copying the two element "evil French winemakers" list into the three element "barflies-at-Moe's" list works. However, going in the reverse direction does not given the size difference.

> **NOTE**   *The* copy() *method copies references between lists. If the underlying object changes, the change would be reflected in what both lists reference.*

Filling Lists

The fill() method of Collections allows you to fill up a list with multiple references to the same element:

```
public static void fill(List list, Object element)
```

The fill() method copies the same object reference to every element of the list. After filling the list, if you then change that one reference, every element of the list will be changed. See Figure 12-2 to visualize this description.

```
List list = new ArrayList(10);
Object anObject = . . .;
Collections.fill(list, anObject);
```

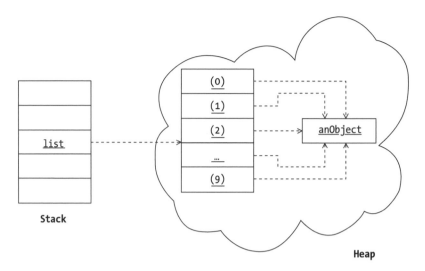

Figure 12-2. How Collections.fill() fills a list with the same object reference.

Multiple-Copy Collections

The nCopies() method of Collections is similar to using fill(), then copy(), with a List:

```
public static List nCopies(int n, Object element)
```

This creates a List with the same element repeated throughout the list. The key difference is that instead of passing in the destination list, nCopies() creates a new one. Another difference is that the nCopies() method creates an immutable collection. Why, you might ask, would you create an immutable collection with the same item present repeatedly? Under most circumstances, the created collection would be immediately passed on to the constructor for another list, one that you can change, as shown here:

```
List list = new LinkedList(Collections.nCopies(10, null));
```

The repeated element does not have to be null. Any value that would serve as a default could be the element. Furthermore, any method (not just a constructor) that accepts a List could be passed this multicopied collection.

> **WARNING**   *Calling the* nCopies() *method with a negative number of copies causes an* IllegalArgumentException *to be thrown.*

Reversing Lists

The reverse() method of Collections is used to reverse the order of the elements in a list:

```
public static void reverse(List list)
```

For instance, if you call reverse with a list of "Barney", "Carl", and "Lenny" as shown here

```
List barFlies = Arrays.asList(new String[] {"Barney", "Carl", "Lenny"});
Collections.reverse(barFlies);
System.out.println(barFlies);
```

you'll get a new list of "Lenny", "Carl", and "Barney" after calling reverse().

Shuffling Lists

The shuffle() method of Collections allows you to randomly reorder the elements of a list:

```
public static void shuffle(List list)
public static void shuffle(List list, Random rnd)
```

As the name may imply, think of it as shuffling a deck of cards.

The Random argument to the method allows you to initialize the seeding of the random number generator. If no Random object is passed into the method, the shuffling is seeded with a number based on the current time, which ensures that subsequent runs of the same program cause different results. If you need repeatability, initialize your own Random object with a specific seed as shown in Listing 12-4.

Listing 12-4. Demonstrating repeatable shuffling.
```
import java.util.*;
public class ShuffleTest {
  public static void main(String args[]) {
    String simpsons[] = {"Bart", "Hugo", "Lisa", "Marge",
                         "Homer", "Maggie", "Roy"};
    List list1 = Arrays.asList(simpsons);
    List list2 = Arrays.asList(simpsons);
    Random rand = new Random(100);
    Collections.shuffle(list1, rand);
    Collections.shuffle(list2, rand);
```

```
      System.out.println(list1);
      System.out.println(list2);
  }
}
```

The results of running Listing 12-4 demonstrate the repeatability of shuffling when the same seed is passed to the Random constructor:

```
[Marge, Bart, Hugo, Roy, Maggie, Homer, Lisa]
[Marge, Bart, Hugo, Roy, Maggie, Homer, Lisa]
```

Sorting Lists

The final two Collections methods named sort() have to do with reordering the elements of a List:

```
public static void sort(List list)
public static void sort(List list, Comparator comp)
```

The one-argument version of sort() requires that the elements of the list implement the Comparable interface. It relies on their natural ordering to order the elements in the list. If the elements don't implement the interface, when you try to sort the list, a ClassCastException will be thrown at runtime.

The two-argument version allows you to ignore the natural ordering or provide a Comparator when the list elements don't implement Comparable. See the earlier Listing 12-1 for an example of using sort().

> **WARNING** *If the* List *passed into* sort() *doesn't support the* set() *operation, you'll see a* UnsupportedOperationException *thrown.*

Both versions of sort() guarantee that the sorting performed is *stable*. This means that if there are two equal elements within the array, they will not be rearranged or reordered. Two elements are equal if their equals() method says so.

> **NOTE** *While the documentation states that a merge sort is performed, this should be considered an implementation note and* not *part of the specification.*

Stability of sorting is important when there are other data elements within an object that are not used for equality checking. For instance, imagine a `Person` object with a first and last name where only the last name is used to check for equality. If the "John Smith" person and the "Jane Smith" person are both in a list, with a stable sort algorithm their original order in the list will not change after sorting that list. Their position may change, but if John appeared before Jane prior to sorting, John will still be before Jane after sorting. Thus, the relative order of equal elements is preserved.

> **NOTE** *For more information on stable sorting, see the white paper "Fast Stable Merging and Sorting in Constant Extra Space" by Bing-Chao Huang and Michael A. Langston available at* `http://lite.ncstrl.org:3803/Dienst/UI/2.0/Describe` `/ncstrl.utk_cs%2fUT-CS-90-106.`

Summary

In this chapter, we examined several specialized implementations of collections in the framework offered by the `Collections` class and saw the many operations you can perform on collections. We saw how the `Collections` class provides factory methods for getting specialized immutable implementations of empty and singleton collections. We also saw how the `Collections` class provides wrappers for creating both unmodifiable and synchronized collections. We explored the specialized sorting and searching functionality added with `Collections` and learned about the generic list operations for creating, copying, and ordering elements in a list. All in all, we learned how to use many of the different utility methods for working with collections to ensure that your Java programs are more maintainable.

In the next chapter, we'll examine the array algorithmic support provided by the `Arrays` class in the Collections Framework. We'll learn how to sort and search arrays as well as explore bulk filling and equality checking.

Array Algorithm Support

The Arrays class introduced with the Collections Framework doesn't manipulate collections. Instead, it provides a series of static methods for manipulating the familiar array type, whose usage is fully described in Chapter 2. As shown in Table 13-1, there are five methods for converting an array to a List: searching, checking for equality, filling, and sorting.

Table 13-1. Summary of the Arrays Class

VARIABLE/METHOD NAME	VERSION	DESCRIPTION
asList()	1.2	Converts an array to a list.
binarySearch()	1.2	Searches for an element within an array.
equals()	1.2	Checks for equality of two arrays.
fill()	1.2	Fills an array with a single element.
sort()	1.2	Sorts the elements of an array.

The asList() method is discussed in Chapter 15; the rest of the methods are described here. While there are only five named methods of the class, because of overloading, there are fifty-five varieties of those five. Only asList() has just one version.

> **NOTE** *While all the methods of the class are static and the constructor is private, the class is not final like the* java.lang.Math *class. Thus, you can subclass it—I can't think of what benefit this would provide, but, technically speaking, you can.*

Filling Arrays

Possibly the simplest of all the Arrays methods to describe is fill().

```
public static void fill(boolean a[], boolean val)
public static void fill(boolean a[], int fromIndex, int toIndex, boolean val)
public static void fill(byte a[], byte val)
public static void fill(byte a[], int fromIndex, int toIndex, byte val)
```

```
public static void fill(char a[], char val)
public static void fill(char a[], int fromIndex, int toIndex, char val)
public static void fill(double a[], double val)
public static void fill(double a[], int fromIndex, int toIndex, double val)
public static void fill(float a[], float val)
public static void fill(float a[], int fromIndex, int toIndex, float val)
public static void fill(int a[], int val)
public static void fill(int a[], int fromIndex, int toIndex, int val)
public static void fill(long a[], long val)
public static void fill(long a[], int fromIndex, int toIndex, long val)
public static void fill(short a[], short val)
public static void fill(short a[], int fromIndex, int toIndex, short val)
public static void fill(Object a[], Object val)
public static void fill(Object a[], int fromIndex, int toIndex, Object val)
```

Of course, with eighteen versions of this method, a little explanation is necessary. Basically, the fill() method allows you to take a single element and fill up an entire array or a subset of that array with copies of the single element. Of the eighteen varieties of this method, two exist for each of the eight primitives types and two for working with Object arrays.

The simplest case is when you do not specify a range. For instance, the following demonstrates how to create an integer array of ten elements and fill it with the number 100.

```
int array[] = new int[10];
Arrays.fill(array, 100);
```

If you were to then examine the contents of each element of the array, you would find 100 in every cell.

> **TIP** *Remember from Chapter 2 that the elements of new, unfilled arrays are initialized with a default value. If you've forgotten what they are, see Table 2-1.*

If, instead of trying to fill an entire array, you only wanted to fill a subset, you can specify a range of cells to fill with a from-index and a to-index. When specifying the indices, the from-index is included in the cells to change and the to-index is *not* included. When the indices are not provided, you can think of the from-index as being zero and the to-index as being the array length. This means that if the from-index is the same as the to-index, nothing will change because the range is empty. For instance, the following will change the contents of cells 3, 4, and 5 of the earlier created array to 50.

```
Arrays.fill(array, 3, 6, 50);
```

As shown in Figure 13-1, elements 0, 1, and 2 are still 100. Elements 3, 4, and 5 are now 50, and elements 6 through 9 are still 100.

array

[0] = 100	[1] = 100	[2] = 100	[3] = 50	[4] = 50
[5] = 50	[6] = 100	[7] = 100	[8] = 100	[9] = 100

Figure 13-1. Results of filling an array of primitives with Arrays.fill().

> **WARNING** *If the from-index is after the to-index, an* IllegalArgumentException *is thrown. If either index is outside the range of indices for the array, then an* ArrayIndexOutOfBoundsException *is thrown.*

There are two questions that may arise when working with fill(). When you try to fill an array with a different type, how are data conversions handled? And when working with objects, is it the same object reference in every cell, or is it a clone or copy of the object?

In the case of data conversions, the fill() method itself doesn't do anything special to convert between different primitive types. Essentially, if the compiler permits the conversion, no casting is necessary. Otherwise, you'll have to manually add a type cast like (*type*) within the method call. For instance, the following requires a cast to fill the byte array as the constant 4 is an integer, even though you can do byte b = 4;:

```
byte array2[] = new byte[10];
Arrays.fill(array2, 4); // illegal
Arrays.fill(array2, (byte)4); // Okay
```

The other case that requires a little extra thought has to do with filling arrays with objects. When filling an object array, the fill() method will copy the same object reference to every cell in the array:

```
Object array[] = new Object[10];
Object anObject = . . .;
Arrays.fill(array, anObject);
```

After filling the array, if you then change that one reference, the attributes of the object in every cell in the array will be changed. See Figure 13-2 for a visualization of this description.

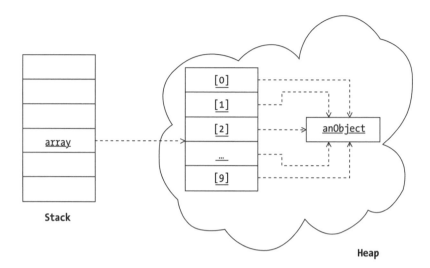

Figure 13-2. How Arrays.fill() fills an array with the same object reference.

> **WARNING** *If you try to* fill() *an object array with something that is not assignment compatible with the array type, an* ArrayStoreException *will be thrown. As the method only accepts an* Object[ ] *and an* Object *argument, it's up to you to ensure the type safety of the call, not the compiler.*

Checking Equality

The second Arrays method is the equals() method:

```
public static boolean equals(boolean a[], boolean array2[])
public static boolean equals(byte array1[], byte array2[])
public static boolean equals(char array1[], char array2[])
public static boolean equals(double array1[], double array2[])
public static boolean equals(float array1[], float array2[])
public static boolean equals(int array1[], int array2[])
public static boolean equals(long array1[], long array2[])
public static boolean equals(short array1[], short array2[])
public static boolean equals(Object array1[], Object array2[])
```

> **NOTE** *The* MessageDigest *class provides an* isEquals() *method. This was the only predefined mechanism to check byte array equality before the addition of the Collections Framework with the Java 2 platform. While it might seem weird to have used this method to compare byte arrays that weren't message digests, it worked.*

There are nine versions of this method, one for each primitive type and one for objects.

Two arrays are defined to be equal if they are the same length and if the elements at corresponding positions in both arrays are equal.

For primitive arrays, this equates to the following: array1.length == array2.length and array1[i] == array2[i] for all i from 0 to array length-1.

For objects arrays, this is almost the same with only a couple of differences. The lengths must still be the same (array1.length == array2.length). However, to check for equality of elements, the equals() method is used instead of the == check: array1[i].equals(array2[i]) for all i from 0 to array length-1. And two elements are equal if they are both null.

There is one other special case worth mentioning: if both array references are null, the arrays are equals.

> **TIP** *To check for equality of a subset of elements in one or both arrays, you'll need to make a copy of the array, most likely with the* arraycopy() *method of* System *described in Chapter 2.*

Sorting Arrays

The sorting methods of the Arrays class are probably the most frequently used methods of this class. We'll look at the different varieties of sorting primitives and objects separately as the differences are a bit more significant than with filling and checking for equality.

Primitive Arrays

There are fourteen methods to sort arrays of primitive values in the `Arrays` class:

```
public static void sort(byte array[])
public static void sort(byte array[], int fromIndex, int toIndex)
public static void sort(char array[])
public static void sort(char array[], int fromIndex, int toIndex)
public static void sort(double array[])
public static void sort(double array[], int fromIndex, int toIndex)
public static void sort(float array[])
public static void sort(float array[], int fromIndex, int toIndex)
public static void sort(int array[])
public static void sort(int array[], int fromIndex, int toIndex)
public static void sort(long array[])
public static void sort(long array[], int fromIndex, int toIndex)
public static void sort(short array[])
public static void sort(short array[], int fromIndex, int toIndex)
```

> **NOTE**   *There is no support for sorting arrays of* boolean *values.*

Like equality checking with `Arrays.equals()`, you can sort the entire array, or perform a sort on a subset of the elements. The from-index is the first cell to sort and is 0 when not specified. The to-index is one beyond the end of cells to sort, or `array.length` when not specified. When the two indices are the same, nothing is sorted.

> **WARNING**   *If the from-index is after the to-index, an* `IllegalArgumentEx-`ception *is thrown. If either index is outside the range of indices for the array, then an* `ArrayIndexOutOfBoundsException` *is thrown.*

To sort an array of primitives, just pass the array into one of the `sort()` methods and you're basically done. The following demonstrates the creation and sorting of an array of integers:

```
int array[] = {2, 5, -2, 6, -3};
Arrays.sort(array);
```

After performing the sort, the array elements will be, in order, –3, –2, 2, 5, 6. Sorting a subset is just as simple:

```
int array2[] = {2, 5, -2, 6, -3, 8, 0, -7, -9, 4};
Arrays.sort(array, 3, 7);
```

Sorting elements 3, 4, 5, and 6 in our new array produces the following order: 2, 5, *–2, –3, 0, 6, 8,* –7, –9, 4. (Notice that the sorted elements are in italic.)

> **NOTE** *According to the class documentation, the sorting algorithm is a tuned quicksort algorithm that was adapted from the article "Engineering a Sort Function,"* Software-Practice and Experience *23, no. 11 (November 1993).*

Object Arrays

While sorting arrays of primitives is very straightforward, sorting arrays of objects can require a little more work. There are four sort() methods for sorting objects:

```
public static void sort(Object array[])
public static void sort(Object array[], int fromIndex, int toIndex)
public static void sort(Object array[], Comparator c)
public static void sort(Object array[], int fromIndex, int toIndex, Comparator c)
```

The first two methods work similar to the primitive array sorting methods. Pass in an array of objects and they'll be sorted. The objects in the array passed in, though, must implement the Comparable interface. If the objects don't implement the interface, when you try to sort the array, a ClassCastException will be thrown at runtime. To demonstrate, the following program will sort the elements passed in from the command line and then print them out:

```
import java.util.*;
public class SortTest {
  public static void main(String args[]) throws Exception {
    Arrays.sort(args);
    for (int i=0, n=args.length; i<n; i++) {
      System.out.println(args[i]);
    }
  }
}
```

When run with a command line of one two three four five, the results of running the program will be:

```
five
four
one
three
two
```

The last two sort() methods exist for circumstances when the object doesn't implement Comparable or when you don't like the natural sort order offered by the object. For instance, the String class implements the Comparable interface. By default, sorting of String objects would be in a case-sensitive, alphabetical order. If you want either a case-insensitive sort or a reverse alphabetical order, you would need to provide your own Comparator.

To demonstrate, the following program will sort the arguments passed in from the command line in reverse alphabetic order, using the reverse Comparator available from Collections:

```java
import java.util.*;
public class SortTest2 {
  public static void main(String args[]) throws Exception {
    Comparator comp = Collections.reverseOrder();
    Arrays.sort(args, comp);
    for (int i=0, n=args.length; i<n; i++) {
      System.out.println(args[i]);
    }
  }
}
```

> **TIP** *For more information on* Comparator *(and* Comparable*), see Chapter 11.*

All four object sorting mechanisms share one thing in common: the sort performed is *stable*. This means that if there are two equal elements within the array, they will not be rearranged or reordered. Two elements are equal if their equals() method says so. For more on stable sorting, see Chapter 12.

> **NOTE** *It's also worth mentioning that while the documentation states that a merge sort is performed, this should be considered an implementation note and not part of the specification.*

Searching Arrays

The final Arrays method, binarySearch(), searches a sorted array for an element. As the name may imply, the search algorithm is based on performing a binary search, repeatedly halving the array to further narrow the part of the array containing the element until found or until there are no more halves to create. If the array is unsorted, the results of calling this method are undefined. It may find the element, but it would be strictly luck. When sorted, the binary search is guaranteed to find the element in no more than log n steps, where n is the array length, or to determine that the element is not present.

Primitive Arrays

There are seven binarySearch() methods for performing a binary search on an array of primitive elements:

```
public static int binarySearch(byte array[], byte key)
public static int binarySearch(char array[], char key)
public static int binarySearch(double array[], double key)
public static int binarySearch(float array[], float key)
public static int binarySearch(int array[], int key)
public static int binarySearch(long array[], long key)
public static int binarySearch(short array[], short key)
```

> **NOTE** *There is no support for performing a binary search on an array of* boolean *values.*

All of these methods will search for key in array, returning the zero-based integer index if found, or a negative number if not. If the key is not found, the returned value can actually be used to determine where in the array to insert the key to have a larger sorted array with the new element present. To find the index, negate the number and subtract one:

```
index = -returnedValue -1;
```

The code in Listing 13-1 demonstrates how to use binarySearch() to try to locate elements and how to insert an element into a sorted array when that search key is not found.

Listing 13-1. Sorting, Searching, and Inserting into a sorted array.

```java
import java.util.*;
public class SearchTest {
  public static void main(String args[]) throws Exception {
    int array[] = {2, 5, -2, 6, -3, 8, 0, -7, -9, 4};

    // Ensure array sorted
    Arrays.sort(array);
    printArray("Sorted array", array);

    // Search for element in array
    int index = Arrays.binarySearch(array, 2);
    System.out.println("Found 2 @ " + index);

    // Search for element not in array
    index = Arrays.binarySearch(array, 1);
    System.out.println("Didn't find 1 @ " + index);

    // Insert
    int newIndex = -index - 1;
    array = insertElement(array, 1, newIndex);
    printArray("With 1 added", array);

  }
  private static void printArray(String message, int array[]) {
    System.out.println(message + ": [length: " + array.length + "]");
    // Print out sorted array elements
    for (int i=0, n=array.length; i<n; i++) {
      if (i != 0) System.out.print(", ");
      System.out.print(array[i]);
    }
    System.out.println();
  }
  private static int[] insertElement(int original[], int element, int index) {
    int length = original.length;
    int destination[] = new int[length+1];
    System.arraycopy(original, 0, destination, 0, index);
    destination[index] = element;
    System.arraycopy(original, index, destination, index+1, length-index);
    return destination;
  }
}
```

The magic of the insertion is found in the `insertElement()` method. Here, the method creates a new, slightly larger array and copies the original array into the new array around the new element.

Object Arrays

There are two `binarySearch()` methods to handle searching for elements in a sorted object array:

```
public static int binarySearch(Object array[], Object key)
public static int binarySearch(Object array[], Object key, Comparator c)
```

As with array sorting, performing a binary search on an array of objects requires a special case. If the array is made up of the objects that implement the `Comparable` interface, you can use the first version of the method. The `compareTo()` method of the object will then be used during the search to pinpoint where in the array the element should be located. If the object doesn't implement `Comparable`, or you don't like the natural sorting order, you can provide your own `Comparator`. Essentially, this says that if you used a `Comparator` when you sorted the array, you should use the same one when you search the array.

As with binary searching for primitive elements, the return value of `binarySearch()` is the index in the array where the element can be found, or, if not found, a negative number. Again, the negative return value can be used to find where in the array the new object can be added to keep the array sorted. One point to add, though, if you find yourself frequently adding elements to an array of objects, thereby causing the array to grow with each addition, perhaps your choice of data structures is not the best. Using a `LinkedList` or maybe a `TreeSet` is probably a better bet. Of course, each has its own performance penalties.

> **WARNING** *Like the* `equals()` *methods, which checks for equality, the* `binarySearch()` *method assumes your array is full. If the array is not full—has null elements—you'll need to create a copy of the array with only those non-null elements in order to search with* `binarySearch()`. *There is no way to use* `binarySearch()` *on a subset of the elements.*

Summary

This chapter explored four of the utility methods for working with Java arrays added with the Collections Framework. We learned how to initialize arrays with a single element through the `fill()` method and how to check for equality between two arrays with the `equals()` method. We also learned how to easily sort an array then search for elements within it, both for arrays of primitives and for arrays of objects with and without a `Comparator`.

You'll learn about creating custom implementations of collections in the next chapter. Starting with classes like `AbstractList` and `AbstractMap`, you'll see how you can extend these classes in order to enhance their functionality to add application-specific capabilities like persistence or just a different type of backing store.

CHAPTER 14

Custom Implementations

All the earlier chapters of the book mention that every concrete implementation class in the Collections Framework extends from an abstract implementation. In fact, there are five abstract classes that form the basis of every system-defined collection introduced by the framework: AbstractCollection, AbstractSet, AbstractList, AbstractSequentialList, and AbstractMap. Some historical collection classes like Hashtable, however, do *not* extend from these classes though. Figure 14-1 shows the relationships between the abstract classes through their class hierarchy. Like the concrete implementations, the map stands alone.

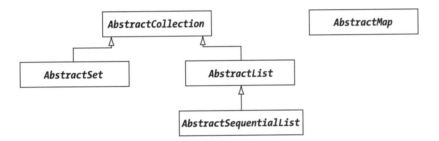

Figure 14-1. Class hierarchy of the abstract collection classes.

These abstract implementations make creating custom implementations very easy. All you have to do is subclass and provide a handful of methods specific to your implementation.

AbstractCollection Class

The AbstractCollection class provides an abstract implementation of the Collection interface. It is essentially a *bag*-type collection, not necessarily a set or a list. Table 14-1 lists the one constructor and the methods of the class.

Table 14-1. Summary of the AbstractCollection Class

VARIABLE/METHOD NAME	VERSION	DESCRIPTION
AbstractCollection()	1.2	Constructs an empty (abstract) collection.
add()	1.2	Adds an element to the collection.
addAll()	1.2	Adds a collection of elements to the collection.
clear()	1.2	Clears all elements from the collection.
contains()	1.2	Checks if the collection contains an element.
containsAll()	1.2	Checks if the collection contains a collection of elements.
isEmpty()	1.2	Checks if the collection is empty.
iterator()	1.2	Returns an object from the collection that allows all of the collection's elements to be visited.
remove()	1.2	Clears a specific element from the collection.
removeAll()	1.2	Clears a collection of elements from the collection.
retainAll()	1.2	Removes all elements from collection not in another collection.
size()	1.2	Returns the number of elements in a collection.
toArray()	1.2	Returns the elements of the collection as an array.
toString()	1.2	Converts the collection contents into a string.

Subclassing AbstractCollection

If you wish to create a concrete implementation based upon the
AbstractCollection class, you must at a minimum implement two constructors
and define two methods.

The AbstractCollection class has only one constructor:

```
protected AbstractCollection()
```

In your custom implementation, you must provide a no-argument constructor and a copy constructor:

```
public MyCollection()
public MyCollection(Collection col)
```

As far as the two methods go, you must implement the abstract iterator()
and size() methods:

```
public abstract iterator Iterator()
public abstract int size()
```

The iterator() method returns an Iterator over the collection. The size() method returns the number of elements in the collection. With these two methods implemented, you have a usable collection, though it isn't modifiable.

Implementing Optional Methods

The Collections Framework relies on optional interface methods to offer additional behavior. If the methods aren't overridden, they provide a default behavior of throwing the UnsupportedOperationException. For your collection to be a little more useful, you need to override the add() method in your collection and provide a remove() method in your iterator:

```
public boolean add(Object element) // In AbstractCollection
public void remove() // In Iterator
```

> **TIP** *Don't override the* remove() *method of* AbstractCollection *unless you are doing it for performance reasons. Remember that you must implement* remove() *in your collection's iterator.*

You do not have to define both methods, although if you are supporting one operation, it usually makes sense to support the other.

The remaining methods of AbstractCollection all rely on size() and iterator() for their behavior. You do not have to override any, though for performance reasons you may choose to do so. The choice is yours.

> **TIP** *For performance reasons, you may wish to override* isEmpty() *so it doesn't rely on* size() *to determine whether the collection is empty. This avoids the* O(n) *cost of calling* size()*.*

AbstractSet Class

The use of an AbstractSet is identical to an AbstractCollection, with the only exception being that, by definition, the set cannot contain duplicates. The class only defines three methods and a constructor with the rest of the behavior directly inherited from AbstractCollection. The methods and constructor of AbstractSet are listed in Table 14-2.

Table 14-2. Summary of the AbstractSet Class

VARIABLE/METHOD NAME	VERSION	DESCRIPTION
AbstractSet()	1.2	Constructs an empty set.
equals()	1.2	Checks for equality with another object.
hashCode()	1.2	Computes a hash code for the set.
removeAll()	1.2	Clears a collection of elements from the set.

Defining an abstract set has the same requirements as defining an abstract collection: two constructors and two methods, or four methods if you wish to support updates. If your custom set also implements SortedSet, then you must provide two additional constructors:

```
public MySet(Comparator comp)
public MySet(SortedSet set)
```

The requirement to enforce uniqueness of elements is placed on your subclass of AbstractSet, not within the abstract class itself.

Creating a Custom Set

Early versions of the Java 2 platform included an ArraySet. This class provided a Set implementation that, compared to HashSet, was rather performance crippled to find an element beyond about five elements. It does, however, provide a good basis for a custom set implementation. Behind the scenes, the class relies on an ArrayList for the actual storage. When adding elements as well as with the copy constructor, be extra careful not to add duplicates.

The set implementation in Listing 14-1 goes beyond the basics necessary to create a custom set. Instead of just defining the minimum, it supports serialization as well as cloning and optimizes several of its operations. It is meant to be a usable set implementation, not just a toy. Also, since ArraySet relies on an ArrayList for its backing store, it isn't necessary to define our own iterator.

Listing 14-1. Custom ArraySet implementation.
```
import java.io.Serializable;
import java.util.*;

public class ArraySet extends AbstractSet
    implements Cloneable, Serializable {

  private ArrayList list;
```

```
public ArraySet() {
  list = new ArrayList();
}

public ArraySet(Collection col) {
  list = new ArrayList();

  // No need to check for dups if col is a set
  Iterator itor = col.iterator();
  if (col instanceof Set) {
    while (itor.hasNext()) {
      list.add(itor.next());
    }
  } else {
    while(itor.hasNext()) {
      add(itor.next());
    }
  }
}

public Iterator iterator() {
  return list.iterator();
}

public int size() {
  return list.size();
}

public boolean add(Object element) {
  boolean modified;
  if (modified = !list.contains(element)) {
    list.add(element);
  }
  return modified;
}

public boolean remove(Object element) {
  return list.remove(element);
}

public boolean isEmpty() {
  return list.isEmpty();
}
```

```
  public boolean contains(Object element) {
    return list.contains(element);
  }

  public void clear() {
    list.clear();
  }

  public Object clone() {
    try {
      ArraySet newSet = (ArraySet)super.clone();
      newSet.list = (ArrayList)list.clone();
      return newSet;
    } catch (CloneNotSupportedException e) {
      throw new InternalError();
    }
  }
}
```

> **NOTE** *Remember that sets are supposed to be unordered, so even though the collection is backed by an array, there is no sequential access outside the iterator. The iterator will return the elements in the order they were added, however, as defined by* ArrayList.

Pulling in an example from Chapter 8, all you have to do is change the constructor call to test our new ArraySet class as shown in Listing 14-2:

Listing 14-2. Testing our new ArraySet implementation.

```
import java.util.*;

public class SetTest {
  public static void main (String args[]) {
    String elements[] = {"Irish Setter", "Poodle",
      "English Setter", "Gordon Setter", "Pug"};
    Set set = new ArraySet(Arrays.asList(elements));
    Iterator iter = set.iterator();
    while (iter.hasNext()) {
```

```
        System.out.println(iter.next());
    }
  }
}
```

AbstractList Class

The AbstractList class forms the basis for creating lists that support random access, partially implementing the List interface and adding some new methods of its own. Table 14-3 lists the methods of the AbstractList class.

Table 14-3. Summary of the AbstractList Class

VARIABLE/METHOD NAME	VERSION	DESCRIPTION
AbstractList()	1.2	Constructs an empty (abstract) list.
modCount	1.2	Used by iterator to check for concurrent modifications of the list.
add()	1.2	Adds an element to the list.
addAll()	1.2	Adds a collection of elements to the list.
clear()	1.2	Clears all elements from the list.
equals()	1.2	Checks for equality with another object.
get()	1.2	Returns an element at a specific position.
hashCode()	1.2	Returns the computed hash code for a list.
indexOf()	1.2	Searches for an element within the list.
iterator()	1.2	Returns an object from the list that allows all of the list's elements to be visited.
lastIndexOf()	1.2	Searches from the end of the list for an element.
listIterator()	1.2	Returns an object from the list that allows all of the list's elements to be visited sequentially.
remove()	1.2	Clears a specific element from the list.
removeRange()	1.2	Clears a range of elements from the list.
set()	1.2	Changes an element at a specific position within the list.
subList()	1.2	Returns a portion of the list.

The protected modcount variable is used to provide support for *fail-fast* iterators. If the list is modified while an iterator is in use, the next call to access an element from the iterator should fail by throwing a ConcurrentModificationException.

Subclassing AbstractList

Creating a concrete implementation based on AbstractList is similar to creating a concrete collection or set: at a minimum, you must implement two constructors and define two methods.

Like AbstractCollection and AbstractSet, the AbstractList class has only one constructor:

```
protected AbstractList()
```

In your custom implementation, you must provide a no-argument constructor and a copy constructor:

```
public MyList()
public MyList(Collection col)
```

As far as the two methods go, you must implement the abstract get() and size() methods:

```
public abstract Object get(int index)
public abstract int size()
```

The get() method returns the element at the specific position and the size() method returns the number of elements in the list. Once you've implemented these two methods you'll have a list, although you can't change its elements.

Implementing Optional Methods

There are three optional methods for an abstract list: add(), remove(), and set().

```
public void add(int index, Object element)
public Object remove(int index)
public Object set(int index, Object element)
```

Which of the three methods you define depends on the operations your list supports. If your list can grow or shrink, you would implement add() or remove(), possibly both. If you want your list to be modifiable, you would implement set(). If you don't override their behavior, they'll throw an UnsupportedOperationException.

The remaining methods of AbstractList all rely on size() and get() for their behavior. Override them when possible to improve performance.

AbstractSequentialList Class

The second partial implementation of the List interface is the
AbstractSequentialList class. As the name may imply, it forms the basis for creating lists that support sequential access like a linked list. Which you choose to
extend depends upon your data storage. As Table 14-4 shows, there are no new
methods added to the AbstractSequentialList.

Table 14-4. Summary of the AbstractSequentialList Class

VARIABLE/METHOD NAME	VERSION	DESCRIPTION
AbstractSequentialList()	1.2	Constructs an empty sequential list.
add()	1.2	Adds an element to the list.
addAll()	1.2	Adds a collection of elements to the list.
get()	1.2	Returns an element at a specific position.
iterator()	1.2	Returns an object from the list that allows all of the list's elements to be visited.
listIterator()	1.2	Returns an object from the list that allows all of the list's elements to be visited sequentially.
remove()	1.2	Clears a specific element from the list.
set()	1.2	Changes an element at a specific position within the list.

> **NOTE** *Remember that the* AbstractSequentialList *class extends from the*
> AbstractList *class.*

Subclassing AbstractSequentialList

The creation of a concrete implementation based on AbstractSequentialList is
like the rest, requiring the implementation of two constructors and the definition
of two methods.

In your custom implementation, you must provide a no-argument constructor and a copy constructor:

```
public MySequentialList()
public MySequentialList (Collection col)
```

As far as the two methods go, you must implement the abstract `listIterator()` and `size()` methods:

```
public abstract ListIterator listIterator(int index)
public abstract int size()
```

The `listIterator ()` method returns an ordered iterator over the elements in the list from the index provided and the `size()` method returns the number of elements in the list. At a minimum, the implementation of `ListIterator` must define `hasNext()`, `next()`, `nextIndex()`, `hasPrevious()`, `previous()`, and `previousIndex()`. As always, implementing these methods is sufficient for the creation of a sequential list but the implementation won't support modification.

Implementing Optional Methods

There are three optional methods *in the iterator* for an abstract sequential list: `add()`, `remove()`, and `set()`:

```
public void add(Object element)
public void remove()
public void set(Object element)
```

Which of the three methods you define depends on the operations your sequential list supports. If your sequential list can grow or shrink, you would implement `add()` or `remove()`, possibly both. If you want your list to be modifiable, you would implement `set()`. If your sequential list doesn't support an operation, the iterator will need to throw an `UnsupportedOperationException`.

Believe it or not, all the remaining methods of `AbstractSequentialList` rely on `size()` and `iterator()` for their behavior, mostly `iterator()`. If your backing support can provide some form of performance improvement, do override as iterating through all elements can be very costly.

AbstractMap Class

The final abstract Collection Framework implementation is the `AbstractMap` class. It provides the basis for implementing the `Map` interface, the methods of which are shown in Table 14-5.

Table 14-5. Summary of the AbstractMap Class

VARIABLE/METHOD NAME	VERSION	DESCRIPTION
AbstractMap()	1.2	Constructs an empty (abstract) map.
clear()	1.2	Removes all the elements from the map.
containsKey()	1.2	Checks to see if an object is a key within the map.
containsValue()	1.2	Checks to see if an object is a value within the map.
entrySet()	1.2	Returns the set of key-value pairs in the map.
equals()	1.2	Checks for equality with another object.
get()	1.2	Retrieves a value for a key in the map.
hashCode()	1.2	Computes a hash code for the map.
isEmpty()	1.2	Checks if the map has any elements.
keySet()	1.2	Retrieves a collection of the keys of the hash table.
put()	1.2	Places a key-value pair into the map.
putAll()	1.2	Places a collection of key-value pairs into the map.
remove()	1.2	Removes an element from the map.
size()	1.2	Returns the number of elements in the map.
toString()	1.2	Converts the map contents into a string.
values()	1.2	Retrieves a collection of the values of the map.

Subclassing AbstractMap

Creating an abstract map is actually simpler than creating all the other collections. Here, you only have to define two constructors and one method entrySet().

In your custom implementation, you must provide a no-argument constructor and a copy constructor:

```
public MyMap()
public MyMap(Collection col)
```

If your custom map also implements SortedMap, then you must provide two additional constructors:

```
public MyMap(Comparator comp)
public MyMap(SortedMap Map)
```

As far as the method goes, you must implement the abstract entrySet() method:

```
public abstract Set entrySet()
```

Because a set knows its size, you don't have to override the size() method of AbstractMap.

Implementing Optional Methods

There are two optional methods, one in the map and one in the *iterators* returned for the entry set, key set, and value set: put() and remove().

```
public Object put(Object key, Object value) // from Map
public void remove() // from Iterator
```

Override the put() method if you want to support adding and replacing elements from the map. Implement the remove() method for all three iterators returned from the map: entrySet().iterator(), keySet().iterator(), and values().iterator().

The remaining methods of AbstractMap all key off of the entrySet() method. For each element in the entry set, remember that it needs to be a Map.Entry object.

Creating a Custom Map

Another collection that didn't make the final cut for the Collections Framework is the ArrayMap class. This is a map implementation that is backed by an array instead of a hash table or balanced tree. It functions fine for very small maps, like five, but fails miserably for look-ups of maps of any large size as all operations provide linear time performance. Like the earlier ArraySet, this too supports serialization and cloning. When used, be sure to utilize the third constructor that takes an initial capacity to size the array data store.

Listing 14-3. Custom ArrayMap implementation.

```
import java.io.Serializable;
import java.util.*;

public class ArrayMap extends AbstractMap
    implements Cloneable, Serializable {

  static class Entry implements Map.Entry {
    protected Object key, value;

    public Entry(Object key, Object value) {
      this.key = key;
      this.value = value;
    }

    public Object getKey() {
      return key;
    }
```

```java
  public Object getValue() {
    return value;
  }

  public Object setValue(Object newValue) {
    Object oldValue = value;
    value = newValue;
    return oldValue;
  }

  public boolean equals(Object o) {
    if (!(o instanceof Map.Entry)) {
      return false;
    }
    Map.Entry e = (Map.Entry)o;
    return (key==null ? e.getKey()==null : key.equals(e.getKey())) &&
      (value==null ? e.getValue()==null : value.equals(e.getValue()));
  }

  public int hashCode() {
    int keyHash = (key==null ? 0 : key.hashCode());
    int valueHash = (value==null ? 0 : value.hashCode());
    return keyHash ^ valueHash;
  }

  public String toString() {
    return key + "=" + value;
  }
}

private Set entries = null;
private ArrayList list;

public ArrayMap() {
  list = new ArrayList();
}

public ArrayMap(Map map) {
  list = new ArrayList();
  putAll(map);
}
```

```
public ArrayMap(int initialCapacity) {
  list = new ArrayList(initialCapacity);
}

public Set entrySet() {
  if (entries==null) {
    entries = new AbstractSet() {
      public void clear() {
        list.clear();
      }
      public Iterator iterator() {
        return list.iterator();
      }
      public int size() {
        return list.size();
      }
    };
  }
  return entries;
}

public Object put(Object key, Object value) {
  int size = list.size();
  Entry entry = null;
  int i;
  if (key==null) {
    for (i=0; i<size; i++) {
      entry = (Entry)(list.get(i));
      if (entry.getKey() == null) {
        break;
      }
    }
  } else {
    for (i=0; i<size; i++) {
      entry = (Entry)(list.get(i));
      if (key.equals(entry.getKey())) {
        break;
      }
    }
  }
  Object oldValue = null;
  if (i<size) {
```

```
      oldValue = entry.getValue();
      entry.setValue(value);
    } else {
      list.add(new Entry(key, value));
    }
    return oldValue;
  }

  public Object clone() {
    return new ArrayMap(this);
  }
}
```

> **NOTE**   *It isn't necessary for us to implement the* remove() *method of the iterator as the iterator returned by the* ArrayList *backing store already does this for us.*

Notice that the entrySet() method returns the same set of entries to every caller. This is possible because the set doesn't actually contain the map entries. Instead, the set indirectly calls the necessary methods of the underlying ArrayList to return a Set. This reduces the number of objects to be created, increasing performance at least a little while using the map.

Pulling in an example from Chapter 10 (and adding a little more to demonstrate the use of our new ArrayMap class), all you have to do is change the constructor call as shown in Listing 14-4:

Listing 14-4. Testing our new ArrayMap implementation.

```
import java.util.*;

public class MapTest {
  public static void main (String args[]) {
    Map map = new ArrayMap(13);
    map.put("Virginia", "Richmond");
    map.put("Massachusetts", "Boston");
    map.put("New York", "Albany");
    map.put("Maryland", "Annapolis");
    map.put("Rhode Island", "Providence");
    map.put("Connecticut", "Hartford");
    map.put("Delaware", "Dover");
    map.put("New Hampshire", "Concord");
```

```
        map.put("North Carolina", "Raleigh");
        map.put("South Carolina", "Columbia");
        map.put("New Jersey", "Trenton");
        map.put("Pennsylvania", "Harrisburg");
        map.put("Georgira", "Atlanta");
        System.out.println(map);
        System.out.println(map.keySet());
        System.out.println(map.values());
    }
}
```

> **NOTE** *For some more interesting implementations of maps and collections, see Chapter 16, which also points out references to existing custom implementations. While you might think you need to create a custom implementation, someone may have already done so. Also, see Part Three of this book for some alternative collection libraries.*

Summary

In this chapter, we examined the creation of custom collections and the abstract framework already provided. Through the subclassing of the existing abstract implementations, you saw how easy it is to create new collections for special purpose needs.

The next chapter explores compatibility issues when using the Collections Framework in a disparate environment with libraries incompatible with the framework. We'll also look into using the framework with JDK 1.1 programs.

CHAPTER 15

Compatibility Issues

There seems to have been great effort spent to ensure that the new Collections Framework works with the historical collections. In this chapter, we'll examine the issues around conversion between the two, as well as how to work with the framework in the older JDK 1.1 release. Lastly, we'll examine the differences within the framework between the 1.2 and 1.3 releases of the Java 2 platform.

Converting from Historical to New Collections

The easiest conversions happen when going from the historical collection support into the new framework. This would entail going from a Vector, Hashtable, array, or Enumeration into one of the new framework pieces—or, more precisely, using one of the older implementations as a new implementation.

Vectors and Hashtables

Of the four conversions from historical to new collections, the simplest conversions are those involving Vector and Hashtable. The designers of the new framework retrofitted these historical classes to be a part of the new framework. The Vector class implements the List interface and acts like a presynchronized ArrayList. The Hashtable implements the Map interface and acts like a presynchronized HashMap. Thus, if you need to work with one of the older classes when a new implementation is needed, just pass along the older class and you're done.

> **NOTE** *This automatic conversion from historical to new collections also holds true for the subclasses of* Vector *and* Hashtable: Stack *and* Properties, *respectively.*

Arrays

There are two different ways to work with arrays in the new framework. The Arrays class offers a series of static methods to perform common functions like sorting and searching, as shown in Chapter 13. Using the sorting and searching methods of the Arrays class isn't converting the array into something that is part of the Collections Framework. In order to convert an array into something that is part of the framework, you need to use the asList() method of Arrays:

```
public static void main (String args[]) {
  List list = Arrays.asList(args);
}
```

When the array is converted by the asList() method, the created List is updateable with the changes reflected in the original array. However, the list will not expand (or shrink) in size. If you try to add or remove an element to or from the returned list, an UnsupportedOperationException will be thrown. In the case of removal, the exception is thrown only if you try to remove something in the list. If the element isn't in the list, the exception will not be thrown.

Enumerations

The final historical conversion is from an Enumeration into the new framework. You can work with an Enumeration in the new framework in two different ways: you can use the Enumeration as an Iterator, or you can create a collection with the Enumeration as the data source.

To use an Enumeration as an Iterator, you must create a wrapper, passing calls through the Iterator methods to the Enumeration methods. The program in Listing 15-1 is one such wrapper.

Listing 15-1. Wrapping an Iterator around an Enumeration.

```
import java.util.*;

public class EnumerationIterator {
  public static Iterator iterator(final Enumeration enum) {
    return new Iterator() {
      public boolean hasNext() {
        return enum.hasMoreElements();
      }

      public Object next() {
        return enum.nextElement();
      }
```

```
      public void remove() {
         throw new UnsupportedOperationException();
      }
    };
  }
  public static void main (String args[]) {
    Vector v = new Vector(Arrays.asList(args));
    Enumeration enum = v.elements();
    Iterator itor = EnumerationIterator.iterator(enum);
    while (itor.hasNext()) {
      System.out.println(itor.next());
    }
  }
}
```

As Enumeration doesn't support element removal, an UnsupportedOperationException will be thrown if called.

The second method of using an Enumeration with the new framework is as the data source for a new collection:

```
Enumeration enum = ...;
Set set = new HashSet();
while (e.hasMoreElements()) {
  set.add(e.nextElement());
}
// use set
```

There is no magic here. Essentially, you just create the new collection instance and loop through the enumeration adding one element at a time. More frequently than not, this construct is unnecessary. Usually, you can return to the original data source of the enumeration and work with that source in a different manner to make it a new collection type.

Converting from New to Historical Collections

The Collections Framework also includes support for backward compatibility. You can go from any collection into a Vector, Hashtable, or array, or you can treat the collection as an Enumeration.

Vectors and Hashtables

For the Vector and Hashtable classes, the conversion is handled by requiring collection implementation classes to have a copy constructor. Since Vector has been retrofitted into the framework, it has a constructor that accepts any Collection object: Vector (Collection c). In the case of Hashtable, it now has a constructor that accepts a Map: Hashtable(Map m). By using these new constructors, you can easily convert a new collection into an old collection.

Arrays

As far as arrays go, the Collection interface includes the toArray() method to convert a new collection into an array. There are two forms of this method. The no argument version will return the elements of the collection in an Object array: public Object[] toArray(). The returned array cannot be cast to any other data type. This is the simplest version and in most cases sufficient. The second version requires you to pass in the data type of the array you'd like returned: public Object[] toArray(Object type[]). If the array passed into this version isn't large enough, a new array will be created of the appropriate type. With this second version, you can cast the returned array to the type passed into the toArray() method. For instance, assuming col represents a collection of Date objects, the following line would succeed:

```
Date stuff[]  = (Date[])col.toArray(new Date[0]);
```

> **NOTE** *In the event that the elements of the collection are not type-compatible with the desired array type, an ArrayStoreException will be thrown when toArray() is called.*

In working with Map collections as an array, you'll need to get either the collection of entries, the keys, or the values for the map and convert that into an array as shown here:

```
String keys[] = (String[])map.keySet().toArray(new String[0]);
```

There are no direct map-to-array conversions available.

Enumerations

The final conversion occurs in going from a `Collection` to an `Enumeration`. There is a helper method in the `Collections` class that does the conversion for us: `Enumeration enumeration(Collection)`. Given any `Collection`, the `enumeration()` method will convert it into an `Enumeration`:

```
List l = Arrays.asList(args);
Enumeration enum = Collections.enumeration(l);
```

As with the `toArray()` method, if you'd like to convert a `Map` to an `Enumeration`, you need to work with the map's specific set of entries, keys, or values:

```
Enumeration enum = Collections.enumeration(map.entrySet());
```

Working with JDK 1.1

To help developers transition their older programs to the Java 2 platform, the designers of the Collections Framework developed a partial backport that would run with the 1.1 release of Java. The classes are essentially source code-equivalent to those delivered with the 1.2 version of Java but include everything in the `com.sun.java.util.collections` package instead of `java.util`. The reason for the package difference is that browsers can't download classes in the `java.*` packages, so the classes needed to move elsewhere.

To get the backport, go to the InfoBus homepage `http://java.sun.com/products/javabeans/infobus/#COLLECTIONS`. The reason for this location is that the backport package was created so InfoBus could run in a Java 1.1 environment. It's available for everyone to use. Once downloaded, unzip the file and add the `collections.jar` file in the `lib` directory to your CLASSPATH.

> **NOTE** *InfoBus is a communications scheme developed by Lotus/IBM for sending messages between JavaBean components. While I have nothing against InfoBus, its usage seems to be dropping in favor of the Java 2 Enterprise Edition (J2EE) standard Java Message Service (JMS) API.*

The backport of the framework only includes all the new classes introduced with the Collections Framework. Any java.lang class like String that was updated for the Java 2 platform to be compatible with the framework has *not* been updated, as you can't randomly replace system classes. This means that classes like Vector and Hashtable have been modified to be part of the framework but what you put into the collections has not. Table 15-1 provides a list of the newly available classes.

Table 15-1. Classes in Collections Backport

NAME	
AbstractCollection	Iterator
AbstractList	LinkedList
AbstractMap	List
AbstractSequentialList	ListIterator
AbstractSet	Map
ArrayList	NoSuchElementException
Arrays	Random
Collection	Set
Collections	SortedMap
Comparable	SortedSet
Comparator	TreeMap
ConcurrentModificationException	TreeSet
HashMap	UnsupportedOperationException
HashSet	Vector
Hashtable	

> **WARNING** *There is a hidden trap in using the backport: you cannot cast (explicitly or implicitly) a* Vector *to a* Vector *if one* Vector *is in* java.util *while the other is in* com.sun.java.util.collections. *This can show up when one developer writes a class with a method that takes a* java.util.Vector *and another calls it from a class that is using the collections backport and is including* com.sun.java.util.collections.Vector. *The compiler will spot this, but it may be a little confusing the first time a developer gets this error message!*

Comparing Objects with JDK 1.1

When comparing system classes for tasks like sorting with the Java 2 platform, you can rely on the fact that many of these core classes implement the Comparable interface. Unfortunately, when using the 1.1 backport, you cannot rely on this. Not only are the classes not comparable, but when you need ordering, you must provide your own Comparator.

While the JDK 1.1 compiler will let you pass arrays or collections of anything to the sorting routines of the Arrays and Collections classes, if you were to pass any of the system classes that are Comparable in the Java 2 platform but aren't in JDK 1.1, you would get a ClassCastException thrown at runtime. In addition, the Collections class offers a reverse order Comparator from its reverseOrder() method. This too is not usable in JDK 1.1 with the system classes as it relies on the natural ordering of the classes (they must implement Comparable). Since the system classes don't have a natural order in JDK 1.1, using the reversing comparator with the system classes will result in a ClassCastException being thrown, too.

In order to sort system classes in JDK 1.1 properly, you must define a custom Comparator and provide a public int compare(Object o1, Object o2) method to order two elements of the appropriate type. If you have trouble figuring out how to properly sort the different classes, a good place to look is in the compareTo() methods of the 1.2 and 1.3 versions of the classes. To help, the utility class in Listing 15-2 provides a Comparator for each of the String, Integer, and Date classes.

Listing 15-2. String, Integer, and Date comparators for JDK 1.1.

```
import com.sun.java.util.collections.*;
import java.util.Date;

public class Comparators {

  public static Comparator stringComparator() {
   return new Comparator() {

     public int compare(Object o1, Object o2) {
       String s1 = (String)o1;
       String s2 = (String)o2;
       int len1 = s1.length();
       int len2 = s2.length();
       int n = Math.min(len1, len2);
       char v1[] = s1.toCharArray();
       char v2[] = s2.toCharArray();
       int pos = 0;

       while (n-- != 0) {
         char c1 = v1[pos];
```

```
            char c2 = v2[pos];
            if (c1 != c2) {
              return c1 - c2;
            }
            pos++;
          }
          return len1 - len2;
      }
    };
  }

  public static Comparator integerComparator() {
    return new Comparator() {

      public int compare(Object o1, Object o2) {
        int val1 = ((Integer)o1).intValue();
        int val2 = ((Integer)o2).intValue();
        return (val1<val2 ? -1 : (val1==val2 ? 0 : 1));
      }
    };
  }

  public static Comparator dateComparator() {
    return new Comparator() {

      public int compare(Object o1, Object o2) {
        long val1 = ((Date)o1).getTime();
        long val2 = ((Date)o2).getTime();
        return (val1<val2 ? -1 : (val1==val2 ? 0 : 1));
      }
    };
  }
}
```

> **NOTE** *While the* Comparator *for the* String *requires a bit of effort to work with each character, the scalar classes* Integer *and* Date *are much easier to deal with. Follow the pattern used for these two classes to extend the utility class for the other missing comparators.*

Listing 15-3 shows a sample program that tests out the String-specific Comparator for sorting a List and an array of String objects.

Listing 15-3. Demonstrating custom comparators.

```java
import com.sun.java.util.collections.*;

public class CompTest {
  public static void main(String args[]) {
    List u2 = new ArrayList();
    u2.add("Beautiful Day");
    u2.add("Stuck In A Moment You Can't Get Out Of");
    u2.add("Elevation");
    u2.add("Walk On");
    u2.add("Kite");
    u2.add("In A Little While");
    u2.add("Wild Honey");
    u2.add("Peace On Earth");
    u2.add("When I Look At The World");
    u2.add("New York");
    u2.add("Grace");

    Comparator comp = Comparators.stringComparator();
    Collections.sort(u2, comp);
    System.out.println(u2);

    Arrays.sort(args, comp);
    System.out.print("[");
    for (int i=0, n=args.length; i<n; i++) {
      if (i != 0) System.out.print(", ");
      System.out.print(args[i]);
    }
    System.out.println("]");
  }
}
```

Running the CompTest program with a command line of java CompTest One Two Three generates the following output:

```
[Beautiful Day, Elevation, Grace, In A Little While, Kite, New York, Peace On
Earth, Stuck In A Moment You Can't Get Out Of, Walk On, When I Look At The World,
Wild Honey]
[One, Three, Two]
```

License Requirements

If you choose to use the backport of the framework, Sun's license does not permit you to run the Java 1.1-compatible program in a Java 1.2 or 1.3 environment. While it should run fine, the license requires you to modify your programs to use the "native" collection support in the java.util package. For more information on the licensing requirements, read the LICENSE.TXT file that comes with the software.

Distinguishing between the 1.2 and 1.3 Releases

There were minimal changes made to the Collections Framework between the 1.2 and 1.3 releases of the Java 2 platform. These changes were made for correctness and completeness. If you use any of the following capabilities, be forewarned that your programs won't work on the older release:

- The WeakHashMap class has a new constructor that accepts a Map. All collection implementations are supposed to have a copy constructor that accepts an instance of the collection interface implemented. The WeakHashMap lacked this constructor. With the newer release, it no longer is lacking.

- The Collections class has a new EMPTY_MAP constant. Previously, the Collections class had only constants for empty lists and sets with EMPTY_LIST and EMPTY_SET. These constants represent immutable empty collections. With the third one added, there are now empty collections for each of the three core interfaces.

- The Collections class has two new methods: singletonList() and singletonMap(). Originally, there was only a singleton() method for sets. Each method provides a simple way to create immutable single-element collections of the appropriate type. There are now methods for creating singleton collections for each of the three core implementation types.

> **NOTE** *The method that returns a singleton* Set *is not* singletonSet(); *it is just plain* singleton().

Summary

This chapter explored the compatibility issues and support you should be aware of when using the Collections Framework. While the new Collections Framework is well thought out, there are times when you can't force it on everyone, possibly because you need to reuse a "standard" library, you don't have the time to upgrade an existing code base, or you need backward compatibility with an older version of Java.

The next chapter demonstrates the flexibility of the Collections Framework by showing off some advanced usage examples. In it, you will see how to create custom collections like priority queues and multimaps.

Advanced Usages

In this final chapter of Part Two, we'll explore extended uses of the Collections Framework. Not only will we create more advanced custom collections, such as priority queues, multimaps, and soft hash maps, but we'll also look at some custom collections that exist out on the Web. These custom collections are different than the complete frameworks discussed in Part Three. They are usually just one or two isolated collection implementations. In conclusion to this section, we'll explore how to pick the right collection to maintain a collection of objects.

Creating Advanced Collections

After digging through the core set of collections, there will come times when the seven predefined general-purpose implementations aren't sufficient. In Chapter 14, we looked at what was necessary to create custom implementations. Here, we'll define three more advanced custom implementations: a priority queue, a multimap, and a soft hash map.

Priority Queue

Queues permit the processing of items in the order in which they arrive. *Priority queues* are a special type of queue where you assign a priority to each item added to the queue and then service queue items in priority order. Items with the same priority revert back to the regular queue behavior of first-in-first-out. This processing is similar to the way hospitals triage patients in an emergency. Hospitals tag those who won't recover without immediate care to be handled first. Patients that will recover with minimal attention go next. Lastly, those who are not expected to recover at all are comforted by support personnel and get little attention from the actual doctors until the end.

Depending upon the number of possible priorities, this abstract data type can be implemented in one of many ways. If the number of possible priorities is low, a separate `List` can be maintained for each priority. If, however, the number of possible priorities is high, then using an ordinary linked list for the entire queue might be the more appropriate data structure. In the following implementation, we'll assume a limited number of priorities and thus rely on an array-based backing store.

The implementation is of type `List` but exhibits the following behavior differences:

- To add elements to the priority queue, use the `public void insert(Object element, int priority)` method instead.

- When you add an element to the queue with either `add()` or `addAll()`, the minimum priority is used for all elements. This includes passing in a collection to the copy constructor.

> **NOTE** *Feel free to extend the behavior to retain priorities when copying a collection.*

- To remove the head element from the queue, use the `public Object removeFirst()` method. You can still use `remove()`, `removeAll()`, `retainAll()`, and `clear()`.

- To fetch but not remove the first element from the queue, use the `public Object getFirst()` method.

Listing 16-1 provides our implementation of a priority queue. It extends from `AbstractList` to get some behavior but much of it is overridden to deal with customizations for our implementation. The priority queue is maintained in an array with one array element per priority. The elements for each priority are maintained in a `LinkedList`, removing elements from the head and adding new elements to the rear. Most operations walk through the array to find where elements are located. Many optimizations can be made to minimize the boundaries checked within the array.

Listing 16-1. PriorityQueue implementation.

```java
import java.io.Serializable;
import java.util.*;

public class PriorityQueue extends AbstractList implements Serializable {

  private final static int DEFAULT_NUM_PRIORITIES = 10;
  private final static int MIN_PRIORITY = 0;

  private List queue[];
```

```java
public PriorityQueue() {
  this(DEFAULT_NUM_PRIORITIES);
}

public PriorityQueue(Collection col) {
  this(col, DEFAULT_NUM_PRIORITIES);
}

public PriorityQueue(int numPriorities) {
  this(null, numPriorities);
}

public PriorityQueue(Collection col, int numPriorities) {
  if (numPriorities <= 0) {
    throw new IllegalArgumentException(
      "Illegal Number of Priorities: "+ numPriorities);
  }
  queue = new List[numPriorities];
  if (col != null) {
    addAll(col);
  }
}

public int size() {
  int size = 0;
  for (int i=0, n=queue.length; i<n; i++) {
    if (queue[i] != null) {
      size += queue[i].size();
    }
  }
  return size;
}

public boolean add(Object element) {
  insert(element, MIN_PRIORITY);
  return true;
}

public void insert(Object element, int priority) {
  if (queue[priority] == null) {
    queue[priority] = new LinkedList();
  }
  queue[priority].add(element);
```

```java
      modCount++;
    }

    public void clear() {
      for (int i=0, n=queue.length; i<n; i++) {
        queue[i].clear();
      }
    }

    public Object get(int index) {
      if (index < 0) {
        throw new IllegalArgumentException(
          "Illegal index: "+ index);
      }
      Iterator iter = iterator();
      int pos = 0;
      while (iter.hasNext()) {
        if (pos == index) {
          return iter.next();
        } else {
          pos++;
        }
      }
      return null;
    }

    public Object removeFirst() {
      Iterator iter = iterator();
      Object obj = iter.next();
      iter.remove();
      return obj;
    }

    public Object getFirst() {
      Iterator iter = iterator();
      Object obj = iter.next();
      return obj;
    }

    public Iterator iterator() {
      Iterator iter = new Iterator() {
        int expectedModCount = modCount;
        int priority = queue.length - 1;
```

```
int count = 0;
int size = size();

int lastRet = -1; // Used to prevent successive remove() calls

Iterator tempIter;

{ // Get iterator for highest priority
  if (queue[priority] == null) {
    tempIter = null;
  } else {
    tempIter = queue[priority].iterator();
  }
}

private final void checkForComodification() {
  if (modCount != expectedModCount) {
    throw new ConcurrentModificationException();
  }
}

public boolean hasNext() {
  return count != size();
}
public Object next() {
  while (true) {
    if ((tempIter != null) && (tempIter.hasNext())) {
      Object next = tempIter.next();
      checkForComodification();
      lastRet = count++;
      return next;
    } else {
      // Get next iterator
      if (-priority < 0) {
        checkForComodification();
        throw new NoSuchElementException();
      } else {
        if (queue[priority] == null) {
          tempIter = null;
        } else {
          tempIter = queue[priority].iterator();
        }
      }
    }
}
```

```
            }
        }

        public void remove() {
          if (lastRet == -1) {
            throw new IllegalStateException();
          }
          checkForComodification();

          tempIter.remove();
          count--;
          lastRet = -1;
          expectedModCount = modCount;
        }
      };
      return iter;
    }

    public String toString() {
      String returnValue = "{";
      for (int i=0, n=queue.length; i<n; i++) {
        if (i!=0) {
          returnValue += ",";
        }
        returnValue += i + ":";
        if ((queue[i] != null) && (queue[i].size() > 0)) {
          returnValue += queue[i].toString();
        }
      }
      returnValue += "}";
      return returnValue;
    }


  }
```

You'll probably want to look closely at the iterator() method as it's the most interesting. It needs to walk through the iterators for each priority ensuring that there are no changes to the queue while it is being processed. The iterator is relied upon to support indexed access in the get() method as there is no direct index to use as a look-up into the multiple priority lists.

The test program for our new priority queue is shown in Listing 16-2. It creates priority queues from command-line arguments as well as manually with different priorities. In the end, all the elements are removed in priority order.

Listing 16-2. PriorityQueue test program.

```java
import java.util.*;

public class TestPriorityQueue {
  public static void main (String args[]) {
    List list = Arrays.asList(args);
    PriorityQueue queue = new PriorityQueue(list);
    System.out.println(queue);
    queue = new PriorityQueue(5);
    try {
      System.out.println(queue.removeFirst());
    } catch (NoSuchElementException e) {
      System.out.println("Got expected Exception");
    }
    queue.insert("Help", 2);
    queue.insert("Me", 2);
    queue.insert("Whazzup", 1);
    queue.insert("Out", 2);
    queue.insert("Of", 2);
    queue.insert("Here", 2);
    System.out.println(queue);
    System.out.println(queue.removeFirst());
    System.out.println(queue);
    queue.addAll(list);
    System.out.println(queue);
    while (queue.size() != 0) {
      System.out.println(queue.removeFirst());
    }
  }
}
```

Running the program produces the output in Listing 16-3. This utilizes our custom toString() version that adds the priority to the display of elements at each priority.

Listing 16-3. PriorityQueue test program output.

```
{0:[one, two, three],1:,2:,3:,4:,5:,6:,7:,8:,9:}
Got expected Exception
{0:,1:[Whazzup],2:[Help, Me, Out, Of, Here],3:,4:}
Help
{0:,1:[Whazzup],2:[Me, Out, Of, Here],3:,4:}
{0:[one, two, three],1:[Whazzup],2:[Me, Out, Of, Here],3:,4:}
Me
```

```
Out
Of
Here
Whazzup
one
two
three
```

> **NOTE** *For another implementation of a priority queue, see the Web page for the* BinHeapPriorityQueue *provided as part of the Flex compiler infrastructure effort at MIT at*
> http://www.flex-compiler.lcs.mit.edu/Harpoon/.

Multimap

A *multimap* is a more general type of priority queue. Where a priority queue internally maps a priority to multiple objects, a multimap permits the external mapping of any key to multiple values. So, for any key, the returned value in a multimap will be another Collection, not a specific value for the key like a normal map. It is actually quite easy to implement and involves very little specialized API, primarily just extending the AbstractMap and adding the extra behavior. The only API additions are the add(key, value) method, which adds the value to the specific key, and remove(key, value), which removes the value from the specific key. Otherwise, all of the methods of the Map interface are valid. If you put() a value into a multi map, it must be a collection, as it will replace the collection for the key, not add something. If you don't like this restriction, combine put() with add() to add a value if the value isn't a Collection. Because the values are stored as a Collection, there is no relative ordering of elements stored for the same key.

The listing for the MultiMap implementation is shown in Listing 16-4.

Listing 16-4. MultiMap implementation.

```java
import java.util.*;

public class MultiMap extends AbstractMap {

  private Map map;

  public MultiMap() {
    this(null);
  }
```

```java
public MultiMap(Map copy) {
  map = new HashMap();
  if (copy != null) {
    Iterator iter = copy.entrySet().iterator();
    while(iter.hasNext()) {
      Map.Entry entry = (Map.Entry)iter.next();
      add(entry.getKey(), entry.getValue());
    }
  }
}

public boolean containsKey(Object key) {
  Collection values = (Collection)map.get(key);
  return ((values != null) && (values.size() != 0));
}

public boolean containsValue(Object value) {
  Iterator iter = map.entrySet().iterator();
  boolean found = false;
  while (iter.hasNext()) {
    Map.Entry entry = (Map.Entry)iter.next();
    Collection values = (Collection)entry.getValue();
    if (values.contains(value)) {
      found = true;
      break;
    }
  }
  return found;
}

public Object get(Object key) {
  return map.get(key);
}

public Object put(Object key, Object value) {
  if (!(value instanceof Collection)) {
    throw new IllegalArgumentException(value.getClass().toString());
  }
  Object original = get(key);
  map.put(key, value);
  return original;
}
```

```
public boolean add(Object key, Object value) {
  return getValues(key).add(value);
}

public boolean addAll(Object key, Collection values) {
  return getValues(key).addAll(values);
}

private Collection getValues(Object key) {
  Collection col = (Collection)map.get(key);
  if (col == null) {
    col = new HashSet();
    map.put(key, col);
  }
  return col;
}

public Object remove(Object key) {
  Object original = get(key);
  map.remove(key);
  return original;
}

public boolean remove(Object key, Object value) {
  Collection values = (Collection)map.get(key);
  if (values == null) {
    return false;
  } else {
    return values.remove(value);
  }
}

public void clear() {
  map.clear();
}

public String toString() {
  StringBuffer buff = new StringBuffer();
  buff.append("{");
  Iterator keys = map.keySet().iterator();
  boolean first = true;
  while (keys.hasNext()) {
    if (first) {
      first = false;
```

```
    } else {
      buff.append(", ");
    }
    Object key = keys.next();
    Collection values = getValues(key);
    buff.append("[" + key + ": " + values + "]");
  }
  buff.append("}");
  return buff.toString();
}

public Set entrySet() {
  int size = 0;
  Iterator iterKeys = map.entrySet().iterator();
  while (iterKeys.hasNext()) {
    Map.Entry entry = (Map.Entry)iterKeys.next();
    Collection values = (Collection)entry.getValue();
    Iterator iterValues = values.iterator();
    while (iterValues.hasNext()) {
      size++;
      iterValues.next();
    }
  }

  final int finalSize = size;

  final Iterator entries = map.entrySet().iterator();

  return new AbstractSet() {
    int pos = 0;
    Map.Entry entry;
    Iterator values;

    public Iterator iterator() {
      return new Iterator() {
        public void remove() {
          throw new UnsupportedOperationException();
        }
        public boolean hasNext() {
          return pos != finalSize;
        }
        public Object next() {
          while(true) {
            if (entry == null) {
```

```
                entry = (Map.Entry)entries.next();
                values = ((Collection)entry.getValue()).iterator();
              }
            Object key = entry.getKey();
            if (values.hasNext()) {
              Object value = values.next();
              pos++;
              return new Entry(key, value);
            } else {
              entry = null;
            }
          }
        }
      };
    }
    public int size() {
      return finalSize;
    }
  };
}

private static class Entry implements Map.Entry {
  Object key;
  Object value;

  Entry(Object key, Object value) {
    this.key = key;
    this.value = value;
  }

  public Object getKey() {
    return key;
  }

  public Object getValue() {
    return value;
  }

  public Object setValue(Object value) {
    Object oldValue = this.value;
    this.value = value;
    return oldValue;
  }
```

```java
    public boolean equals(Object o) {
      if (!(o instanceof Map.Entry)) {
        return false;
      } else {
        Map.Entry e = (Map.Entry)o;
        return (key==null ? e.getKey()==null : key.equals(e.getKey())) &&
          (value==null ? e.getValue()==null : value.equals(e.getValue()));
      }
    }

    public int hashCode() {
      return ((value==null) ? 0 : value.hashCode());
    }

    public String toString() {
      return key+"="+value;
    }
  }

}
```

The most interesting of these methods is entrySet(), which must iterate through all of the elements of the map creating a proper Map.Entry for each element. Since there is no predefined class for the entries, the private, inner Entry class is defined. There *is* support in the multimap for null keys and values.

The test program for the MultiMap class is shown in Listing 16-5. It creates a HashMap, copies the HashMap into a MultiMap, then adds and removes elements from the MultiMap.

Listing 16-5. MultiMap test program.

```java
import java.util.*;

public class TestMultiMap {
  public static void main (String args[]) {
    Map map = new HashMap();
    map.put("one", "two");
    map.put("three", "four");
    map.put("five", "six");
    MultiMap multi = new MultiMap(map);
    System.out.println(multi);
    multi.add("five", "seven");
    multi.add("five", "eight");
    multi.add("five", "nine");
    multi.add("five", "ten");
```

```
        multi.add("three", "seven");
        System.out.println(multi);
        multi.remove("three");
        System.out.println(multi);
    }
}
```

The following is the output of running the test program shown in Listing 16-5. Notice how the map key of "five" has multiple values associated with it:

```
{[five: [six]], [one: [two]], [three: [four]]}
{[five: [ten, eight, six, nine, seven]], [one: [two]], [three: [seven, four]]}
{[five: [ten, eight, six, nine, seven]], [one: [two]]}
```

Soft Hash Map

A *soft hash map* is like the WeakHashMap implementation found in the Collections Framework but instead of relying on weak references for the keys of the map, it uses soft references. A hash map where the keys are soft references is good for caches, for as memory gets tight, the SoftHashMap can arbitrarily reduce its size. Thus, if you needed what had been in the map again, you would just need to refetch or recalculate the value.

Listing 16-6 provides the source for the SoftHashMap implementation.

Listing 16-6. SoftHashMap implementation.
```
Import java.util.*;
import java.lang.ref.*;

public class SoftHashMap extends AbstractMap implements Map {

    private Set entrySet = null;
    private Map hash;
    private ReferenceQueue queue = new ReferenceQueue();

    static private class SoftKey extends SoftReference {
        private int hash;

        private SoftKey(Object k) {
            super(k);
            hash = k.hashCode();
        }
        private static SoftKey create(Object k) {
```

```
      if (k == null) {
        return null;
      } else {
        return new SoftKey(k);
      }
    }
    private SoftKey(Object k, ReferenceQueue q) {
      super(k, q);
      hash = k.hashCode();
    }
    private static SoftKey create(Object k, ReferenceQueue q) {
      if (k == null) {
        return null;
      } else {
        return new SoftKey(k, q);
      }
    }
    public boolean equals(Object o) {
      if (this == o) {
        return true;
      } else if (!(o instanceof SoftKey)) {
        return false;
      }
      Object t = this.get();
      Object u = ((SoftKey)o).get();
      if ((t == null) || (u == null)) {
        return false;
      } else if (t == u) {
        return true;
      } else {
        return t.equals(u);
      }
    }
    public int hashCode() {
      return hash;
    }
  }

  private void processQueue() {
    SoftKey sk;
    while ((sk = (SoftKey)queue.poll()) != null) {
      hash.remove(sk);
    }
  }
}
```

```java
public SoftHashMap() {
  hash = new HashMap();
}

public SoftHashMap(Map t) {
  this(Math.max(2*t.size(), 11), 0.75f);
  putAll(t);
}

public SoftHashMap(int initialCapacity) {
  hash = new HashMap(initialCapacity);
}

public SoftHashMap(int initialCapacity, float loadFactor) {
  hash = new HashMap(initialCapacity, loadFactor);
}

public int size() {
  return entrySet().size();
}

public boolean isEmpty() {
  return entrySet().isEmpty();
}

public boolean containsKey(Object key) {
  return hash.containsKey(SoftKey.create(key));
}

public Object get(Object key) {
  return hash.get(SoftKey.create(key));
}

public Object put(Object key, Object value) {
  processQueue();
  return hash.put(SoftKey.create(key, queue), value);
}

public Object remove(Object key) {
  processQueue();
  return hash.remove(SoftKey.create(key));
}

public void clear() {
```

```java
    processQueue();
    hash.clear();
  }

  private static class Entry implements Map.Entry {
    private Map.Entry ent;
    private Object key;

    Entry(Map.Entry ent, Object key) {
      this.ent = ent;
      this.key = key;
    }

    public Object getKey() {
      return key;
    }

    public Object getValue() {
      return ent.getValue();
    }

    public Object setValue(Object value) {
      return ent.setValue(value);
    }

    public boolean equals(Object o) {
      if (!(o instanceof Map.Entry)) {
        return false;
      } else {
        Map.Entry e = (Map.Entry)o;
        Object value = getValue();
        return (key==null ? e.getKey()==null : key.equals(e.getKey())) &&
               (value==null ? e.getValue()==null : value.equals(e.getValue()));
      }
    }

    public int hashCode() {
      Object value = getValue();
      return (((key == null) ? 0 : key.hashCode())
        ^ ((value == null) ? 0 : v.hashCode()));
    }

  }
```

```java
            public Set entrySet() {
              if (entrySet == null) {
                entrySet = new EntrySet();
              }
              return entrySet;
            }

            private class EntrySet extends AbstractSet {
              Set set = hash.entrySet();

              public Iterator iterator() {

                return new Iterator() {
                  Iterator iter = set.iterator();
                  Entry next = null;

                  public boolean hasNext() {
                    while (iter.hasNext()) {
                      Map.Entry ent = (Map.Entry)iter.next();
                      SoftKey sk = (SoftKey)ent.getKey();
                      Object k = null;
                      if ((sk != null) && ((k = sk.get()) == null)) {
                        /* Soft key has been cleared by GC */
                        continue;
                      }
                      next = new Entry(ent, k);
                      return true;
                    }
                    return false;
                  }

                  public Object next() {
                    if ((next == null) && !hasNext()) {
                      throw new NoSuchElementException();
                    }
                    Entry element = next;
                    next = null;
                    return element;
                  }

                  public void remove() {
                    hashIterator.remove();
                  }
                };
```

```
  }
  public boolean isEmpty() {
    return !(iterator().hasNext());
  }

  public int size() {
    int size = 0;
    for (Iterator i = iterator(); i.hasNext(); i.next(), size++); {
    return size;
  }

  public boolean remove(Object o) {
    processQueue();
    if (!(o instanceof Map.Entry)) {
      return false;
    }
    Map.Entry e = (Map.Entry)o;
    Object ev = e.getValue();
    SoftKey sk = SoftKey.create(e.getKey());
    Object hv = hash.get(sk);
    if ((hv == null)
        ? ((ev == null) && hash.containsKey(sk)) : hv.equals(ev)) {
      hash.remove(sk);
      return true;
    }
    return false;
  }

  public int hashCode() {
    int h = 0;
    for (Iterator i = hashEntrySet.iterator(); i.hasNext();) {
      Map.Entry ent = (Map.Entry)i.next();
      SoftKey sk = (SoftKey)ent.getKey();
      Object v;
      if (sk == null) {
        continue;
      }
      h += (sk.hashCode()
        ^ (((v = ent.getValue()) == null) ? 0 : v.hashCode()));
    }
    return h;
  }
  }
}
}
```

The code for the SoftHashMap is very similar to that of the WeakHashMap. A great deal of the magic is found in the SoftKey class definition, which extends from the SoftReference class. Much of the rest of the code defines the Set returned by the entrySet() method.

> **NOTE** *An interesting second* SoftHashMap *would have the values as soft references instead of the keys—and the map knew how to regenerate the values based on the keys. The map entries would always stay around but if a look-up discovered a value being lost, it would just regenerate it. This only works when you can easily regenerate a value from a key, as in the case of a filename for an image. If memory was tight, the image could be lost but it could be retrieved again at a later time.*

The test program for the SoftHashMap shown in Listing 16-7 tries to eat up a lot of memory, displaying the size and contents of the SoftHashMap each time through the loop. The size should decrease as the amount of memory used by the program increases. The program does eventually stop once the map has emptied.

Listing 16-7. SoftHashMap test program.

```java
import java.util.*;

public class TestSoftMap {
  public static void main (String args[]) {
    final Map map = new SoftHashMap();
    map.put(new String("one"), "two");
    map.put(new String("three"), "four");
    map.put(new String("five"), "six");
    boolean end = false;
    for (int i=0; i<1000000000; i++) {
      Map maps = new HashMap(map);
      System.out.println("Size: " + map.size());
      System.out.println("Elements: " + map);
      if (end) {
        break;
      }
      if (map.size() == 0) {
        end = true;
      }
    }
  }
}
```

When running the program, you'll get many lines that look like this:

```
Size: 3
Elements: {five=six, one=two, three=four}
```

. . .before the output changes to the following:

```
Size: 0
Elements: {}
```

> **NOTE** *When running the test program, it is possible to get an intermediate result that displays only one or two elements in the* SoftHashMap.

Finding Additional Collections

The implementations found in the Collections Framework were created because they fill the general-purpose needs of most developers for collections. However, there are times when the general-purpose collections aren't enough. If you discover you need a special-purpose collection, you can either build it yourself or find someone else who already has. A good place to get started in finding additional collection implementations is the Java Collections Clearinghouse Web site at `http://www.javacollections.org/`. The maintainers keep a list of third-party implementations you can readily reuse, the licenses of which vary considerably, though many are open source. Before creating your own collection implementations, consider looking there first. You'll even find special-purpose Comparator objects predefined, such as those for comparing file sizes.

One word of caution about reusing other people's work: be sure to read the documentation for any special requirements. For instance, you'll find an implementation of a FastHashMap at `http://www.crionics.com/projects/fhm/fhm.html`. Designed purely for speed, it breaks under certain conditions, such as when you don't have unique hash codes. If your requirements happen to match needs that a predesigned collection fills, you can save yourself plenty of time. If, however, it doesn't or if you miss the warnings about the usage of a collection, you could be paddling for a long time. Be sure to bring a paddle.

Choosing the Right Collection

To close this chapter, let's take a quick look at some deciding factors in how to pick which standard collection implementation to use. These are not meant to be hard and fast rules but rather general guidelines to help you along.

- If you need to store primitive elements, you must use an array unless you want to place every item into a wrapper class like Integer or Float. Consider using a BitSet instead of an array of booleans.

- Rarely, if ever, should you use an historical collection class like Hashtable or Vector. Sometimes you need to use a Properties object, which is a type of Hashtable. Unless explicitly called for—as when using the JavaMail API—the historical collection class should be avoided in favor of the newer framework implementations.

- Use a List if you need ordered access. Pick an ArrayList for indexed access. Definitely use a LinkedList when you need to add and remove elements from the beginning or middle of the list. If you only need ordered access through an Iterator, believe it or not, LinkedList is actually faster. Lists are also good if your collection requires the storing of duplicates, triplicates, or more.

- Sets are for storing unique items in a collection. If you need ordered access, use a TreeSet. Otherwise, use a HashSet. If you only need ordered access after all the elements have been added, consider creating the set with a HashSet, then copying all the elements into a TreeSet.

- Use a Map if you need to store key-value pairs and the key isn't an integer. (Consider using an array or List for indexed access.) Like Set, you should always use the hashed version of the collection (HashMap) unless you need sorted access (TreeMap).

- Rely on the Collections class to make collections and maps read-only and thread-safe.

- Use the WeakHashMap if you need to maintain weak references to keys stored in the map.

If you find the standard collections insufficient for your needs, don't fret. As shown here and in Chapter 14, it's relatively easy to build your own. Or, just find some other sucker who has already done it!

Summary

This chapter explored the creation of more advanced custom creations. You saw how to create a priority queue, a multimap, and a soft hash map—three collection implementations not found in the standard Collections Framework. We also discussed how to go about finding other collection implementations and how best to choose the right collection for your data structure. As we close Part Two of the book, consider yourself an expert on the use of the Collections Framework.

The next chapter begins Part Three of the book where we explore third party collection libraries, some built around the Collections Framework and others not. The first library examined is the JGL Libraries from ObjectSpace.

Part Three

Alternative
Collection Libraries

JGL Libraries

The JGL Libraries are a Java add-on from ObjectSpace modeled after the C++ Standard Template Libraries (STL). While the standard Java Development Kit was evolving, and prior to the now standard Collections Framework, there was limited support for data collections in the core libraries. `Vector` and `Hashtable` primarily provided this support. Since ObjectSpace worked considerably with STL, they naturally ported their work over to Java. The libraries were then licensed to practically all of the early Java IDE vendors and became a de facto standard for Java collections support.

> **NOTE** *The original name was the Java Generic Library, abbreviated to JGL. After the Sun legal team was through with ObjectSpace, the product was renamed to the Generic Library for Java but the acronym JGL Libraries stuck.*

Unfortunately (or fortunately, depending on how you look at it), the people at Sun weren't buying into the JGL Libraries. Besides the fact that the original product name violated Sun's Java trademark, the general consensus was that it was too large and bulky for general usage and it took too much time and effort to understand. So, Josh Bloch and company at Sun developed the more lightweight Collections Framework. For more information on the reasons behind the decision not to use the JGL Libraries, see the Collections Design FAQ at `http://java.sun.com/products/jdk/1.2/docs/guide/collections/designfaq.html#23`.

> **TIP** *While the rest of this chapter describes how to use the JGL Libraries, I personally would not recommend that any new development use them. They haven't been updated since before Java 2, version 1.2 went beta and it seems that the standard Collections library has won out in the minds of developers.*

Getting Started

The JGL Libraries are made up of classes and interfaces that support handling data collections and processing the algorithms or functions that apply to all elements of such collections. Split across eight packages, the `com.objectspace.jgl` libraries both provide collection classes and predicate support that is completely oblivious to the Collections Framework.

Acquisition

To get the JGL Libraries, visit ObjectSpace's download area at `http://www.objectspace.com/products/voyager/downloads.asp`. The product's home is now buried under their Voyager product at `http://www.objectspace.com/products/voyager/libraries.asp`. It is no longer considered an independent product at ObjectSpace.

Once on the download page, select the JGL 3.1 link. You'll be presented with a form you must fill out before you can download. Select the file format, provide an email address, hit next, and then fill out their lengthy form. Be sure to supply a valid email address on the first page as you will be emailed a URL from which you can download the software.

> **WARNING** *ObjectSpace's Web site has a serious security problem. That is, you can enter* anyone's *email address—if that person has already registered, a phone number and address will appear prefilled within the form. So, when filling out the form, don't enter any information you don't mind giving out publicly—aside from your own valid email address. Without it, you will not get the download URL.*

After receiving the email, follow the link to download the software. Depending on which format you choose, the size will vary. Expect about a 2 MB download, although the gzip version is less than 1 MB.

Installation

How you install the software depends upon which file type you download. Basically, you need to unpack it. If you download either the Generic Zip, the Unix Tarred & Compressed, or the Unix Tarred & GZipped, you'll need the appropriate tools to unpack it. For instance, for the Generic Zip format, you can use the `jar` utility that comes with the JDK. This will unpack the files into a directory named `jgl3.1.0`:

```
jar xvf jgl3_1_0.zip
```

The self-extracting version is meant for the Windows platforms only. If you don't mind the extra bandwidth required to download (it's the largest of the bunch), you can go through a common set of InstallShield prompts to install the JGL Libraries as shown in Figures 17-1 through 17-5.

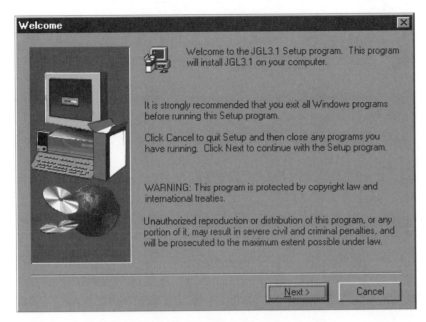

Figure 17-1. The JGL Libraries installation startup screen.

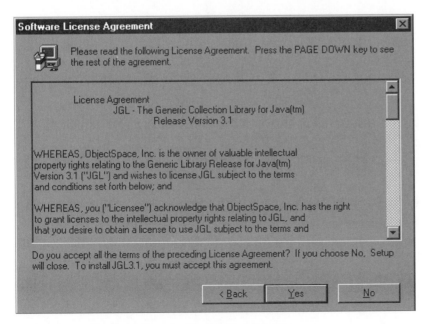

Figure 17-2. The JGL Libraries license agreement screen.

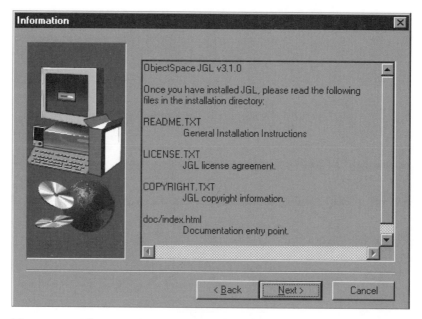

Figure 17-3. The JGL Libraries information screen.

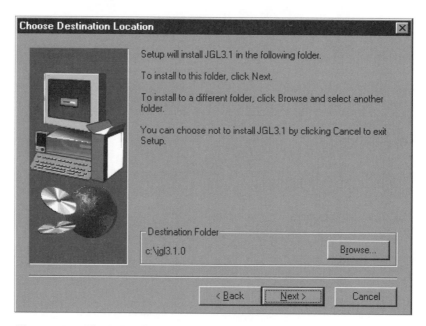

Figure 17-4. The JGL Libraries installation destination screen.

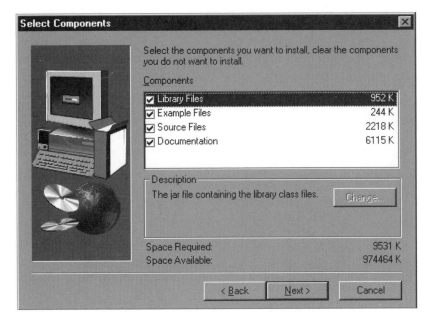

Figure 17-5. The JGL Libraries component selection screen.

Just select "Next" or "Yes" on each screen. If you don't want to install onto the default device or directory (usually `C:\jgl3.1.0`), you'll need to choose a different location on the fourth screen (see Figure 17-5). After selecting "Next" on the fifth screen, the installation occurs.

> **NOTE** *Given the complexity of the libraries, you'll probably want to select the Documentation option shown in Figure 17-5. However, if disk space is tight, you can read it online at* `http://support.objectspace.com/`. *You don't really need the source files unless you like digging through code to better understand things.*

Before the self-extractor completes, you'll be prompted to update your CLASSPATH. If you select "Yes," your CLASSPATH will be adjusted to contain the JGL Libraries (along with the main JGL directory, which is superfluously added into your CLASSPATH). On Windows 95/98 platforms, the following is added to a line at the end of your AUTOEXEC.BAT file:

```
%CLASSPATH%;.;c:\jgl3.1.0;c:\jgl3.1.0\lib\jgl3.1.0.jar
```

On Windows NT/2000 platforms, the setting will be added or appended to your existing CLASSPATH in the user's System Environment.

> **WARNING** *Not everyone prefers to have the current directory (.) in their CLASSPATH. If you didn't have it there before, it will be added whether you like it or not. Also, the automated setting of CLASSPATH does not always preserve the current CLASSPATH, sometimes not prepending %CLASSPATH% in the AUTOEXEC.BAT file.*

The safest precaution is to manually set the CLASSPATH. If you select "No" during the running of the self-extractor, or you manually unpacked one of the other installation formats, you must manually place the JGL Libraries into your CLASSPATH. When programming with the Java 2 platform, it is easiest to place the jgl3.1.0.jar file (found in the lib directory) into an appropriate directory for the Java Extensions Framework, in order to load the .jar file without mucking with the CLASSPATH environment variable. You will need to place the .jar file in the /jre/lib/ext directory of your Java Runtime Environment (JRE) so that the standard Java extension mechanism can find the file. In the case of a Win32 user with the JDK 1.3 installed in C:\jdk1.3, copying the .jar file translates into execution of the following command from the jgl3.1.0 directory:

```
copy lib\jgl3.1.0.jar c:\jdk1.3\jre\lib\ext
```

Once you've copied the file, you can use the com.objectspace.jgl.* classes in your programs.

Usage

The current version of the JGL Libraries comes with eight primary packages and includes a ninth for usage examples as shown in Table 17-1.

Table 17-1. Packages of the JGL Libraries

PACKAGE NAME	DESCRIPTION
com.objectspace.jgl	The core interfaces and collection classes.
com.objectspace.jgl.adapters	Adapters for working with native arrays within the JGL framework.
com.objectspace.jgl.algorithms	The JGL Libraries' algorithm implementations.
com.objectspace.jgl.functions	Functions for altering the algorithms.
com.objectspace.jgl.predicates	Predicates for altering element order in a collection.
com.objectspace.jgl.util:	The set of utility classes.
com.objectspace.jgl.voyager, com.objectspace.jgl.voyager.algorithms	The classes for connecting to Voyager.
com.objectspace.jgl.examples	Examples of library usage.

When it comes time to actually use the classes, be sure to import the appropriate packages:

```
import com.objectspace.jgl.*;
import com.objectspace.jgl.util.*;
```

In addition to the javadoc .html files, the distribution comes with a User Guide (see Figure 17-6) and links to online support.

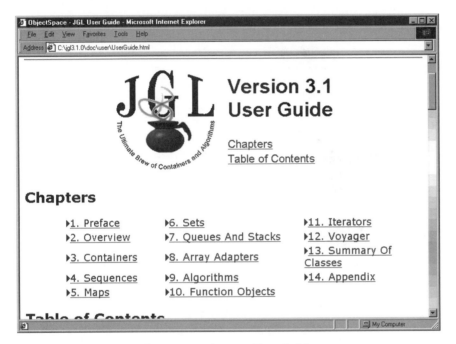

Figure 17-6. The JGL Libraries version 3.1 User Guide.

NOTE *Since the JGL Libraries were last updated in 1997, the generated javadoc comes in the older format. You may wish to regenerate it with a newer javadoc tool to get the newer style. If you do, you'll see things such as which classes implement which interfaces. Also, when using the classes with the Java 2 platform, you may run across classes and interfaces with duplicate names within the JGL Libraries. Be careful with your import statements.*

Licensing and Redistribution Rights

While the JGL Libraries are freely available, they are neither open source nor public domain. If you didn't read it before downloading, be sure to read the LICENSE.TXT file that comes with the distribution. The license essentially states that you can include the .class files as part of your distribution, as long as your tool is not a Java development environment or development tool and as long as they are not a documented part of the distribution. Any desire to redistribute the source, help files, documentation, examples, and benchmarks requires prior written consent from ObjectSpace.

Product Support

The key resource for product support is the User Guide. The guide is rather complete and should help you get started using the JGL product. ObjectSpace product support is available from `http://support.objectspace.com`. There, you'll find reference to a JGL Libraries FAQ and a JGL-specific mailing list (JGL-INTEREST), none of which you can get to until you register for support. The mailing list traffic is relatively light and has received only one or two messages a month in the year or so I've been on it. To subscribe to the mailing list, send a message to objectlist@objectspace.com with "join jgl-interest foo@bar.none" as the message content (include your email address).

If you need to report a bug, send email to jgl@objectspace.com.

> **NOTE** *Archives of the mailing list are not available.*

As of this writing, the current version of the product is 3.1, released in December 1997.

Key Classes and Interfaces

The JGL Libraries are made up of classes and interfaces to work with data structures and algorithms. Basically, you pick an appropriate abstract data type (ADT) to work with. When you want to do something with the elements of the collection, tell the ADT what to do for each element (rather than getting an `Enumeration` and doing it yourself). You'll find descriptions in the following sections of the key capabilities broken up into logical groupings.

Collection Classes

All of the classes that are collections of elements in the JGL Libraries implement the Container interfaces. Unlike the core Collections Framework where there are two root interfaces for the collection implementations (Collection and Map), the JGL Libraries' framework provides a single root interface. In addition to the root interface, there are Sequence and Set interfaces and abstract Map and ArrayAdapter classes, which serve as the base collection architecture. The ArrayAdapter class provides support for converting between historical collection implementations (such as arrays and Vector) and their JGL counterparts. The basic class hierarchy is shown in Figure 17-7.

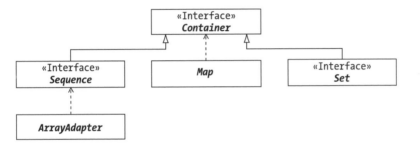

Figure 17-7. The base JGL Libraries collections hierarchy diagram.

The Container Interface

Due to the JGL Libraries being rooted by a single interface, the basic operations for working with the JGL Libraries are defined within the Container interface. In addition to the methods from the Object class included in the interface definition, the basic collection operations are shown here:

* Adding elements: add()

* Removing elements: clear() and remove()

* Working with the collection size: isEmpty(), maxSize(), and size()

* Accessing elements: elements(), start(), and finish()

The concrete Container implementations in the JGL Libraries' framework are Stack, Queue, and PriorityQueue. You'll find that most of the JGL Libraries' class names are fairly self-explanatory.

The following example demonstrates Stack usage:

```
import com.objectspace.jgl.*;

public class StackTest {
  public static void main(String args[]) {
    Stack stack = new Stack();
    for (int i=0, n=args.length; i<n; i++) {
      stack.push(args[i]);
    }
    System.out.println(stack);
    System.out.println("Pop elements: ");
    while (!stack.isEmpty()) {
      System.out.println("\t" + stack.pop());
    }
  }
}
```

Notice that most concrete implementations provide methods in addition to the basic Container methods for working with the collection.

The following output is the result of the prior program run with the command line java StackTest one two three:

```
Stack( Array( one, two, three ) )
Pop elements:
        three
        two
        one
```

The Sequence Interface

The Sequence interface adds operations for working with containers where elements can be accessed sequentially. Besides overloading some of the Container methods, it adds some of its own:

- Adding elements: pushFront() and pushBack()

- Removing elements: popFront(), popBack(), and remove()

- Replacing elements: put() and replace()

- Checking containment: `contains()`, `count()`, `indexOf()`

- Accessing elements: `at()`, `front()`, and `back()`

You'll find twenty-three concrete `Sequence` implementations, including `Array` (which is growable like a `java.util.Vector`), `SList` and `DList` (singly and doubly linked lists), `Deque` (a double-ended queue), and several others, all of which serve to integrate with basic Java types. Those that integrate with the Java objects almost all have two implementations, one a growable buffer and one not—an array:

BooleanArray and BooleanBuffer

ByteArray and ByteBuffer

CharArray and CharBuffer

DoubleArray and DoubleBuffer

FloatArray and FloatBuffer

IntArray and IntBuffer

LongArray and LongBuffer

ObjectArray

ShortArray and ShortBuffer

VectorArray

> **NOTE**   *A* deque *is a double-ended queue that permits easy insertion and deletion at both ends.*

The following example demonstrates the usage of an ObjectArray, converting into a Sequence the String array passed to main():

```
import java.util.Enumeration;
import com.objectspace.jgl.adapters.*;

public class ObjectArrayTest {
  public static void main(String args[]) {
    Sequence sequence = new ObjectArray(args);

    Enumeration enum = sequence.elements();
    while (enum.hasMoreElements()) {
      System.out.println(enum.nextElement());
    }
  }
}
```

> **TIP** *Don't let class names like* ObjectArray *fool you. The concrete* Sequence *implementations for integrating with the older collections do not subclass the* Array *class. Instead, they subclass* ArrayAdapter, *which is a direct* Object *subclass.*

The Set Interface

The Set interface is like the java.util.Set interface and defines an unordered collection of elements. Like java.util.Set, the JGL interface includes methods to add and remove elements and check for their existence.

* Adding elements: put()

* Removing elements: remove()

* Checking existence: get() and count()

There are just two concrete sets found in the JGL Libraries: HashSet and OrderedSet.

The following example demonstrates using a HashSet:

```
import com.objectspace.jgl.*;

public class HashSetTest {
  public static void main(String args[]) {
    Set set = new HashSet();
    for (int i=0, n=args.length; i<n; i++) {
      set.put(args[i]);
    }
    System.out.println(set);
  }
}
```

To print out the individual values, walk through the elements with an Enumeration just like you did in the previous ObjectArrayTest example.

The following output occurs if you run the prior program with the command line, java HashSetTest one two three four five six:

```
HashSet( six, four, three, two, one, five )
```

The Map Class

In the JGL Libraries, Map is an abstract class, not an interface. Thus, it can extend the java.util.Dictionary class. It is utilized like Dictionary and Hashtable to work with sets of key-value pairs in the JGL Libraries. The Map class adds methods to work explicitly with keys and values, otherwise everything comes from Container:

- Checking containment: count() and countValues()

- Accessing elements: keys(), values()

Those methods that are not abstract in the class will throw an AbstractMethodError and expect the subclasses to override them.

Like Set, there are two concrete Map implementations found in the JGL Libraries: HashMap and OrderedMap. Unlike the java.util.Hashtable class, the JGL HashMap allows duplicates. And similar to the java.util.TreeMap, an OrderedMap is backed by an internal tree structure.

When working with a HashMap or OrderedMap, you can add elements to the map as separate key and value objects, or as a joined Pair object. The Pair object, as its name implies, holds a pair of objects. When working with maps, the first object in the Pair is the key and the second is the value.

The following example demonstrates the usage of Pair and HashMap:

```
import com.objectspace.jgl.*;

public class HashMapTest {
  public static void main(String args[]) {
    HashMap map = new HashMap();
    for (int i=0, n=args.length; i<n; i+=2) {
      Pair pair = new Pair(args[i], args[i+1]);
      map.add(pair);
    }
    System.out.println(map);
    System.out.println(map.get(args[0]));
    System.out.println(map.get("Foo"));
  }
}
```

For each pair of elements from the command line, a Pair is created and added to the HashMap. The map is then printed. The first command-line argument is searched for in the map, as is a fixed key, which is likely *not* in the map. When there is no value for a key, null is returned.

If you run the previous program with the command line, java HashMapTest one two three four five six five seven, the following output will occur:

```
HashMap( Pair( three, four ), Pair( one, two ), Pair( five, six ) )
two
null
```

Notice that the value for "five" is not replaced with "seven" in the output. This is different than the Hashtable behavior. There are separate methods to add and replace versus just add. To add with replacement, use the put() method instead of add(). On the other hand, in order to have "five" paired with both "six" and "seven," you would need to use a different constructor that allows duplicates: new HashMap(true).

> **NOTE** *Aside from the concrete implementation classes listed above, there are also several in the* com.objectspace.jgl.voyager *package to use with ObjectSpace's Voyager product and Application Server and Object Request Broker (ORB).*

Algorithm Support

Once you get a feel for the different collection classes, it's time to move on to the algorithmic support found in the `com.objectspace.jgl.algorithms` package. This package is made up of twenty-two classes, all of which are `final` classes full of `static` methods, as shown in Table 17-2.

Table 17-2. The JGL Libraries' Algorithms Classes

CLASS	ALGORITHMS
Applying	forEach, inject
Comparing	equal, lexicographicalCompare, median, mismatch
Copying	copy, copyBackward
Counting	accumulate, adjacentDifference, count, countIf
Filling	fill, fillN
Filtering	reject, select, unique, uniqueCopy
Finding	adjacentFind, detect, every, find, findIf, some
Hashing	orderedHash, unorderedHash
Heap	makeHeap, popHeap, pushHeap, sortHeap
MinMax	maxElement, minElement
OrderedSetOperations and SetOperations	includes, setDifference, setIntersection, setSymmetricDifference, setUnion
Permuting	nextPermutation, prevPermutation
Printing	print, println, toString
Removing	remove, removeCopy, removeCopyIf, removeIf
Replacing	replace, replaceCopy, replaceCopyIf, replaceIf
Reversing	reverse, reverseCopy
Rotating	rotate, rotateCopy
Shuffling	randomShuffle
Sorting	iterSort, sort
Swapping	iterSwap, swapRanges
Transforming	collect, transform

To work with different algorithms, find the appropriate class in the package and call the specific method in the class to perform the operation you want. For instance, in the earlier `ObjectArrayTest` example, an `Enumeration` was used to iterate through the collection. We could have just as easily used the `println()` method of the `Printing` class, as shown here:

```
import com.objectspace.jgl.*;
import com.objectspace.jgl.adapters.*;
import com.objectspace.jgl.algorithms.*;

public class ObjectArrayTest {
  public static void main(String args[]) {
    Sequence sequence = new ObjectArray(args);
    Printing.println(sequence);
    }
  }
}
```

However, there is one key difference: `Printing.println()` does not add a new line at the end of each element, it only adds one at the end of all of the elements (and even places them in parenthesis). As shown in Listing 17-1, to add a new line at the end of *each* element, use the `forEach()` method of the `Applying` class:

Listing 17-1. Printing the elements of a Sequence.
```
import com.objectspace.jgl.*;
import com.objectspace.jgl.adapters.*;
import com.objectspace.jgl.algorithms.*;

public class ObjectArrayTest3 {
  static class UnaryPrintFunction implements UnaryFunction {
    public Object execute(Object element) {
      System.out.println(element);
      return null;
    }
  }
  public static void main(String args[]) {
    Sequence sequence = new ObjectArray(args);
    UnaryFunction print = new UnaryPrintFunction();
    Applying.forEach(sequence, print);
  }
}
```

This allows you to create a `UnaryFunction` that calls the `System.out.println()` method on each element.

While printing individual elements isn't a particularly complicated task, you can create common unary functions to establish a useful container task library.

That way, you won't have to continually enumerate through all the elements. You can also collect the results of running the UnaryFunction on all of the elements by using the collect() method of Transformation. Moreover, there are BinaryFunction algorithms that allow you to pass a second argument to each element in the container.

Functions and Predicates

You can create your own custom functions with all the different algorithm classes. Thankfully, the JGL Libraries predefine some for you, which are found in the com.objectspace.jgl.functions package. You'll find the functions that accept a single argument in Table 17-3 and those that accept two in Table 17-4.

Table 17-3. UnaryFunction Implementations

FUNCTION	
BindFirst	Print
BindSecond	SelectFirst
ConstantFunction	SelectSecond
Hash	ToString
IdentifyFunction	UnaryCompose
LengthString	UnaryPredicateFunction
NegateNumber	

Table 17-4. BinaryFunction Implementations

FUNCTION	
ConstantFunction	BinaryPredicateFunction
PlusString	TimesNumber
ModulusNumber	BinaryCompose
SwappedBinaryFunction	MinusNumber
PlusNumber	DividesNumber

The JGL Libraries also support something called a predicate. A predicate is a boolean function that, when performed against an element in the sequence, lets the algorithm decide whether it should perform that specific function. Say, for instance, that instead of performing a function for all elements, you want to perform the function for all elements less than or equal to the "John" object. The predefined predicates are found in the com.objectspace.jgl.predicate package. Table 17-5 lists the predefined unary predicates. Table 17-6 displays the binary ones.

Table 17-5. UnaryPredicate Implementations

PREDICATE

PositiveNumber	LogicalNot
UnaryOr	BindSecondPredicate
UnaryNot	InstanceOf
NegativeNumber	ConstantPredicate
UnaryTern	BindFirstPredicate
UnaryComposePredicate	UnaryAnd

Table 17-6. BinaryPredicate Implementations

PREDICATE

BinaryAnd	HashComparator
BinaryComposePredicate	IdenticalTo
BinaryNot	LessCollationKey
BinaryOr	LessCollator
BinaryTern	LessEqualCollationKey
ConstantPredicate	LessEqualCollator
EqualCollationKey	LessEqualNumber
EqualCollator	LessEqualString
EqualNumber	LessNumber
EqualString	LessString
EqualTo	LogicalAnd
GreaterCollationKey	LogicalOr
GreaterCollator	NotEqualCollationKey
GreaterEqualCollationKey	NotEqualCollator
GreaterEqualCollator	NotEqualNumber
GreaterEqualNumber	NotEqualString
GreaterEqualString	NotEqualTo
GreaterNumber	NotIdenticalTo
GreaterString	SwappedBinaryPredicate

To demonstrate the use of functions and predicates, Listing 17-2 calculates the product of a set of values and then performs the same operations on the positive numbers only:

Listing 17-2. Using JGL functions and predicates.

```
import com.objectspace.jgl.*;
import com.objectspace.jgl.algorithms.*;
import com.objectspace.jgl.functions.*;
import com.objectspace.jgl.predicates.*;

public class AlgTest {
  public static void main(String args[]) {
    Array array = new Array();
    array.add(new Integer(10));
    array.add(new Integer(-10));
    array.add(new Integer(23));
    Integer product = (Integer)Applying.inject(
      array, new Integer(1), new TimesNumber());
    System.out.println("Array = " + array + " / Product = " + product);
    Array posArray = (Array)Filtering.select(array, new PositiveNumber());
    Integer product2 = (Integer)Applying.inject(
      posArray, new Integer(1), new TimesNumber());
    System.out.println("Array = " + posArray + " / Pos Product = " + product2);
  }
}
```

The inject() method of Applying works by building up the return values: it passes the results of executing the function on the first element along to the next execution of the binary function, thus returning the final calculated value.

Summary

This chapter examined the JGL framework from ObjectSpace. You learned how the libraries provide a framework for using abstract data structures and the algorithms to work within those structures. You learned about the different collection classes the JGL Libraries support, from the common, growable array classes to the less common double-ended queue (Deque) class, including many new classes in between. You also saw how the product provides support to execute algorithms across all of the collection elements as well as its predefined set of functions and predicates to perform such algorithms. While the JGL Libraries are very rich libraries and, due to their STL roots, somewhat familiar for developers who transition to Java from C++, the framework seems to be little used for new development efforts today. When creating new systems, you're better off using the Collections

Framework defined in the earlier parts of this book. Of course, if you can't transition to the Java 2 platform yet, the JGL Libraries may be a viable option for collections support.

In the next chapter, we'll explore Doug Lea's util.concurrent library. You'll learn how to utilize this library to improve performance when using the standard Collections Framework.

CHAPTER 18

util.concurrent

Doug Lea was a man on a mission. Having noticed a severe lack of collections support in the early Java releases, in the fall of 1995, Doug released a "standard" collections library. If you don't know Doug, he is, according to his latest book (*Concurrent Programming in Java*, Addison-Wesley, 2000), "one of the foremost experts on object-oriented technology and software reuse. He has been doing collaborative research with Sun labs for more than five years. Lea is Professor of Computer Science at SUNY Oswego, Co-director of the Software Engineering Lab at the New York Center for Advanced Technology in Computer Applications, and Adjunct Professor of Electrical and Computer Engineering at Syracuse University." Doug also serves on the Java Community Process (JCP) Executive Committee for J2SE/J2EE.

This collections library became widely used over the next year or so. While still freely available from `http://gee.cs.oswego.edu/dl/classes/collections/`, it was superceded by the now standard Collections Framework of the Java 2 platform.

In addition to his collections library, Doug worked on a second library for concurrent Java development called util.concurrent, which I'll describe in this chapter. Here, you'll learn about the makeup of the library and what you can do with it to make yourself more productive.

The util.concurrent library is not truly a collections library. In fact, it is part of a library supporting concurrent programming, which Doug describes more fully in *Concurrent Programming in Java*. For more detailed information about the classes described in this chapter or the underlying classes they utilize, consider Doug's book. It's an excellent addition to any serious Java developer's library.

Getting Started

The util.concurrent library is comprised of classes and interfaces that help you develop multithreaded Java applications. Instead of spending your time developing thread-safe support structures, you can grab the util.concurrent library and focus on your business issues. Where does all this fit in the context of a book on collections? Several of the classes in the library are extensions to the classes in the Collections Framework.

Acquisition

Getting the util.concurrent library is rather simple. Go to Doug Lea's Web site at http://gee.cs.oswego.edu/dl/classes/EDU/oswego/cs/dl/util/concurrent /intro.html and download. Doug provides the source code in either a tar.gz format or a .zip file. It is your responsibility to compile the code.

Installation

Once you download and uncompress the file, you'll need to compile the source code and add the class files to your CLASSPATH. Within the Java 2 platform, it is easiest to package the classes into a .jar file, then place it into the appropriate directory for the Java Extensions Framework to load the .jar file without mucking with the CLASSPATH environment variable.

To compile all the classes, go to the concurrent directory created when you uncompressed the downloaded file and execute the following command:

```
javac -d . *.java
```

This will create all the .class files in the appropriate directory structure under the current directory. You can now either add this directory to your CLASSPATH or create the .jar file.

To create the .jar file, execute the following command from the concurrent directory:

```
jar cvf concurrent.jar EDU
```

Now that you've created the .jar file, you can copy it into the appropriate directory. In order for the standard Java extension mechanism to find the file, you'll need to place it in the /jre/lib/ext directory of your Java Runtime Environment (JRE). In the case of a Win32 user with the JDK 1.3 installed in C:\jdk1.3, copying the .jar file translates into execution of the following command from the concurrent directory:

```
copy concurrent.jar c:\jdk1.3\jre\lib\ext
```

Now that you've copied the .jar file, you can use the util.concurrent classes in your programs.

Usage

Before actually learning what classes and interfaces are available, let's take a quick look at how you can use them in your program. All classes are in a single package:

```
EDU.oswego.cs.dl.util.concurrent
```

> **NOTE** *Yes, the first level package is EDU in all caps. This is a remnant from the package's original creation when the language specification showed all caps for the first-level package structure.*

In order to use any of the util.concurrent interfaces or classes in your program, you'll need to import the necessary package with the following line:

```
import EDU.oswego.cs.dl.util.concurrent.*;
```

> **NOTE** *If you'd like the javadoc documentation for the library, you'll need to generate the complete set yourself. You can also view it online at* http://gee.cs.oswego.edu/dl/classes/index.html.

Licensing and Redistribution Rights

The library has been placed into the public domain by the author. This means that you are free to redistribute it with your own applications and you don't need to get or pay for licenses from the library's maintainer.

Product Support

Since the library is in the public domain, you use it at your risk. In answer to the question, "Can I get commercial support for this package?" the library's FAQ states, "I don't know of any place to get it. I can't think of any technical reason that you'd want it." If you're having problems using the library, try to read the necessary descriptions in Doug Lea's book. You can check out the book's online supplement at http://gee.cs.oswego.edu/dl/cpj/. You might also look at a set of slides that provide an overview of the package at http://gee.cs.oswego.edu/dl/cpjslides/util.pdf.

As of this writing, the current version of the library is 1.3, released in January 2001. Judging from the maintenance history of the library, it seems that the author is responsive to bug reports. If you happen to be the first to report a specific coding error in the current release of the library, you can get a free copy of the latest edition of Doug Lea's book, *Concurrent Programming in Java.*

Key Classes and Interfaces

The key parts of the util.concurrent library are not the collections-related classes. Instead, the library is made up of a core set of interfaces related to concurrent programming and their implementations.

The collections-related classes are implementations that utilize other parts of the library. The collections-related classes use two key interfaces from the library: Sync and ReadWriteLock. There are several other key interfaces in the library. For information on the Channel, Barrier, SynchronizedVariable, and Executor interfaces, please see their appropriate online documentation or Doug Lea's book.

Sync Interface

The Sync interface defines a basic acquire-release locking mechanism. There are twelve implementations of this interface within the library as shown in Figure 18-1. Table 18-1 provides a brief description of each.

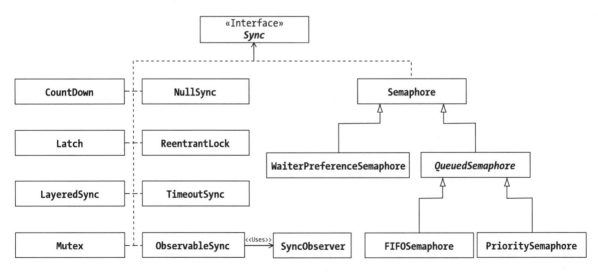

Figure 18-1. Sync interface implementation hierarchy.

Table 18-1. Summary of Sync Implementations

IMPLEMENTATION	DESCRIPTION
CountDown	Blocks until 'n' objects try to acquire lock.
FIFOSemaphore	Maintains a first-in, first-out semaphore queue.
Latch	Once released, forever acquirable.
LayeredSync	Combines multiple syncs.
Mutex	Basic non-reentrant locking mechanism.
NullSync	A no-op sync implementation.
ObservableSync	Notifies a SyncObserver when lock acquire or release is attempted, does no locking (combine use in LayeredSync with appropriate implementation).
PrioritySemaphore	Maintains semaphore queue in thread priority order.
ReentrantLock	Permits per-thread access.
Semaphore	Permits multiple objects to acquire lock.
TimeoutSync	All lock acquisition is done with at least a default timeout.
WaiterPreferenceSemaphore	Maintains semaphore objects in a manner to avoid starvation.

Once you pick which implementation to use, you tend to just call the methods of the Sync interface. As Table 18-2 shows, the Sync interface consists of three methods and several constants.

Table 18-2. Summary of Sync Interface

VARIABLE/METHOD NAME	DESCRIPTION
acquire()	Called to acquire a lock.
attempt()	Called to attempt to acquire a lock in a certain period.
release()	Called to release a lock.
ONE_CENTURY	Number of milliseconds in one century.
ONE_DAY	Number of milliseconds in one day.
ONE_HOUR	Number of milliseconds in one hour.
ONE_MINUTE	Number of milliseconds in one minute.
ONE_SECOND	Number of milliseconds in one second.
ONE_WEEK	Number of milliseconds in one week.
ONE_YEAR	Number of milliseconds in one year.

When using the collections-oriented classes in the library, you'll need to pick the appropriate Sync implementation (or ReadWriteLock) to use with the collection. The basic usage of the locking mechanism is to acquire the lock with either acquire() or attempt(), and then to release the lock with release(). The

attempt() method has an argument for the number of milliseconds to wait to try
to get the lock:

```
public void acquire() throws InterruptedException
public boolean attempt(long msecs) throws InterruptedException
public void release()
```

Upon timeout or failure, false is returned; otherwise, upon successful acquisition, true is returned.

Listing 18-1 demonstrates this, where the following class utilizes a Sync to
provide access synchronization to an internal variable. Similar code using standard Java syntax would use a synchronized block, where the block was synchronized on the object passed in to the constructor.

Listing 18-1. Demonstrating the use of Sync.

```
public class UseSync {
  private It it;
  private final Sync lock;
  public UseSync(Sync lock) {
    this.lock = lock;
  }
  public void setIt(It it) {
    try {
      lock.acquire();
      try {
        this.it = updateIt(it);
      } finally {
        lock.release();
      }
    } catch (InterruptedException e) {
    }
  }
  public It getIt() {
    It it = null;
    try {
      lock.acquire();
      try {
        it = this.it.clone()
      } catch (CloneNotSupportedException e) {
      } finally {
        lock.release();
      }
    } catch (InterruptedException e) {
```

```
    }
    return it;
  }
}
```

While the use of this code might seem like overkill when compared to a synchronized block, you have more control over the order of lock acquisition. And when dealing with multiple levels of locks, you have better control in avoiding deadlocks. The first lock acquisition would use the acquire() method, as shown in Listing 18-1. Later lock acquisitions would use the attempt() method, where you specify the number of milliseconds to wait before giving up:

```
if (otherLock.attempt(500)) {
  try {
    // do stuff
  } finally {
    otherLock.release();
  }
}
```

Remember that attempt() returns true or false to signify whether the lock was actually acquired.

There are interface constants for several predefined periods:

```
public static long ONE_CENTURY
public static long ONE_YEAR
public static long ONE_WEEK
public static long ONE_DAY
public static long ONE_HOUR
public static long ONE_MINUTE
public static long ONE_SECOND
```

You can pass these constants into the attempt() calls.

> **NOTE** *Some* Sync *implementations add additional methods, such as to* attach() *and* detail() *observers with the* ObservableSync, release(count) *with the* QueuedSemaphore, *or to check the* initialCount()/currentCount() *with the* CountDown. *In most cases, their usage should be fairly obvious. In the event they are not, feel free to look up their usage in the javadoc documentation.*

ReadWriteLock Interface

The ReadWriteLock interface defines a special dual-locking mechanism with separate read and write locks. They basically permit multiple readers to access a critical code area but only one writer at a time, and not while there are any readers. The util.concurrent library offers four implementations of this interface, as shown by Figure 18-2. Table 18-3 provides a brief description of each.

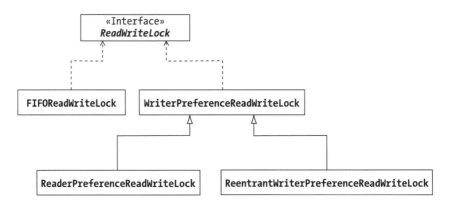

Figure 18-2. ReadWriteLock interface implementation hierarchy.

Table 18-3. Summary of ReadWriteLock Implementations

IMPLEMENTATION	DESCRIPTION
FIFOReadWriteLock	Maintains a pair of first-in, first-out (FIFO) semaphore queues. The writer access is first-in, first-out. For the writer lock attempt to succeed, there must be no holders of the read lock. If there are readers holding the read lock and another reader asks for the lock, the reader will succeed even if there is a waiting write lock request.
ReaderPreferenceReadWriteLock	Prefers waiting readers to writers (limited use), not FIFO access.
ReentrantWriterPreference ReadWriteLock	Prefers waiting writers, and permits reentrant access from same thread, like ReentrantLock.
WriterPreferenceReadWriteLock	Similar to a FIFOReadWriteLock, however, if there are waiting write lock requests when a new read lock request comes in, the reader must wait for the waiting writer to get and release the write lock.

The ReadWriteLock interface is a little simpler than the Sync interface, offering just the two methods shown in Table 18-4.

Table 18-4. Summary of ReadWriteLock Interface

VARIABLE/METHOD NAME	DESCRIPTION
readLock()	Gets the read lock.
writeLock()	Gets the write lock.

The two methods of the ReadWriteLock interface each let you get one of the locks:

```
public Sync readLock()
public Sync writeLock()
```

An example of the basic usage of the interface is shown in Listing 18-2.

Listing 18-2. Using a ReadWriteLock.

```
public class RWDemo {
  ReadWriteLock lock;

  public void readIt() throws InterruptedException {
    lock.readLock().acquire();
    try {
      // read data
    } finally {
      lock.readlock().release()
    }
  }
  public void writeIt() throws InterruptedException {
    rw.writeLock().acquire();
    try {
      // set data
    } finally {
      rw.writelock().release()
    }
  }
}
```

> **NOTE** *When using the collection classes in the util.concurrent library, you won't have to worry about calling the* Sync *or* ReadWriteLock *methods. The collection classes will call them for you. All you'll have to do is figure out which interface implementation to use.*

Collection Classes

There are three sets of collections objects in the util.concurrent library: copy-on-write collections, collections synchronized on either Sync or ReadWriteLock objects, and optimized hash maps for concurrent access. Figure 18-3 shows the ten implementations and how they fit into the Collections Framework.

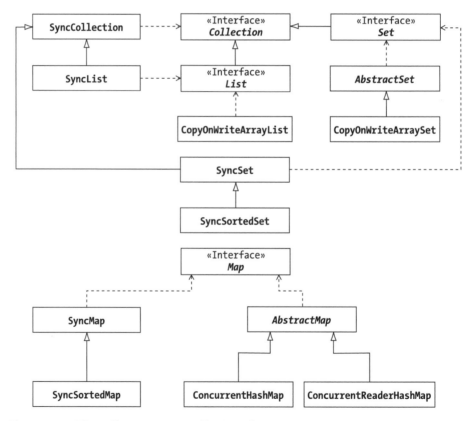

Figure 18-3. The util.concurrent collection classes.

Copy-on-Write Collections

The copy-on-write implementations, CopyOnWriteArraySet and CopyOnWriteArrayList, allow you to maintain groups of immutable objects. When it is time for the group to change, they change en masse with no possible way to see the intermediate group or with only some of the elements changed. This is important when you are iterating through the set of objects, as it is impossible for the group of objects to be corrupted even if the collection simultaneously changes the items in the group.

There are three constructors for CopyOnWriteArrayList:

```
public CopyOnWriteArrayList()
public CopyOnWriteArrayList(Collection c)
public CopyOnWriteArrayList(Object[] arrayToCopyIn)
```

...and two for CopyOnWriteArraySet:

```
public CopyOnWriteArraySet()
public CopyOnWriteArraySet(Collection c)
```

To demonstrate their usage, look at the CopyOnWriteArrayList class. CopyOnWriteArrayList is a useful collection to store your listener lists in. If you remember Chapter 3, we used a Vector to store our list of listeners in the ExceptionCatcherThread class. We can rewrite that class to use a CopyOnWriteArrayList instance to store the list. Our new fireExceptionHappened() method no longer needs to clone() the listener list before notifying the listeners, as the iterator returned by the CopyOneWriteArrayList is guaranteed to not change the set of listeners that were in the collection when the iterator was created. Listing 18-3 shows the new class implementation:

Listing 18-3. Using a CopyOnWriteArrayList.

```
import EDU.oswego.cs.dl.util.concurrent.*;
import java.util.Iterator;
public class ExceptionCatcherThread extends ThreadGroup {

  private Runnable runnable;
  private Thread runner;
  private CopyOnWriteArrayList listenerList = new CopyOnWriteArrayList();

  /* For autonumbering our group. */
  private static int threadInitNumber;
  private static synchronized int nextThreadNum() {
```

```
              return threadInitNumber++;
        }

        public ExceptionCatcherThread(Runnable r) {
          super("ExceptionCatcherThread-" + nextThreadNum());
          runnable = r;
          // Create thread in this group
          runner = new Thread(this, runnable);
        }

        public void start() {
          runner.start();
        }

        /* Listener registration methods */

        public synchronized void
            addThreadExceptionListener(ThreadListener t) {
          listenerList.add(t);
        }
        public synchronized void
            removeThreadExceptionListener(ThreadListener t) {
          listenerList.remove(t);
        }

        public void uncaughtException(Thread source, Throwable t) {
          fireExceptionHappened(t);
          super.uncaughtException(source, t);
        }

        protected void fireExceptionHappened(Throwable t) {
          ThreadException e = (t instanceof ThreadException) ?
            (ThreadException)t : new ThreadException(runnable, t);
          Iterator iterator = listenerList.iterator();
          while (iterator.hasNext()) {
            ThreadListener tl = (ThreadListener) iterator.next();
            tl.exceptionHappened(e);
          }
        }
      }
```

> **NOTE** *There are two specialized classes that utilize the* CopyOnWriteArrayList *class for this very behavior:* PropertyChangeMulticaster *and* VetoableChangeMulticaster. *They are direct replacements for the* PropertyChangeSupport *and* VetoableChangeSupport *classes, respectively, found in the* java.beans *package. Feel free to use them to take advantage of this behavior.*

Synchronized Collections

There are six wrapper collections in the util.concurrent library that let you use Sync and ReadWriteLock objects for synchronization of the collections: SyncCollection, SyncList, SyncMap, SyncSet, SyncSortedMap, and SyncSortedSet. You would use these collections when the basic collection synchronization provided by the methods in the Collections class wasn't sufficient. (For more on synchronization with the Collections class, see Chapter 12.)

When you use any of these six collections, you create the Sync/ReadWriteLock object first and then pass it into the constructor. The collection then deals with all the synchronization for you internally as instructed by the specific Sync/ReadWriteLock object you created.

Each of the specialized collections has three constructors. You specify a ReadWriteLock object or either one or two Sync objects for synchronization:

```
public SyncCollection(Collection c, ReadWriteLock readWriteLock)
public SyncCollection(Collection c, Sync sync)
public SyncCollection(Collection c, Sync readLock, Sync writeLock)
public SyncList(List l, ReadWriteLock readWriteLock)
public SyncList(List l, Sync sync)
public SyncList(List l, Sync readLock, Sync writeLock)
public SyncMap(Map m, ReadWriteLock readWriteLock)
public SyncMap(Map m, Sync sync)
public SyncMap(Map m, Sync readLock, Sync writeLock)
public SyncSet(Set s, ReadWriteLock readWriteLock)
public SyncSet(Set s, Sync sync)
public SyncSet(Set s, Sync readLock, Sync writeLock)
public SyncSortedMap(SortedMap sm, ReadWriteLock readWriteLock)
public SyncSortedMap(SortedMap sm, Sync sync)
public SyncSortedMap(SortedMap sm, Sync readLock, Sync writeLock)
public SyncSortedSet(SortedSet c, ReadWriteLock readWriteLock)
public SyncSortedSet(SortedSet c, Sync sync)
public SyncSortedSet(SortedSet c, Sync readLock, Sync writeLock)
```

The basic usage of any of these classes is to create the lock then wrap the set. You don't have to create the internal set at the same time. You can pass to the constructor one that has already been created and filled:

```
ReadWriteLock lock = new FIFOReadWriteLock();
Set s = new SyncSet(new HashSet(), lock);
```

If you need your lock attempts to timeout, you'll have to simulate this yourself by using a TimeoutSync. The Sync collections do not call the attempt() method directly. The following code frame implements timeouts:

```
ReadWriteLock readWriteLock = new FIFOReadWriteLock();
Sync readLock = new TimeoutSync(readWriteLock.readLock(), 250);
Sync writeLock = new TimeoutSync(readWriteLock.writeLock(), 250);
Set s = new SyncSet(new HashSet(), readlock, writelock);
```

Optimized Hash Maps

Added to the 1.3 release of the library are two optimized map implementations: ConcurrentReaderHashMap and ConcurrentHashMap. Under most circumstances they can be used as a direct replacement to the Hashtable class. And as long as you don't have null keys or values, they can also be used as HashMap replacements.

For the ConcurrentReaderHashMap class, "under most circumstances" refers to its ability to perform concurrent reading and writing operations. As long as your Hashtable or synchronized HashMap usage don't rely on readers getting blocked during write operations, you can use ConcurrentReaderHashMap. If reading and writing happen in different threads, they can perform simultaneously. ConcurrentReaderHashMap is useful if one thread creates and fills the map while several others read from the map after creating and filling.

With the ConcurrentHashMap you get even more interesting behavior. The concurrent reader behavior doesn't change with regards to writing. Both can happen at the same time. The ConcurrentHashMap class adds the ability to have up to thirty-two concurrent updates happening simultaneously. With ConcurrentHashMap, there is absolutely no way to lock an entire table to prevent updates.

Neither class relies on Sync or ReadWriteLock for synchronization. Instead, their own custom mechanism is used.

> **WARNING** *The iterators returned from* `keySet().iterator()`, `entrySet().iterator()`, `values.iterator()`, `keys()`, *and* `elements()` *are not fail-fast. They will not throw a ConcurrentModificationException. You'll never get the same element multiple times but it is possible that a key may have been removed or its value replaced after creating the iterator.*

Summary

In this chapter, we examined the collections support found in Doug Lea's util.concurrent library. We discovered his specialized copy-on-write collections, to process a collection's elements while they can still be modified. We also saw how this library provides specialized support for improving collection performance with extended synchronization to support multiple readers and one or many writers. Feel free to use this public domain library to improve your concurrent programming efforts.

In the next chapter, we'll examine Colt, a high performance, scientific and technical computing library with support for specialized data structures beyond the core framework.

Colt

Colt is both an open source library designed for scientific computing, and the distribution of a specific set of third-party Java libraries, one of which is the Colt library. The end goal of the distribution is to make technical computing easier with Java by creating a baseline of utilities for common tasks in the scientific community. Originally written by Wolfgang Hoschek for the European Organization for Nuclear Research (CERN), you'll find that the Colt distribution provides, for the right audience, a useful collection of Java utilities.

Getting Started

The basics of the Colt library are packaged into the `cern.colt.*` package structure. Here you'll find classes and interfaces for data collections as well as specialized support for numerical manipulations. Besides the core Colt library, the Colt distribution includes many other libraries that you may choose to use.

Acquisition

To get the Colt library, visit The Colt Distribution Web site at:

`http://tilde-hoschek.home.cern.ch/~hoschek/colt/index.htm`.

After agreeing to their license agreement, download the latest version. The download includes the Colt library and all the other libraries (mentioned in the "Other Libraries" section later in this chapter). The download size of the current version is over 6 MB. You can only get it as a .zip file. Unlike Doug Lea's library, you are given the binaries (.class files) and the documentation files (generated javadoc) as well as the source code.

Installation

After downloading the .zip file, you need to unpack it. This can be done with either the WinZip tool or the `jar` command-line tool that comes with the Java

Development Kit. Be sure to create a top-level directory that you wish to unpack everything into first as there is no top-level directory defined for you in the .zip. The following shows one way of unpacking:

```
md colt
cd colt
jar xvf colt1.0.1.zip
```

After unpacking everything, place the `colt.jar` file into your CLASSPATH. Within the Java 2 platform, it is easiest to place the .jar file into an appropriate directory for the Java Extensions Framework to load the .jar file without mucking with the CLASSPATH environment variable. In order for the standard Java extension mechanism to find the file, place it in the `/jre/lib/ext` directory of your Java Runtime Environment (JRE). In the case of a Win32 user with the JDK 1.3 installed in `C:\jdk1.3`, copying the .jar file translates into the execution of the following command from the newly created `colt` directory:

```
copy colt.jar c:\jdk1.3\jre\lib\ext
```

Now that you've copied the .jar file, you can use the `cern.colt.*` classes in your programs as well as all the third-party libraries that come with Colt.

Usage

As with using all libraries in Java programs, it is necessary to import the appropriate packages when you need to use them. The standard Colt classes are found in one of thirteen different packages:

`cern.colt`: The core sorting and partitioning classes are found here.

`cern.colt.bitvector`: For the bit vector and matrix classes.

`cern.colt.list`, `cern.colt.list.adapter`: For the primitive, list-like data structures and their adapters that make them compatible with the Java Collections Framework.

`cern.colt.buffer`: The streaming buffer support classes.

`cern.colt.function`: The core functional interfaces are here.

`cern.colt.map`: For the primitive map-like data structures.

cern.colt.matrix, cern.colt.matrix.bench, cern.colt.matrix.doublealgo, cern.colt.matrix.impl, cern.colt.matrix.linalg, cern.colt.matrix.objectalgo: The multidimensional array classes and their supporting libraries.

When it comes time to actually use the library, be sure to import the appropriate package or packages:

```
import cern.colt.*;
import cern.colt.buffer.*;
```

> **TIP** *Remember, importing only* cern.colt.* *does not automatically import all the subpackages. You must import each package separately.*

Since the javadoc .html files come with the distribution, there is no need to generate these files yourself. To view them, just open the README.html file that comes with the distribution. Besides the javadoc files, you'll also get a few other pointers to help you get started. Figure 19-1 shows what the Colt distribution homepage looks like.

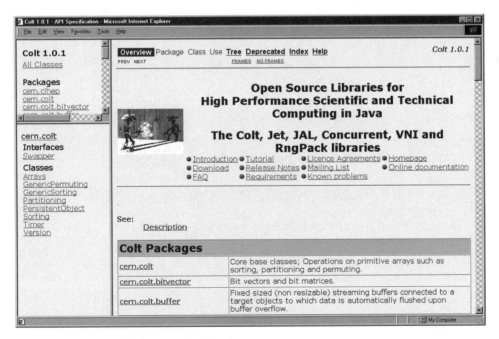

Figure 19-1. The Colt documentation homepage.

> **NOTE**   *Don't be fooled by the Tutorial link. There is nothing behind it besides a TBD (to be done) note.*

Licensing and Redistribution Rights

While the library is open source, the complete distribution includes several libraries from third-party sources. For the complete license agreement and copyright, see `http://tilde-hoschek.home.cern.ch/~hoschek/colt/download/v1.0.1/download.htm` (or following the License Agreements link from the documentation homepage shown in Figure 19-1). The basic Colt libraries are provided as is, free of charge. Each of the other included libraries has their own separate copyright notice and redistribution clause. They vary, from not for commercial use for the libraries from the book, *Core Java 1.1: Fundamentals* (by Gary Cornell and Cay Horstmann, SunSoft Press Java Series, 1997) to some with the more familiar GNU public licenses and even public domain. Be sure to read the usage restrictions for the specific piece you are using.

> **NOTE**   *The online link for the license agreement is version specific. See* `http://tilde-hoschek.home.cern.ch/~hoschek/colt/download.htm` *for a list of the available versions and be sure to read the latest licensing agreement. Or just read the downloaded agreement.*

Product Support

While the licensing agreement states that the Colt library is provided as is, there is some support available. Besides the brief FAQ that comes with the documentation, you can utilize the Colt mailing list. Subscription information is available by following the Mailing List link shown in Figure 19-1 or by going to `http://tilde-hoschek.home.cern.ch/~hoschek/colt/V1.0.1/doc/cern/colt/doc-files/mailing.html`.

To subscribe to the mailing list, send a message to ListServer@listbox.cern.ch, where the content of the message is "subscribe colt" (no quotes). The subject of the message is ignored.

> **NOTE**   *Archives of the mailing list are available at* `https://wwwlistbox.cern.ch/earchive/colt/`. *However, it is not a very active mailing list—there are less than fifty total messages listed since early 1999.*

For a list of known bugs, go to `http://tilde-hoschek.home.cern.ch/ ~hoschek/colt/V1.0.1/doc/cern/colt/doc-files/problems.html`. While there are no known bugs listed, there is a list of patches for 1.0.1 available from `http://nicewww.cern.ch/~hoschek/colt/patches/patches.html`. If you find any new bugs, you can email the author at wolfgang.hoschek@cern.ch.

As of this writing, the current version of the library is 1.0.1, released in May 2000 with the patches from June 2000.

Other Libraries

What's the deal with all these other libraries included with the Colt distribution? Reading into what's included with the introduction of the package, apparently there was a desire to "provide an infrastructure for scalable scientific and technical computing in Java." Instead of just creating and delivering a single library (COLT), the group at CERN decided to package up a bunch of libraries to solve their problems, and hopefully yours.

The following is a list of all the libraries provided with the Colt distribution besides the basic Colt library.

> package `cern.clhep`: CLHEP is a port of a C++ Class Library for High Energy Physics (CLHEP). For a user and reference guide on the package, see `http://wwwinfo.cern.ch/asd/lhc++/clhep/`.

> package `cern.jet`: The Jet packages are a set of math libraries that go well beyond the basic `Math` class for working with probabilities, the Chebyshev series, and pseudo-random numbers, among many other tasks.

> package `corejava`: The `corejava` package is from *Core Java 1.1: Fundamentals* by Gary Cornell and Cay Horstmann (SunSoft Press Java Series, 1997). The copyright notice shows a date of 1997, so it's an old version of the package. The only class present is a `Format` class that offers functionality similar to the C/C++ `printf()` function (or the Java `NumberFormat` class).

> package `com.imsl.math`: This library seems to be an old version of what is now JNL, a Numerical Library for Java from Visual Numerics. It includes support for complex numbers and a library of math functions missing from the `Math` class. Information on the old library seems to be available at `http://www.vni.com/corner/garage/grande/`, while the new library is referenced at `http://www.vni.com/products/wpd/jnl/`.

> package `edu.cornell.lassp.houle.RngPack`: RngPack is a specialized library for Random Number Generation (RNG). It isn't recommended for secure

random number generation. However, it is supposed to be better than the basic random() method of the Math class. For additional information on RngPack see http://www.honeylocust.com/RngPack/.

package edu.oswego.cs.dl.util.concurrent: This is Doug Lea's concurrent programming library. See Chapter 18 for details.

> **WARNING** *Judging from the package name, I can't tell what version of Doug's library this is. Somebody changed the package names from EDU.* to edu.* and it wasn't Doug. Possibly, this was done to avoid conflicts if you already had Doug's libraries installed before installing the Colt distribution.*

package hep.aida: The High Energy Physics (HEP) interactive data analysis libraries are used to add performant histogramming functionality to your Java programs. The JavaHEP homepage is located at http://java.freehep.org/.

> **NOTE** *For those interested in the topic, you can sign up for the HEP-JAVA mailing list at* http://www.slac.stanford.edu/cgi-bin/lwgate/HEP-JAVA/, *although this mailing list is even less popular than the Colt one, with no traffic since June of 2000.*

package jal: The Java Algorithm Library (JAL) is a collection of algorithms modeled after the C++ Standard Template Library (STL). The JAL homepage is at http://reality.sgi.com/austern_mti/java/.

> **NOTE** *I'm not exactly sure how JAL was able to keep its name of Java Algorithm Library and the JGL product couldn't. It's possible that JAL is used so little that it stayed under the radar of the Sun legal team. Either that or Sun already contacted the authors and told them to rename the next version. The libraries haven't been updated since 1996.*

package ViolinStrings: The ViolinStrings package is a set of utility functions (138 in all) for string manipulation. You can find out more about it from http://users.aol.com/MSchmelng/Home.html.

> **NOTE** *I guess if you were working in the numerical programming field these extra packages might prove helpful, though you might double-check that you have the latest versions. This chapter only looks at the Colt libraries for the purpose of using their collection-like capabilities.*

Key Classes and Interfaces

Similar to the util.concurrent library, the key parts of the Colt library are not related to collections. They are meant for numerical computations. In the following sections, you'll find a description of each package separately, with extra details spent on the collections-related implementations.

Package `cern.colt`

Almost all of the classes in the `cern.colt` package are made up of only static methods. Table 19-1 provides a brief description of each. The only exceptions to the static rule are `Timer` and `PersistentObject`.

Table 19-1. The cern.colt Package Classes

CLASS/INTERFACE	DESCRIPTION
Arrays	Provides three methods [ensureCapacity(), toString(), and trimToCapacity()] for arrays of each of the eight primitive data types and for Object.
GenericPermuting	Reorders an array of elements with the help of an array of indices and a Swapper implementation.
GenericSorting	Performs a quick sort on an array with the help of a Swapper and IntComparator.
Partitioning	Partitions array elements such that elements within a programmer-specified interval are adjacent.
PersistentObject	Provides a common base class for all persistent-capable Colt classes.
Sorting	Supports binary searches, quick sorts, and merge sorts on arrays of the eight primitive types and of Object. Uses either the standard Java Comparator or a Colt-specific type-safe one found in the cern.colt.function package.
Timer	Provides a basic timing class that works to the nearest millisecond.
Version	Reports the current version of the library.

The following program demonstrates the use of the Timer and Arrays classes:

```
import cern.colt.*;

public class TimeIt {
  public static void main (String args[]) {
    Timer timer = new Timer();
    timer.start();
    System.out.println(args);
    System.out.println(Arrays.toString(args));
    timer.stop();
    System.out.println(timer);
  }
}
```

When working with Timer, don't forget to start() it after you create it. When working with the Arrays class, the nice thing about its nine toString() methods is that each converts an array to a comma-delimited list. There is one version for each primitive type and one for Object arrays.

> **WARNING**   *There is a name clash between the Timer class here and the two provided with the core Java classes. Functionally, think of this Timer as a free-running clock, not a scheduler-type timer that runs some code at a later time.*

Running the program with the command java TimeIt One Two Three produces the following output:

```
[Ljava.lang.String;@129206
[One, Two, Three]
Time=0.01 secs
```

Package cern.colt.bitvector

The cern.colt.bitvector package provides alternate implementations of the
java.util.BitSet class. Instead of supporting dynamic sizing, they offer fixed-
size collections of states. Table 19-2 lists and describes the three classes.

Table 19-2. The cern.colt.bitvector Package Classes

CLASS/INTERFACE	DESCRIPTION
BitMatrix	A matrix of bit states in which you get() or put() elements with two dimensions instead of one.
BitVector	A vector of bit states in which you get() or put() elements with one dimension like BitSet.
QuickBitVector	A vector of bit states that doesn't perform bounds checking for optimal performance. Use with caution.

Package cern.colt.list and cern.colt.list.adapter

The cern.colt.list and cern.colt.list.adapter packages provide the actual
data structures in the Colt library. In the cern.colt.list package, you'll find the
custom classes for the Colt library. In the cern.colt.list.adapter package, you'll
find classes that fit into the Collections Framework. They are basically Vector or
ArrayList implementations that let you specify a particular type of primitive to
store in the structure besides the generic Object type. Figure 19-2 shows the hierarchy of the base package.

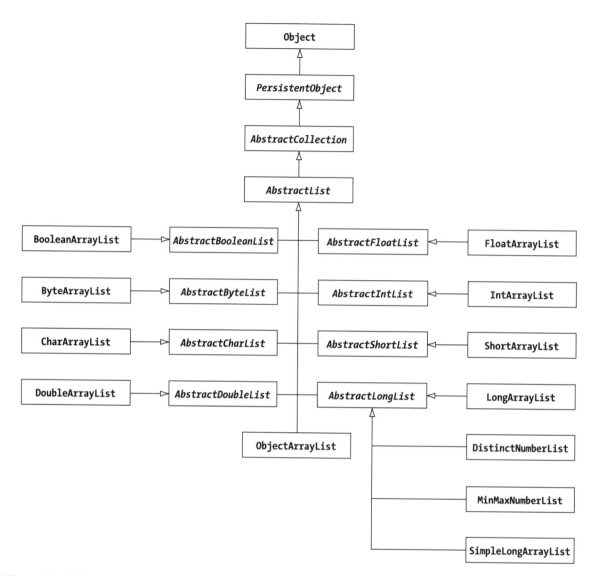

Figure 19-2. The cern.colt.list class hierarchy.

The classes found in the cern.colt.list.adapter package (see Figure 19-3) are similar to their cern.colt.list counterparts. However, instead of subclassing the AbstractList class found in the cern.colt.list package, they subclass the AbstractList class found in the java.util package. As such, they can be used in place of any of the core collection classes.

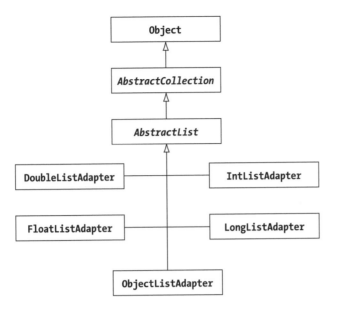

Figure 19-3. The cern.colt.list.adapter class hierarchy.

The chief purpose of this package is to provide better type-safe numeric collections classes. There is no magic in the ObjectListAdapter class that truly differentiates it from an ArrayList. However, with the other four classes, you must pass a java.lang.Number into the setter methods or risk an exception being thrown at runtime.

Package cern.colt.buffer

In the cern.colt.buffer package, you'll find seven paired up sets of interfaces and classes that offer type-safe, producer-consumer-like buffering implementations. Table 19-3 lists the seven pairs.

Table 19-3. The cern.colt.buffer Package Classes

CLASS/INTERFACE	DESCRIPTION
DoubleBuffer/DoubleBufferConsumer	Allows you to buffer elements of type double.
DoubleBuffer2D/DoubleBuffer2DConsumer	Allows you to buffer two-dimensional points where each coordinate is specified as a double.
DoubleBuffer3D/DoubleBuffer3DConsumer	Allows you to buffer three-dimensional points where each coordinate is specified as a double.
IntBuffer/IntBufferConsumer	Allows you to buffer elements of type int.
IntBuffer2D/IntBuffer2DConsumer	Allows you to buffer two-dimensional points where each coordinate is specified as an int.
IntBuffer3D/IntBuffer3DConsumer	Allows you to buffer three-dimensional points where each coordinate is specified as an int.
ObjectBuffer/ObjectBufferConsumer	Allows you to buffer elements of type Object.

To demonstrate, the following `ObjectBufferConsumer` implementation stores objects in an `ObjectArrayList`. These new elements to store are passed in periodically when the `public void addAllOf(ObjectArrayList list)` method of the `ObjectBufferConsumer` interface implementation is called. To provide notification when elements are added, you'll need to add in your own JavaBeans-style notification. In Listing 19-1, registered `ActionListener` objects are notified when elements are added:

Listing 19-1. Defining an ObjectBufferConsumer.

```
import cern.colt.buffer.*;
import cern.colt.list.*;
import java.awt.AWTEventMulticaster;
import java.awt.event.ActionEvent;
import java.awt.event.ActionListener;

public class MyConsumer implements ObjectBufferConsumer {
  private ObjectArrayList list;
  private ActionListener listenerList;
  public synchronized void
      addActionListener(ActionListener t) {
    listenerList = AWTEventMulticaster.add(listenerList, t);
  }
  public synchronized void
      removeActionListener(ActionListener t) {
    listenerList = AWTEventMulticaster.remove(listenerList, t);
  }
  public MyConsumer(ObjectArrayList list) {
    this.list = list;
  }
  public void addAllOf(ObjectArrayList list) {
    int size = list.size();
    this.list.addAllOfFromTo(list, 0, size-1);
    ActionEvent event = new ActionEvent (
      list, ActionEvent.ACTION_PERFORMED, "Adding " + size);
    listenerList.actionPerformed(event);
  }
}
```

Utilizing the above consumer, Listing 19-2 demonstrates the use of the consumer by filling up a three-element ObjectBuffer with arguments passed in from the command-line. Since the buffer size is three, as every three elements are added, a call to the action listener is triggered:

Listing 19-2. Using our ObjectBufferConsumer.

```java
import cern.colt.buffer.*;
import cern.colt.list.*;
import java.awt.event.*;

public class BuffIt {
  public static void main (String args[]) {
    ObjectArrayList list = new ObjectArrayList();
    MyConsumer consumer = new MyConsumer(list);
    ObjectBuffer buffer = new ObjectBuffer(consumer, 3);
    ActionListener listener = new ActionListener() {
      public void actionPerformed(ActionEvent e) {
        System.out.println(e.getActionCommand());
      }
    };
    consumer.addActionListener(listener);
    for (int i=0, n=args.length; i<n; i++) {
      buffer.add(args[i]);
    }
    buffer.flush();
  }
}
```

Package cern.colt.function

The cern.colt.function package provides a core set of interfaces that offer type-safe comparators, and procedures as well as functions for iterating across all of the elements in a collection, which are listed in Table 19-4.

Table 19-4. The cern.colt.function Package Classes

INTERFACE		
BooleanProcedure	DoubleIntProcedure	IntIntProcedure
ByteComparator	DoubleProcedure	IntObjectProcedure
ByteProcedure	FloatComparator	IntProcedure
CharComparator	FloatProcedure	LongComparator
CharProcedure	IntComparator	LongObjectProcedure
Double27Function	IntDoubleFunction	LongProcedure
Double5Function	IntDoubleProcedure	ObjectFunction
Double9Function	IntFunction	ObjectObjectFunction
DoubleComparator	IntIntDoubleFunction	ObjectProcedure
DoubleDoubleFunction	IntIntDoubleProcedure	ShortComparator
DoubleDoubleProcedure	IntIntFunction	ShortProcedure
DoubleFunction	IntIntIntProcedure	

Package `cern.colt.map`

In the `cern.colt.map` package, you'll find special collections for key-value pairs where the key is a primitive data type and the value can be either a primitive or an object.

There are five concrete collections here, none of which fit into the core collections framework:

`OpenDoubleIntHashMap`: Supports a map of `double` keys to `int` values.

`OpenIntDoubleHashMap`: Supports a map of `int` keys to `double` values.

`OpenIntIntHashMap`: Supports a map of `int` keys to `int` values.

`OpenIntObjectHashMap`: Supports a map of `int` keys to `Object` values.

`OpenLongObjectHashMap`: Supports a map of `long` keys to `Object` values.

Besides the concrete implementation classes and their abstract parents, Table 19-5 lists the support classes found in the package.

Table 19-5. The cern.colt.map Support Classes

CLASS	DESCRIPTION
Benchmark	For benchmarking the maps in the package.
HashFunctions	For generating hash codes on primitives and objects.
PrimeFinder	For locating prime numbers to increase hash table capacity.

Package `cern.colt.matrix.*`

The `cern.colt.matrix` package and its supporting `cern.colt.matrix.bench`, `cern.colt.matrix.doublealgo`, `cern.colt.matrix.impl`, `cern.colt.matrix.linalg`, and `cern.colt.matrix.objectalgo` packages provide support for manipulating dense and sparse matrices holding either primitives or objects. My intention is not to short-change the matrix packages as they are rich in capabilities, however, their functionality really goes beyond the scope of the book. If you need to do things like linear algebra matrix computations, it's sufficient to say that support is definitely there.

Summary

In this chapter, we examined the Colt library and the rest of the Colt distribution. We learned about their many different custom collection classes. We saw how their libraries extend the basic BitSet capabilities to their own BitMatrix and BitVector classes. We saw how to use their buffering classes to limit the propagation of data to an eventual consumer. And, we explored how to use their custom list and map implementations to work with type-safe collections of primitives.

This ends Part Three of the book. In Appendix A, you'll find an API reference to the standard collection classes; a class, method, and field index; and a class-level API index. The appendix should serve as a quick reference to the classes in the Collections Framework.

APPENDIX A

Collections API Reference

This appendix presents information to help you navigate through the classes in the Java Collections Framework.

Class, Method, and Field Index

Table A-1 provides an index to all the classes, methods, and fields in the Java Collections Framework. Classes specify which package they are in, while methods and fields specify what classes they belong to. For detailed information about the classes, methods, and fields, see the chapters that describe them.

Table A-1. Summary of Collection Framework Classes, Methods, and Fields

CLASS/METHOD/FIELD NAME	PACKAGE/CLASS FOR CLASS/METHOD/FIELD
A	
AbstractCollection	java.util
AbstractList	java.util
AbstractMap	java.util
AbstractSequentialList	java.util
AbstractSet	java.util
add()	AbstractCollection, AbstractList, AbstractSequentialList, ArrayList, Collection, HashSet, LinkedList, List, ListIterator, Set, TreeSet, Vector
addAll()	AbstractCollection, AbstractList, AbstractSequentialList, ArrayList, Collection, LinkedList, List, Set, TreeSet, Vector
addElement()	Vector
addFirst()	LinkedList
addLast()	LinkedList
and()	BitSet
andNot()	BitSet
ArrayList	java.util
Arrays	java.util

Table A-1. Continued

CLASS/METHOD/FIELD NAME	PACKAGE/CLASS FOR CLASS/METHOD/FIELD
asList()	Arrays
B	
binarySearch()	Arrays, Collections
BitSet	java.util
C	
capacity()	Vector
capacityIncrement	Vector
clear()	AbstractCollection, AbstractList, AbstractMap, ArrayList, BitSet, Collection, HashMap, HashSet, Hashtable, LinkedList, List, Map, Set, TreeMap, TreeSet, Vector, WeakHashMap
clone()	ArrayList, BitSet, HashMap, HashSet, Hashtable, LinkedList, TreeMap, TreeSet, Vector
Collection	java.util
Collections	java.util
Comparable	java.lang
Comparator	java.util
comparator()	SortedMap, SortedSet, TreeMap, TreeSet
compare()	Comparator
compareTo()	Comparable
contains()	AbstractCollection, ArrayList, Collection, HashSet, Hashtable, LinkedList, List, Set, TreeSet, Vector
containsAll()	AbstractCollection, Collection, List, Set, Vector
containsKey()	AbstractMap, HashMap, Hashtable, Map, TreeMap, WeakHashMap
containsValue()	AbstractMap, HashMap, Hashtable, Map, TreeMap
copy()	Collections
copyInto()	Vector
D	
defaults	Properties
Dictionary	java.util
E	
elementAt()	Vector
elementCount	Vector
elementData	Vector
elements()	Dictionary, Hashtable, Vector
empty()	Stack
EMPTY_LIST	Collections
EMPTY_MAP	Collections
EMPTY_SET	Collections
ensureCapacity()	ArrayList, Vector

Table A-1. Continued

CLASS/METHOD/FIELD NAME	PACKAGE/CLASS FOR CLASS/METHOD/FIELD
entrySet()	AbstractMap, HashMap, Hashtable, Map, TreeMap, WeakHashMap
Enumeration	java.util
enumeration()	Collections
equals()	AbstractList, AbstractMap, AbstractSet, Arrays, BitSet, Collection, Comparator, Hashtable, List, Map, Map.Entry, Set, Vector
F	
fill()	Arrays, Collections
first()	SortedSet, TreeSet
firstElement()	Vector
firstKey()	SortedMap, TreeMap
G	
get()	AbstractList, AbstractMap, AbstractSequentialList, ArrayList, BitSet, Dictionary, HashMap, Hashtable, LinkedList, List, Map, TreeMap, Vector, WeakHashMap
getFirst()	LinkedList
getKey()	Map.Entry
getLast()	LinkedList
getProperty()	Properties
getValue()	Map.Entry
H	
hashCode()	AbstractList, AbstractMap, AbstractSet, BitSet, Collection, Hashtable, List, Map, Map.Entry, Set, Vector
HashMap	java.util
HashSet	java.util
Hashtable	java.util
hasMoreElements()	Enumeration
hasNext()	Iterator, ListIterator
hasPrevious()	ListIterator
headMap()	SortedMap, TreeMap
headSet()	SortedSet, TreeSet
I	
indexOf()	AbstractList, ArrayList, LinkedList List, Vector
insertElementAt()	Vector
isEmpty()	AbstractCollection, AbstractMap, ArrayList, Collection, Dictionary, HashMap, HashSet, Hashtable, List, Map, Set, TreeSet, Vector, WeakHashMap

Table A-1. Continued

CLASS/METHOD/FIELD NAME	PACKAGE/CLASS FOR CLASS/METHOD/FIELD
Iterator	java.util
iterator()	AbstractCollection, AbstractList, AbstractSequentialList, Collection, HashSet, List, Set, TreeSet
K	
keys()	Dictionary, Hashtable
keySet()	AbstractMap, HashMap, Hashtable, Map, TreeMap
L	
last()	SortedSet, TreeSet
lastElement()	Vector
lastIndexOf()	AbstractList, ArrayList, LinkedList, List, Vector
lastKey()	SortedMap, TreeMap
length()	BitSet
LinkedList	java.util
List	java.util
list()	Properties
ListIterator	java.util
listIterator()	AbstractList, AbstractSequentialList, LinkedList, List
load()	Properties
M	
Map	java.util
Map.Entry	java.util
max()	Collections
min()	Collections
modCount	AbstractList
N	
nCopies()	Collections
next()	Iterator, ListIterator
nextElement()	Enumeration
nextIndex()	ListIterator
O	
or()	BitSet
P	
peek()	Stack
pop()	Stack
previous()	ListIterator
previousIndex()	ListIterator
Properties	java.util
propertyNames()	Properties

Table A-1. Continued

CLASS/METHOD/FIELD NAME	PACKAGE/CLASS FOR CLASS/METHOD/FIELD
push()	Stack
put()	AbstractMap, Dictionary, HashMap, Hashtable, Map, TreeMap, WeakHashMap
putAll()	AbstractMap, HashMap, Hashtable, Map, TreeMap
R	
rehash()	Hashtable
remove()	AbstractCollection, AbstractList, AbstractMap, AbstractSequentialList, ArrayList, Collection, Dictionary, HashMap, HashSet, Hashtable, Iterator, LinkedList, List, ListIterator, Map, Set, TreeMap, TreeSet, Vector, WeakHashMap
removeAll()	AbstractCollection, AbstractSet, Collection, List, Set, Vector
removeAllElements()	Vector
removeElement()	Vector
removeElementAt()	Vector
removeFirst()	LinkedList
removeLast()	LinkedList
removeRange()	AbstractList, ArrayList, Vector
retainAll()	AbstractCollection, Collection, List, Set, Vector
reverse()	Collections
reverseOrder()	Collections
S	
save()	Properties
search()	Stack
Set	java.util
set()	AbstractList, AbstractSequentialList, ArrayList, BitSet, LinkedList, List, ListIterator, Vector
setElementAt()	Vector
setProperty()	Properties
setSize()	Vector
setValue()	Map.Entry
shuffle()	Collections
singleton()	Collections
singletonList()	Collections
singletonMap()	Collections
size()	AbstractCollection, AbstractMap, ArrayList, BitSet, Collection, Dictionary, HashMap, HashSet, Hashtable, LinkedList, List, Map, Set, TreeMap, TreeSet, Vector, WeakHashMap

Table A-1. Continued

CLASS/METHOD/FIELD NAME	PACKAGE/CLASS FOR CLASS/METHOD/FIELD
sort()	Arrays, Collections
SortedMap	java.util
SortedSet	java.util
Stack	java.util
store()	Properties
subList()	AbstractList, List, Vector
subMap()	SortedMap, TreeMap
subSet()	SortedSet, TreeSet
synchronizedCollection()	Collections
synchronizedList()	Collections
synchronizedMap()	Collections
synchronizedSet()	Collections
synchronizedSortedMap()	Collections
synchronizedSortedSet()	Collections
T	
tailMap()	SortedMap, TreeMap
tailSet()	SortedSet, TreeSet
toArray()	AbstractCollection, ArrayList, Collection, LinkedList, List, Set, Vector
toString()	AbstractCollection, AbstractMap, BitSet, Hashtable, Vector
TreeMap	java.util
TreeSet	java.util
trimToSize()	ArrayList, Vector
U	
unmodifiableCollection()	Collections
unmodifiableList()	Collections
unmodifiableMap()	Collections
unmodifiableSet()	Collections
unmodifiableSortedMap()	Collections
unmodifiableSortedSet()	Collections
V	
values()	AbstractMap, HashMap, Hashtable, Map, TreeMap
Vector	java.util
W	
WeakHashMap	java.util
X	
xor()	BitSet

Class-Level API Index

In the tables that follow, you'll find the class summary tables from the earlier chapters recreated in a common location for easy reference. They list the constructors, methods, and fields of each class in the Collections Framework. For those constructors, methods, and fields that are protected, you'll find them listed in italic. In all cases, the version of Java that the constructor, method, or field was introduced is mentioned as well as a short description.

AbstractCollection Class

Table A-2. Summary of the AbstractCollection Class

VARIABLE/METHOD NAME	VERSION	DESCRIPTION
AbstractCollection()	1.2	Constructs an empty (abstract) collection.
add()	1.2	Adds an element to the collection.
addAll()	1.2	Adds a collection of elements to the collection.
clear()	1.2	Clears all elements from the collection.
contains()	1.2	Checks if the collection contains an element.
containsAll()	1.2	Checks if the collection contains a collection of elements.
isEmpty()	1.2	Checks if the collection is empty.
iterator()	1.2	Returns an object from the collection that allows all of the collection's elements to be visited.
remove()	1.2	Clears a specific element from the collection.
removeAll()	1.2	Clears a collection of elements from the collection.
retainAll()	1.2	Removes all elements from collection not in another collection.
size()	1.2	Returns the number of elements in a collection.
toArray()	1.2	Returns the elements of the collection as an array.
toString()	1.2	Converts the collection contents into a string.

AbstractList Class

Table A-3. Summary of the AbstractList Class

VARIABLE/METHOD NAME	VERSION	DESCRIPTION
AbstractList()	1.2	Constructs an empty (abstract) list.
modCount	1.2	Used by iterator to check for concurrent modifications of the list.
add()	1.2	Adds an element to the list.
addAll()	1.2	Adds a collection of elements to the list.
clear()	1.2	Clears all elements from the list.
equals()	1.2	Checks for equality with another object.
get()	1.2	Returns an element at a specific position.
hashCode()	1.2	Returns the computed hash code for a list.
indexOf()	1.2	Searches for an element within the list.
iterator()	1.2	Returns an object from the list that allows all of the list's elements to be visited.
lastIndexOf()	1.2	Searches from the end of the list for an element.
listIterator()	1.2	Returns an object from the collection that allows all of the list's elements to be visited sequentially.
remove()	1.2	Clears a specific element from the list.
removeRange()	1.2	Clears a range of elements from the list.
set()	1.2	Changes an element at a specific position within the list.
subList()	1.2	Returns a portion of the list.

AbstractMap Class

Table A-4. Summary of the AbstractMap Class

VARIABLE/METHOD NAME	VERSION	DESCRIPTION
AbstractMap()	1.2	Constructs an empty (abstract) map.
clear()	1.2	Removes all the elements from the map.
containsKey()	1.2	Checks to see if an object is a key within the map.
containsValue()	1.2	Checks to see if an object is a value within the map.
entrySet()	1.2	Returns the set of key-value pairs in the map.
equals()	1.2	Checks for equality with another object.
get()	1.2	Retrieves a value for a key in the map.
hashCode()	1.2	Computes a hash code for the map.
isEmpty()	1.2	Checks if the map has any elements.
keySet()	1.2	Retrieves a collection of the keys of the hash table.
put()	1.2	Places a key-value pair into the map.
putAll()	1.2	Places a collection of key-value pairs into the map.
remove()	1.2	Removes an element from the map.
size()	1.2	Returns the number of elements in the map.
toString()	1.2	Converts the map contents into a string.
values()	1.2	Retrieves a collection of the values of the map.

AbstractSequentialList Class

Table A-5. Summary of the AbstractSequentialList Class

VARIABLE/METHOD NAME	VERSION	DESCRIPTION
AbstractSequentialList()	1.2	Constructs an empty sequential list.
add()	1.2	Adds an element to the list.
addAll()	1.2	Adds a collection of elements to the list.
get()	1.2	Returns an element at a specific position.
iterator()	1.2	Returns an object from the list that allows all of the list's elements to be visited.
listIterator()	1.2	Returns an object from the list that allows all of the list's elements to be visited sequentially.
remove()	1.2	Clears a specific element from the list.
set()	1.2	Changes an element at a specific position within the list.

AbstractSet Class

Table A-6. Summary of the AbstractSet Class

VARIABLE/METHOD NAME	VERSION	DESCRIPTION
AbstractSet()	1.2	Constructs an empty set.
equals()	1.2	Checks for equality with another object.
hashCode()	1.2	Computes a hash code for the set.
removeAll()	1.2	Clears a collection of elements from the set.

ArrayList Class

Table A-7. Summary of the ArrayList Class

VARIABLE/METHOD NAME	VERSION	DESCRIPTION
ArrayList()	1.2	Constructs an empty list backed by an array.
add()	1.2	Adds an element to the list.
addAll()	1.2	Adds a collection of elements to the list.
clear()	1.2	Clears all elements from the list.
clone()	1.2	Creates a clone of the list.
contains()	1.2	Checks to see if an object is a value within the list.
ensureCapacity()	1.2	Ensures capacity of internal buffer is at least a certain size.
get()	1.2	Returns an element at a specific position.
indexOf()	1.2	Searches for an element within the list.
isEmpty()	1.2	Checks if list has any elements.
lastIndexOf()	1.2	Searches from end of list for an element.
remove()	1.2	Clears a specific element from the list.
removeRange()	1.2	Clears a range of elements from the list.
set()	1.2	Changes an element at a specific position within the list.
size()	1.2	Returns the number of elements in the list.
toArray()	1.2	Returns elements of the list as an array.
trimToSize()	1.2	Trims capacity of internal buffer to actual size.

Arrays Class

Table A-8. Summary of the Arrays Class

VARIABLE/METHOD NAME	VERSION	DESCRIPTION
asList()	1.2	Converts an array to a list.
binarySearch()	1.2	Searches for an element within an array.
equals()	1.2	Checks for equality of two arrays.
fill()	1.2	Fills an array with a single element.
sort()	1.2	Sorts the elements of an array.

BitSet Class

Table A-9. Summary of the BitSet Class

VARIABLE/METHOD NAME	VERSION	DESCRIPTION
BitSet()	1.0	Creates a bit set with all bits clear.
and()	1.0	Performs a logical AND operation with another bit set.
andNot()	1.2	Performs a logical NOT operation of another bit set, then performs a logical AND operation with this bit set.
clear()	1.0	Clears a specific bit from the set.
clone()	1.0	Copies the bit set.
equals()	1.0	Checks for equality with another object.
get()	1.0	Gets the setting of a specific bit from the set.
hashCode()	1.0	Returns computed hash code for the bit set.
length()	1.2	Returns the logical size of the set.
or()	1.0	Performs a logical OR operation with another bit set.
set()	1.0	Sets a specific bit of the set.
size()	1.0	Returns the internal space used to represent the bit set.
toString()	1.0	Converts the bit set contents into a string.
xor()	1.0	Performs a logical XOR operation with another bit set.

Collection Interface

Table A-10. Summary of the Collection Interface

VARIABLE/METHOD NAME	VERSION	DESCRIPTION
add()	1.2	Adds an element to the collection.
addAll()	1.2	Adds a collection of elements to the collection.
clear()	1.2	Clears all elements from the collection.
contains()	1.2	Checks if a collection contains an element.
containsAll()	1.2	Checks if a collection contains a collection of elements.
equals()	1.2	Checks for equality with another object.
hashCode()	1.2	Returns the computed hash code for the collection.
isEmpty()	1.2	Checks if a collection is empty.
iterator()	1.2	Returns an object from the collection that allows all of the collection's elements to be visited.
remove()	1.2	Clears a specific element from collection.
removeAll()	1.2	Clears a collection of elements from the collection.
retainAll()	1.2	Removes all elements from the collection not in another collection.
size()	1.2	Returns the number of elements in the collection.
toArray()	1.2	Returns the elements of a collection as an array.

Collections Class

Table A-11. Summary of the Collections Class

VARIABLE/METHOD NAME	VERSION	DESCRIPTION
EMPTY_LIST	1.2	Represents an empty immutable list.
EMPTY_MAP	1.3	Represents an empty immutable map.
EMPTY_SET	1.2	Represents an empty immutable set.
binarySearch()	1.2	Searches for an element in the list with a binary search.
copy()	1.2	Copies elements between two lists.
enumeration()	1.2	Converts a collection to an enumeration.
fill()	1.2	Fills a list with a single element.
max()	1.2	Searches for the maximum value within a collection.
min()	1.2	Searches for the minimum value within a collection.
nCopies()	1.2	Creates an immutable list with multiple copies of an element.
reverse()	1.2	Reverses elements within a list.
reverseOrder()	1.2	Returns a comparator for reversing the order of comparable elements.
shuffle()	1.2	Randomly reorders elements in a list.
singleton()	1.2	Returns an immutable set of one element.
singletonList()	1.3	Returns an immutable list of one element.
singletonMap()	1.3	Returns an immutable map of one element.
sort()	1.2	Reorders the elements in a list.
synchronizedCollection()	1.2	Creates a thread-safe collection.
synchronizedList()	1.2	Creates a thread-safe list.
synchronizedMap()	1.2	Creates a thread-safe map.
synchronizedSet()	1.2	Creates a thread-safe set.
synchronizedSortedMap()	1.2	Creates a thread-safe sorted map.
synchronizedSortedSet()	1.2	Creates a thread-safe sorted set.
unmodifiableCollection()	1.2	Creates a read-only collection.
unmodifiableList()	1.2	Creates a read-only list.
unmodifiableMap()	1.2	Creates a read-only map.
unmodifiableSet()	1.2	Creates a read-only set.
unmodifiableSortedMap()	1.2	Creates a read-only sorted map.
unmodifiableSortedSet()	1.2	Creates a read-only sorted set.

Comparable Interface

Table A-12. Summary of the Comparable Interface

VARIABLE/METHOD NAME	VERSION	DESCRIPTION
compareTo()	1.2	Checks for ordering with another object.

Comparator Interface

Table A-13. Summary of the Comparator Interface

VARIABLE/METHOD NAME	VERSION	DESCRIPTION
compare()	1.2	Checks for ordering between two elements.
equals()	1.2	Checks for equality with another Comparator

ConcurrentModificationException Class

Table A-14. Summary of the ConcurrentModificationException Class

VARIABLE/METHOD NAME	VERSION	DESCRIPTION
ConcurrentModificationException	1.2	Constructs a ConcurrentModificationException.

Dictionary Class

Table A-15. Summary of the Dictionary Class

VARIABLE/METHOD NAME	VERSION	DESCRIPTION
Dictionary()	1.0	Empty constructor, implicitly called by subclass.
elements()	1.0	Returns an object from the dictionary that allows all of the dictionary's keys to be visited.
get()	1.0	Retrieves a specific element from the dictionary.
isEmpty()	1.0	Checks if dictionary is empty.
keys()	1.0	Returns a collection of the keys in the dictionary.
put()	1.0	Places a key-value pair into the dictionary.
remove()	1.0	Removes an element from the dictionary.
size()	1.0	Returns the number of elements in the dictionary.

Enumeration Interface

Table A-16. Summary of the Enumeration Interface

VARIABLE/METHOD NAME	VERSION	DESCRIPTION
hasMoreElements()	1.0	Checks for more elements in enumeration.
nextElement()	1.0	Fetches next element of the enumeration.

HashMap Class

Table A-17. Summary of the HashMap Class

VARIABLE/METHOD NAME	VERSION	DESCRIPTION
HashMap()	1.2	Constructs an empty hash map.
clear()	1.2	Removes all the elements from the hash map.
clone()	1.2	Creates a clone of the hash map.
containsKey()	1.2	Checks to see if an object is a key for the hash map.
containsValue()	1.2	Checks to see if an object is a value within the hash map.
entrySet()	1.2	Returns a set of key-value pairs in the hash map.
get()	1.2	Retrieves the value for a key in the hash map.
isEmpty()	1.2	Checks if hash map has any elements.
keySet()	1.2	Retrieves a collection of the keys of the hash map.
put()	1.2	Places a key-value pair into the hash map.
putAll()	1.2	Places a collection of key-value pairs into the hash map.
remove()	1.2	Removes an element from the hash map.
size()	1.2	Returns the number of elements in the hash map.
values()	1.2	Retrieves a collection of the values of the hash map.

HashSet Class

Table A-18. Summary of the HashSet Class

VARIABLE/METHOD NAME	VERSION	DESCRIPTION
HashSet()	1.2	Constructs a hash set.
add()	1.2	Adds an element to the set.
clear()	1.2	Removes all elements from the set.
clone()	1.2	Creates a clone of the set.
contains()	1.2	Checks if an object is in the set.
isEmpty()	1.2	Checks if the set has any elements.
iterator()	1.2	Returns an object from the set that allows all of the set's elements to be visited.
remove()	1.2	Removes an element from the set.
size()	1.2	Returns the number of elements in the set.

Hashtable Class

Table A-19. Summary of the Hashtable Class

VARIABLE/METHOD NAME	VERSION	DESCRIPTION
Hashtable()	1.0/1.2	Constructs a hash table.
clear()	1.0	Removes all the elements from the hash table.
clone()	1.0	Creates a clone of the hash table.
contains()	1.0	Checks to see if an object is a value within the hash table.
containsKey()	1.0	Checks to see if an object is a key for the hash table.
containsValue()	1.2	Checks to see if an object is a value within the hash table.
elements()	1.0	Returns an object from the hash table that allows all of the hash table's keys to be visited.
entrySet()	1.2	Returns set of key-value pairs in hash table.
equals()	1.2	Checks for equality with another object.
get()	1.0	Retrieves value for key in hash table.
hashCode()	1.2	Computes hash code for hash table.
isEmpty()	1.0	Checks if hash table has any elements.
keys()	1.0	Retrieves a collection of the keys of the hash table.
keySet()	1.2	Retrieves a collection of the keys of the hash table.
put()	1.0	Places a key-value pair into the hash table.
putAll()	1.2	Places a collection of key-value pairs into the hash table.
rehash()	1.0	For increasing the internal capacity of the hash table.
remove()	1.0	Removes an element from the hash table.
size()	1.0	Returns the number of elements in the hash table.
toString()	1.0	Converts hash table contents into string.
values()	1.2	Retrieves a collection of the values of the hash table.

Iterator Interface

Table A-20. Summary of the Iterator Interface

VARIABLE/METHOD NAME	VERSION	DESCRIPTION
hasNext()	1.2	Checks for more elements in the iterator.
next()	1.2	Fetches the next element of the iterator.
remove()	1.2	Removes an element from the iterator.

LinkedList Class

Table A-21. Summary of the LinkedList Class

VARIABLE/METHOD NAME	VERSION	DESCRIPTION
LinkedList()	1.2	Constructs an empty list backed by a linked list.
add()	1.2	Adds an element to the list.
addAll()	1.2	Adds a collection of elements to the list.
addFirst()	1.2	Adds an element to beginning of the list.
addLast()	1.2	Adds an element to end of the list.
clear()	1.2	Clears all elements from the list.
clone()	1.2	Creates a clone of the list.
contains()	1.2	Checks to see if an object is a value within the list.
get()	1.2	Returns an element at a specific position.
getFirst()	1.2	Returns the first element in a list.
getLast()	1.2	Returns the last element in a list.
indexOf()	1.2	Searches for an element within the list.
lastIndexOf()	1.2	Searches from end of the list for an element.
listIterator()	1.2	Returns an object from the list that allows all of the list's elements to be visited sequentially.
remove()	1.2	Clears a specific element from the list.
removeFirst()	1.2	Removes the first element from the list.
removeLast()	1.2	Removes the last element from the list.
set()	1.2	Changes an element at a specific position within the list.
size()	1.2	Returns the number of elements in the list.
toArray()	1.2	Returns the elements of the list as an array.

List Interface

Table A-22. Summary of the List Interface

VARIABLE/METHOD NAME	VERSION	DESCRIPTION
add()	1.2	Adds an element to the list.
addAll()	1.2	Adds a collection of elements to the list.
clear()	1.2	Clears all elements from the list.
contains()	1.2	Checks to see if an object is a value within the list.
containsAll()	1.2	Checks if the list contains a collection of elements.
equals()	1.2	Checks for equality with another object.
get()	1.2	Returns an element at a specific position.
hashCode()	1.2	Computes hash code for the list.
indexOf()	1.2	Searches for an element within the list.
isEmpty()	1.0	Checks if the list has any elements.
iterator()	1.2	Returns an object from the list that allows all of the list's elements to be visited.
lastIndexOf()	1.2	Searches from the end of the list for an element.
listIterator()	1.2	Returns an object from the list that allows all of the list's elements to be visited sequentially.
remove()	1.2	Clears a specific element from the list.
removeAll()	1.2	Clears a collection of elements from the list.
retainAll()	1.2	Removes all elements from the list not in another collection.
set()	1.2	Changes an element at a specific position within the list.
size()	1.2	Returns the number of elements in the list.
subList()	1.2	Returns a portion of the list.
toArray()	1.2	Returns the elements of the list as array.

ListIterator Interface

Table A-23. Summary of the ListIterator Interface

VARIABLE/METHOD NAME	VERSION	DESCRIPTION
add()	1.2	Adds an element to the list.
hasNext()	1.2	Checks in the forward direction for more elements in the iterator.
hasPrevious()	1.2	Checks in the reverse direction for more elements in the iterator.
next()	1.2	Fetches the next element of the iterator.
nextIndex()	1.2	Returns the index of the next element of the iterator.
previous()	1.2	Fetches the previous element of the iterator.
previousIndex()	1.2	Returns the index of the previous element of the iterator.
remove()	1.2	Removes an element from the iterator.
set()	1.2	Changes the element at a specific position within the list.

Map Interface

Table A-24. Summary of the Map Interface

VARIABLE/METHOD NAME	VERSION	DESCRIPTION
clear()	1.2	Removes all the elements from the map.
containsKey()	1.2	Checks to see if an object is a key for the map.
containsValue()	1.2	Checks to see if an object is a value within the map.
entrySet()	1.2	Returns the set of key-value pairs in the map.
equals()	1.2	Checks for equality with another object.
get()	1.2	Retrieves a value for a key in the map.
hashCode()	1.2	Computes a hash code for the map.
isEmpty()	1.2	Checks if hash map has any elements.
keySet()	1.2	Retrieves a collection of the keys of the map.
put()	1.2	Places a key-value pair into the map.
putAll()	1.2	Places a collection of key-value pairs into the map.
remove()	1.2	Removes an element from the map.
size()	1.2	Returns the number of elements in the map.
values()	1.2	Retrieves a collection of the values of the map.

Map.Entry Interface

Table A-25. Summary of the Map.Entry Interface

VARIABLE/METHOD NAME	VERSION	DESCRIPTION
equals()	1.2	Checks for equality with another object.
getKey()	1.2	Retrieves the key for a map entry.
getValue()	1.2	Retrieves the value for a map entry.
hashCode()	1.2	Computes the hash code for a map entry.
setValue()	1.2	Changes the value for a map entry.

Properties Class

Table A-26. Summary of the Properties Class

VARIABLE/METHOD NAME	VERSION	DESCRIPTION
Properties()	1.0	Constructs a properties list.
getProperty()	1.0	Retrieves a value for a key in the properties list.
list()	1.0	Lists all the properties and their values.
load()	1.0	Loads the properties list from a stream.
propertyNames()	1.0	Returns a collection of the keys in the properties list.
setProperty()	1.2	Places a key-value pair into the properties list.
store()	1.2	Saves the properties list to a stream.
defaults	1.0	A default set of the property values.

Set Interface

Table A-27. Summary of the Set Interface

VARIABLE/METHOD NAME	VERSION	DESCRIPTION
add()	1.2	Adds an element to the set.
addAll()	1.2	Adds a collection of elements to the set.
clear()	1.2	Clears all elements from the set.
contains()	1.2	Checks if the set contains an element.
containsAll()	1.2	Checks if the set contains a collection of elements.
equals()	1.2	Checks for equality with another object.
hashCode()	1.2	Returns a computed hash code for the set.
isEmpty()	1.2	Checks if the set is empty.
iterator()	1.2	Returns an object from the set that allows all of the set's elements to be visited.
remove()	1.2	Clears a specific element from the set.
removeAll()	1.2	Clears a collection of elements from the set.
retainAll()	1.2	Removes all elements from the set not in another collection.
size()	1.2	Returns the number of elements in the set.
toArray()	1.2	Returns the elements of set as an array.

SortedMap Interface

Table A-28. Summary of the SortedMap Interface

VARIABLE/METHOD NAME	VERSION	DESCRIPTION
comparator()	1.2	Retrieves the comparator from the map.
firstKey()	1.2	Retrieves the first key from the map.
headMap()	1.2	Retrieves a sub map from the beginning of the entire map.
lastKey()	1.2	Retrieves the last key from the map.
subMap()	1.2	Retrieves a sub map of the entire map.
tailMap()	1.2	Retrieves a sub map from the end of the entire map.

SortedSet Interface

Table A-29. Summary of the SortedSet Interface

VARIABLE/METHOD NAME	VERSION	DESCRIPTION
comparator()	1.2	Retrieves the comparator for the set.
first()	1.2	Retrieves the first element of the set.
headSet()	1.2	Retrieves a subset from the beginning of the entire set.
last()	1.2	Retrieves the last element of the set.
subSet()	1.2	Retrieves a subset of the entire set.
tailSet()	1.2	Retrieves a subset from the end of the entire set.

Stack Class

Table A-30. Summary of the Stack Class

VARIABLE/METHOD NAME	VERSION	DESCRIPTION
Stack()	1.0	Constructs an empty stack.
empty()	1.0	Checks if the stack is empty.
peek()	1.0	Fetches an element at the top of the stack.
pop()	1.0	Removes an element from the top of the stack.
push()	1.0	Adds an element to the top of the stack.
search()	1.0	Checks if an element is on the stack.

TreeMap Class

Table A-31. Summary of the TreeMap Class

VARIABLE/METHOD NAME	VERSION	DESCRIPTION
TreeMap()	1.2	Constructs an empty tree map.
clear()	1.2	Removes all the elements from the tree map.
clone()	1.2	Creates a clone of the tree map.
comparator()	1.2	Retrieves the comparator for the map.
containsKey()	1.2	Checks to see if an object is a key for the tree map.
containsValue()	1.2	Checks to see if an object is a value within the tree map.
entrySet()	1.2	Returns a set of key-value pairs in the tree map.
firstKey()	1.2	Retrieves the first key of the map.
get()	1.2	Retrieves a value for a key in the tree map.
headMap()	1.2	Retrieves the sub map at the beginning of the entire map.
keySet()	1.2	Retrieves a collection of keys from the tree map.
lastKey()	1.2	Retrieves the last key of the map.
put()	1.2	Places a key-value pair into the tree map.
putAll()	1.2	Places a collection of key-value pairs into the tree map.
remove()	1.2	Removes an element from the tree map.
size()	1.2	Returns the number of elements in the tree map.
subMap()	1.2	Retrieves a sub map of the entire map.
tailMap()	1.2	Retrieves a sub map at the end of the entire map.
values()	1.2	Retrieves a collection of values from the tree map.

TreeSet Class

Table A-32. Summary of the TreeSet Class

VARIABLE/METHOD NAME	VERSION	DESCRIPTION
TreeSet()	1.2	Constructs a tree set.
add()	1.2	Adds an element to the set.
addAll()	1.2	Adds a collection of elements to the set.
clear()	1.2	Removes all elements from the set.
clone()	1.2	Creates a clone of the set.
comparator()	1.2	Retrieves a comparator for the set.
contains()	1.2	Checks to see if an object is in the set.
first()	1.2	Retrieves the first element of the set.
headSet()	1.2	Retrieves a subset at the beginning of the entire set.
isEmpty()	1.2	Checks if the set has any elements.
iterator()	1.2	Returns an object from the set that allows all of the set's elements to be visited.
last()	1.2	Retrieves the last element of the set.
remove()	1.2	Removes an element from the set.
size()	1.2	Returns the number of elements in the set.
subSet()	1.2	Retrieves a subset of the entire set.
tailSet()	1.2	Retrieves a subset at the end of the entire set.

UnsupportedOperationException Class

Table A-33. Summary of the UnsupportedOperationException Class

VARIABLE/METHOD NAME	VERSION	DESCRIPTION
UnsupportedOperationException	1.2	Constructs an UnsupportedOperationException.

Vector Class

Table A-34. Summary of the Vector Class

VARIABLE/METHOD NAME	VERSION	DESCRIPTION
Vector()	1.0/1.2	Constructs an empty vector of the appropriate initial size.
capacityIncrement	1.0	Size increment for increasing vector capacity.
elementCount	1.0	Number of elements within a vector.
elementData	1.0	Internal buffer for vector elements.
modCount	1.2	From `AbstractList`: used by iterator to check for concurrent modifications.
add()	1.2	Adds an element to a vector.
addAll()	1.2	Adds a collection of elements to a vector.
addElement()	1.0	Adds an element to the end of a vector.
capacity()	1.0	Returns the capacity of an internal buffer for a vector.
clear()	1.2	Clears all elements from a vector.
clone()	1.0	Creates a clone of a vector.
contains()	1.0	Checks if the vector contains an element.
containsAll()	1.2	Checks if the vector contains a collection of elements.
copyInto()	1.0	Copies elements of the vector into an array.
elementAt()	1.0	Returns an element at a specific position.
elements()	1.0	Returns an object from the vector that allows all of the vector's elements to be visited.
ensureCapacity()	1.0	Ensures the capacity of an internal buffer is at least a certain size.
equals()	1.2	Checks for equality with another object.
firstElement()	1.0	Returns the first element within a vector.
get()	1.2	Returns an element at a specific position.
hashCode()	1.2	Returns the computed hash code for a vector.
indexOf()	1.0	Searches for an element within a vector.
insertElementAt()	1.0	Inserts an element into the vector.
isEmpty()	1.0	Checks if the vector is empty.
iterator()	1.2	Returns an object from the vector that allows all of the vector's elements to be visited.
lastElement()	1.0	Returns the last element within a vector.
lastIndexOf()	1.0	Searches from the end of a vector for an element.
listIterator()	1.2	Returns an object from the vector that allows all of the vector's elements to be visited sequentially.
remove()	1.2	Clears a specific element from the vector.
removeAll()	1.2	Clears a collection of elements from the vector.
removeAllElements()	1.0	Clears all elements from the vector.
removeElement()	1.0	Clears a specific element from the vector.

Table A-34. Continued

VARIABLE/METHOD NAME	VERSION	DESCRIPTION
removeElementAt()	1.0	Clears an element at specific position from the vector.
removeRange()	1.2	Clears a range of elements from the vector.
retainAll()	1.2	Removes all elements from the vector not in another collection.
set()	1.2	Changes an element at a specific position within the vector.
setElementAt()	1.0	Changes an element at a specific position within the vector.
setSize()	1.0	Changes the size of an internal vector buffer.
size()	1.0	Returns the number of elements in a vector.
subList()	1.2	Returns a portion of the vector.
toArray()	1.2	Returns the elements of a vector as an array.
toString()	1.0	Converts vector contents into a string.
trimToSize()	1.0	Trims the capacity of internal buffer to actual size.

WeakHashMap Class

Table A-35. Summary of the WeakHashMap Class

VARIABLE/METHOD NAME	VERSION	DESCRIPTION
WeakHashMap()	1.2/1.3	Creates an empty weak hash map.
clear()	1.2	Removes all elements from the hash map.
containsKey()	1.2	Checks to see if an object is a key for the hash map.
entrySet()	1.2	Returns a set of key-value pairs in the hash map.
get()	1.2	Retrieves a value for a key in the hash map.
isEmpty()	1.2	Checks if the hash map has any elements.
put()	1.2	Places a key-value pair into the hash map.
remove()	1.2	Removes an element from the hash map.
size()	1.2	Returns the number of elements in the hash map.

Collections Resources

This appendix is meant to provide a useful collection of resources on the Collections Framework and related libraries discussed in this book. While I'd like to say it is exhaustive, I'm sure I missed something worthwhile given the nature of the Web. For an online version of this list, see
http://www.apress.com/catalog/book/1893115925/.

Collections Implementations

http://java.sun.com/j2se/1.3/docs/guide/collections/

    The Collections Framework from Sun.

http://www.objectspace.com/products/voyager/libraries.asp

    The Generic Collection Library for Java (JGL) from ObjectSpace.

http://gee.cs.oswego.edu/dl/classes/EDU/oswego/cs/dl/util
/concurrent/

    Doug Lea's util.concurrent library.

http://gee.cs.oswego.edu/dl/classes/collections/

    Doug Lea's (outdated) collections package.

http://tilde-hoschek.home.cern.ch/~hoschek/colt/index.htm

    The Colt Distribution.

http://www.cs.bell-labs.com/who/wadler/pizza/gj/

    GJ: Generic Java.

`http://www.pmg.lcs.mit.edu/polyj/`

PolyJ: Java with Parameterized Types.

`http://www.cs.rpi.edu/projects/STL/stl/stl.html`

The C++ Standard Template Library.

`http://www.cs.brown.edu/cgc/jdsl/`

The Data Structures Library in Java.

`http://reality.sgi.com/austern_mti/java/`

The Java Algorithm Library (JAL).

`http://www.alphaworks.ibm.com/ab.nsf/bean/Collections`

alphaWorks Collection Bean Suit.

`http://www.javacollections.org/`

Java Collections Clearinghouse.

Collections FAQs and Tutorials

`http://java.sun.com/j2se/1.3/docs/guide/collections/designfaq.html`

Collections Framework design FAQ.

`http://www.jguru.com/faq/Collections`

Collections FAQ from jGuru.com.

`http://www.cs.bell-labs.com/who/wadler/pizza/gj/FAQ/`

GJ: Generic Java FAQ.

`http://www.pmg.lcs.mit.edu/polyj/comparison.html`

PolyJ Design FAQ.

`http://developer.java.sun.com/developer/onlineTraining/collections/`

Introduction to Collections Framework tutorial from the Java Developer Connection.

`http://java.sun.com/docs/books/tutorial/collections/index.html`

The Java Tutorial trail on the Collections Framework.

`http://www.javaworld.com/javaworld/jw-01-1999/jw-01-jglvscoll-2.html`

"The battle of the container frameworks: which should you use?" A *Java-World* article comparing JGL and the Collections Framework.

`http://www.javaworld.com/javaworld/jw-11-1998/jw-11-collections.html`

"Get started with the Java Collections Framework." Another *JavaWorld* article to get you started.

`http://www.cs.brown.edu/cgc/jdsl/tutorial/tutorial.html`

JDSL Tutorials.

`http://www.phrantic.com/scoop/tocmed.htm`

Richard Baldwin's Java Programming Tutorials, includes collections lessons.

Mailing Lists and Newsgroups

`http://www.egroups.com/group/advanced-java`

Advanced-java email list for technical discussions about full-blown Java applications.

`news:comp.lang.java.help` and `news:comp.lang.java.programmer`

The main Usenet news groups do not have a discussion group specific to the Collections Framework. Your best bet for finding help are these two general-purpose groups.

Collections-Related Web Sites and Information

http://java.sun.com/aboutJava/communityprocess/jsr/jsr_014_gener.html

Java Specification Request (JSR) 14: For adding generic types to the Java Programming Language.

http://developer.java.sun.com/developer/bugParade/bugs/4064105.html

Bug parade for adding parameterized types.

http://java.sun.com/beans/infobus/index.html#DOWNLOAD_COLLECTIONS

Partial Collections Framework library for use with Java 1.1.

http://developer.java.sun.com/developer/Books/MasteringJava/Ch17/

Collections chapter from my *Mastering Java 2* book (Sybex Inc., 1998) at the Java Developer Connection.

APPENDIX C

Generic Types

Generic types, parameterized types, or *templates* are essentially different names for the same thing. (Though some will argue that generic types are not templates.) They represent the ability to work with collections of objects in a type-safe manner where, instead of working with a collection of Object instances, you work with a collection of a specific type. They are not presently a part of the Java programming language. At the time Java was introduced back in 1995, James Gosling, the father of Java, was strongly interested in keeping things simple and getting things right. The concept of templates was not simple and sufficient resources couldn't be spent on getting things designed properly, thus templates were left out of the initial release of Java.

Turn the clocks ahead a few years and there is strong desire from the user community to have generic types added into Java. Looking at the "Top 25 Requests for Enhancements" (RFEs) in the Java Bug Database at http://developer.java.sun.com/developer/bugParade/top25rfes.html, you'll see template support as the second most requested feature below support for porting Java to FreeBSD and just above support for assertions. Because adding generic types would require language-level changes and can't be done just by adding on another class library, the process of adding support has been going through the Java Community Process (JCP) as JSR #14.

While I haven't personally been involved with the JCP for this Java Specification Request (JSR), rumor has it that support for generic types will be added to some upcoming release of the Java 2 platform. In what specific form this will be available is completely unknown. What follows in the rest of this appendix is a review of two publicly available implementations that were used as the basis of the JSR submission: Generic Java (GJ) and PolyJ. I hope that this appendix will get you primed for the changes and enable you to use them more easily once they are available.

> **NOTE** *In an earlier lifetime, the GJ implementation was known as Pizza.*

Generic Type Basics

The basic concept of working with generic types is that when you define a class, you specify where the generic type fits in. For instance, the following defines a Vector of some type T, the type parameter:

```
Vector<T>
```

When the class is later used, the actual type is specified, either in a variable declaration:

```
Vector<String> stringVector;
```

. . .or in calling its constructor:

```
new Vector<String>()
```

Now, whenever you add elements to the collection or get items out, the only datatype that works is that which was passed to the template, in this case, String. If, when using the object, you pass in an incompatible datatype, you'll get a compile-type error, instead of waiting for a runtime exception when you try to cast to an improper type.

While you can create a type-safe container without generic types, you cannot create one that is a subclass of Vector as the rules of overridden methods don't let you return a more specific subtype. In addition, while you can create methods that only accept the type you want, you cannot hide the methods that accept an Object, so essentially you haven't changed or hidden anything.

With generic types, you can create type-safe specific containers easily by simply replacing the type parameter. For instance, in addition to vectors of type String, you can also have Button, Integer, or classes that you knew nothing about when you defined your custom, template-friendly class but the person using your class defined instead:

```
Vector<Button>
Vector<Integer>
Vector<MyClass>
```

That's really all there is to templates. Behind the scenes, it is a little more involved than that and the exact syntax that will be introduced (assuming the JSR is implemented) is still to be determined. Templates essentially add the ability to define generic constructs that accept arbitrary types without using inheritance or composition.

Getting generic types to work without changing the Java Virtual Machine (JVM) and with nongeneric libraries requires a bit of thought, as do issues like support for primitive types and dealing with run-time type data (for instance, with casting and `instanceof`). Besides just the syntax, these are the issues that the working group is actually working on.

Generic Java

Generic Java (GJ) is one such implementation for adding parameterized-type support into Java. It relies on a preprocessor to work and provides a custom set of parameterized core library classes that need to be properly installed into the `bootclasspath` before the system libraries in order to run. GJ was designed by Gilad Bracha of Sun Microsystems, Martin Odersky of the University of South Australia, David Stoutamire of Sun Microsystems, and Philip Wadler of Bell Labs, Lucent Technologies. The following demonstrates how to create and use classes with GJ.

Defining Generic Classes and Interfaces

Classes and interfaces designed to support templates are defined by specifying the type parameter with the class definition. GJ uses angle brackets to surround the type parameter, as in `<A>`. For example, the following demonstrates the creation of a `LinkedList` class that implements a `Collection` interface, which supports an `Iterator` for iterating through the elements:

```
interface Collection<A> {
  public void add(A x);
  public Iterator<A> iterator();
}
interface Iterator<A> {
  public A next();
  public boolean hasNext();
}
class NoSuchElementException extends RuntimeException {}
```

In the `LinkedList` definition, notice in Listing C-1 that using a parameter of the generic type is like using any other parameter:

Listing C-1. A parameterized class for GJ.

```
class LinkedList<A> implements Collection<A> {
  protected class Node {
    A elt;
    Node next = null;
    Node (A elt) { this.elt = elt; }
  }
  protected Node head =null, tail = null;
  public LinkedList() {}
  public void add(A elt) {
    if (head == null) {head=new Node(elt); tail=head; }
    else { tail.next=new Node(elt); tail=tail.next; }
  }
  public Iterator<A> iterator() {
    return new Iterator<A> () {
      protected Node ptr=head;
      public boolean hasNext () { return ptr!=null; }
      public A next () {
        if (ptr!=null) {
          A elt=ptr.elt; ptr=ptr.next; return elt;
        } else throw new NoSuchElementException ();
      }
    };
  }
}
```

NOTE *The GJ examples are taken from the "GJ: Extending the Java Programming Language with type parameters" tutorial available at* http://www.cs.bell-labs.com/who/wadler/pizza/gj/Documents/. *While the interface and class names are identical to those in the Collections Framework, these examples are outside of the framework.*

Using Generic Classes

Now, when you need to use the generalized class, you conveniently don't have to cast the objects returned when retrieved from the collection. The other benefit is that at compile time, you will find out if there are any class conversion errors. This lets you avoid getting a ClassCastException thrown at runtime when you try to convert between improper types.

Listing C-2 demonstrates the just-defined `LinkedList` class. The last usage would result in a compile-time error:

Listing C-2. Using a parameterized GJ class.

```
class Test {
  public static void main (String args[]) {
    // byte list
    LinkedList<Byte> xs = new LinkedList<Byte>();
    xs.add(new Byte(0)); xs.add(new Byte(1));
    Byte x = xs.iterator().next();

    // string list
    LinkedList<String> ys = new LinkedList<String>();
    ys.add("zero"); ys.add("one");
    String y = ys.iterator().next();

    // string list list
    LinkedList<LinkedList<String> zss
      = new LinkedList<LinkedList<String>();
    zss.add(ys);
    String z = zs.iterator().next().iterator().next();

    // string list treated as byte list
    Byte w = ys.iterator.next(); // compile-time error
  }
}
```

For complete information on using Generic Java, visit the GJ homepage at Bell Labs (`http://www.cs.bell-labs.com/who/wadler/pizza/gj/`) or one of the mirror sites.

PolyJ

PolyJ is another implementation of a "proof of concept" for adding generic types into Java. It came out of MIT's Laboratory for Computer Science (LCS), though the latest version is from Cornell University. The syntax is different, essentially using square brackets ([ ]) instead of angle brackets (< >) to specify type. And there are some functional differences, such as supporting generic primitive usage like a Vector of int elements (`Vector[int]`). Effectively, the two projects add the same thing in a different way with different supported capabilities. Both rely on a pre-compiler to work.

Defining Generic Classes and Interfaces

Listing C-3 demonstrates the use of PolyJ by converting the previous GJ example:

Listing C-3. A parameterized class for PolyJ.

```
interface Collection [A] {
  public void add(A x);
  public Iterator[A] iterator();
}
interface Iterator[A] {
  public A next();
  public boolean hasNext();
}
class NoSuchElementException extends RuntimeException {}
class LinkedList[A] implements Collection[A] {
  protected class Node {
    A elt;
    Node next = null;
    Node (A elt) { this.elt = elt; }
  }
  protected Node head =null, tail = null;
  public LinkedList() {}
  public void add(A elt) {
    if (head == null) {head=new Node(elt); tail=head; }
    else { tail.next=new Node(elt); tail=tail.next; }
  }
  public Iterator[A] iterator() {
    return new Iterator[A] () {
      protected Node ptr=head;
      public boolean hasNext () { return ptr!=null; }
      public A next () {
        if (ptr!=null) {
          A elt=ptr.elt; ptr=ptr.next; return elt;
        } else throw new NoSuchElementException ();
      }
    };
  }
}
```

While it looks like the only differences are the use of different brackets, PolyJ provides some interesting capabilities by adding a new where keyword to the language. Its usage is kind of like saying that the generic type implements a pseudo-interface. For instance, the following class definition shows a generic type with equals() and hashCode() methods. Thus, within the HashMap definition, these methods of the Key generic type are directly callable:

```
public class HashMap[Key,Value]
    where Key {
        boolean equals(Key k);
        int hashCode();
    }
    implements Map[Key,Value] {
. . .
}
```

You can find out more on PolyJ at its MIT homepage at http://www.pmg.lcs.mit.edu/polyj/. From a syntax perspective, it appears as though GJ is winning out. From a capabilities perspective, however, some of the PolyJ extensions will be part of the eventual implementation.

JSR 14

The Java Specification Request for generic types is still in committee. How it appears once it gets out and if it will ever be added to the language are still essentially up in the air. If you are interested in following the JSR that can extend the Java programming language to support generic types, you may want to watch the following sites:

http://java.sun.com/aboutJava/communityprocess/jsr/jsr_014_gener.html

Java Community Process homepage for JSR #000014: "Add Generic Types to the Java Programming Language."

http://java.sun.com/people/gbracha/generics-update.html

Gilad Bracha is the JSR specification head. He maintains this resource, which provides information on the specific JSR members, a not-so-current status of the JSR, and a link to a JavaOne presentation on adding genericity.

Index

O

P

About Apress

Apress, located in Berkeley, CA, is an innovative publishing company devoted to meeting the needs of existing and potential programming professionals. Simply put, the "A" in Apress stands for the "Author's Press™." Apress' unique author-centric approach to publishing grew from conversations between Dan Appleman and Gary Cornell, authors of best-selling, highly regarded computer books. In 1998, they set out to create a publishing company that emphasized quality above all else, a company with books that would be considered the best in their market. Dan and Gary's vision has resulted in over 30 widely acclaimed titles by some of the industry's leading software professionals.

Do You Have What It Takes to Write for Apress?

Apress is rapidly expanding its publishing program. If you can write and refuse to compromise on the quality of your work, if you believe in doing more then rehashing existing documentation, and if you're looking for opportunities and rewards that go far beyond those offered by traditional publishing houses, we want to hear from you!

Consider these innovations that we offer all of our authors:

- **Top royalties with *no* hidden switch statements**
  Authors typically only receive half of their normal royalty rate on foreign sales. In contrast, Apress' royalty rate remains the same for both foreign and domestic sales.

- **A mechanism for authors to obtain equity in Apress**
  Unlike the software industry, where stock options are essential to motivate and retain software professionals, the publishing industry has adhered to an outdated compensation model based on royalties alone. In the spirit of most software companies, Apress reserves a significant portion of its equity for authors.

- **Serious treatment of the technical review process**
  Each Apress book has a technical reviewing team whose remuneration depends in part on the success of the book since they too receive royalties.

Moreover, through a partnership with Springer-Verlag, one of the world's major publishing houses, Apress has significant venture capital behind it. Thus, we have the resources to produce the highest quality books *and* market them aggressively. If you fit the model of the Apress author who can write a book that gives the "professional what he or she needs to know™. . .," then please contact one of our Editorial Directors, Gary Cornell (gary_cornell@apress.com), Dan Appleman (dan_appleman @apress.com), Karen Watterson (karen_watterson@apress.com) or Jason Gilmore (jason_gilmore@apress.com) for more information.